P L A T E D
ECSTASY

One Man's Culinary Passion

Vincent DiLoreto

Fulton Books
Meadville, PA

Published by Fulton Books 2021

ISBN 978-1-63985-074-7 (paperback)
ISBN 978-1-63985-075-4 (digital)

Printed in the United States of America

CONTENTS

INTRODUCTION

I am obsessed with fine dining. I am neither boasting nor apologizing for my obsession. It is simply who I am. In this biographical memoir, I will attempt to describe my passion through the prism of gourmet food, fine wine, and stimulating travel. But the solitary word *passion* is not strong enough nor comprehensive enough. At the risk of being overly dramatic, let me expand with the descriptors sensual, sexual, and hedonistic to intensify the breadth of my passion.

I have never worked in the culinary industry. My obsession didn't evolve out of practical necessity to make a living or a family lineage of chefs or association with culinary professionals. I have come to believe that it is a manifestation of my inherent sensitivity to sensory stimuli. I will refer back to this belief throughout this tome. If sensory sensitivity could be measured, I would expect that I would be an outlier on the normal distribution bell curve. Sight, scent, and taste activate the pleasure centers of my brain to a degree that borders on magical. The sum of superior ingredients prepared with professional expertise and presented artistically is the catalyst to activate a high level of plated ecstasy. There is a cliché that simplistically classifies people into two categories: the majority who eat to live and the fortunate few who live to eat. I align myself with the latter group.

We have all read about or have possibly known gifted people with extraordinary sensory talents. Mozart had the ability to hear a piece of music for the first time and then was able to play the piece from memory minutes, months, or years later. Michelangelo could look at a piece of Carrera marble and see the statue inside, and he would chip away the excess with perfection to reveal his vision. Antonin Carême, an innovative French chef from the post-French Revolution era, was reputed to be able to distinguish the ingredients in a dish down to a pinch of spice. No less extraordinary in the current era is Robert Parker, a master wine evaluator. Parker could taste one hundred wines a week, describe the characteristics of each, document his perceptions, and record all this in his prodigious memory for future recall. Let me be clear. I do not profess to have a scintilla of the sensory talents of these geniuses, but I may have a specialized, minor variation of a rare memory condition called hyperthymesia where I can recall with clarity a number of truly remarkable meals and amazing fine wines that I have experienced. When I say "recall," I do not mean that I recall just the names of the courses in the meal. I can vividly recall the sight of the colorful, contrasting artistic presentation, the sound of silverware ringing against china, the aroma, texture, and taste of the meticulously prepared dish, if it was truly remarkable. I close my eyes, it is in front of me, and I salivate like the day I ate it. I can say the same about the memory of a fine wine whose bouquet returns to my nose and whose taste is a spiritual experience that defies description. As I describe my personal encounters with exceptional food and wine in this narrative, please try to move beyond the words to share with me in your imagination the sensory pleasure.

I do not need any memory aids to vividly recall the details of those handfuls of truly exceptional dinners I have been privileged to enjoy. However, for countless other superb dinners that rank slightly below the pinnacle of the truly exceptional dinners, I documented some in photographs and others in a journal to assist my memory. The specifics of dinners over years of vacations, dining out, and entertaining at home are stored in file folders on my PC, on numerous CDs, and in my journal. For example, I have a one-year record of every dinner I prepared at home during the COVID-19 pandemic in 2020, and many of those were gourmet quality. As I write this narrative, I will frequently refer to my notes to share with the reader some of my dining experiences that cover the spectrum from exceptional to routine. In some cases where the years have fogged my memory, I have reconstructed scenes and dialogue with some creativity in an attempt to clear the fog. I have also juxtaposed or expanded vignettes to assist with story continuity and to dramatize events. Is this obsessive behavior? Or is it just the lifestyle of a passionate culinarian? I will leave that judgment to the reader.

I do not view fine dining as a solitary undertaking. Quite the contrary, a meal is something that brings people together. Whether it is an intimate romantic dinner with someone special or a large holiday gathering with family and friends, good food is the glue that strengthens bonds, creates friendship, and offers memorable milestones on our path through life. There is great satisfaction in consuming an exquisite meal, but that satisfaction is considerably amplified by the preparation of that exquisite meal. The great French chef Jacques Pépin famously said, "Food, for me, is inseparable from sharing. There is no great meal unless it is shared with family or friends." To be the gatekeeper for such an event and for a chef or dinner host to be able to say "I'm preparing a meal that is bringing people together" is truly awesome.

I have liberally sprinkled a few of my recipes throughout the passages of this book, but this is not a cookbook. The recipes are intended to simply add emphasis to a specific topic in the narrative. If you want to find a reference that aligns with my passion for culinary excellence, I recommend the publication titled *The Professional Chef* by the Culinary Institute of America, which offers an encyclopedic compilation of all aspects of culinary art.

PART 1

Earliest
Recollections

CHAPTER 1

The Formative Years

Why am I so obsessed with fine dining? Is it part of my DNA? Did it gradually evolve as the aggregate of lifelong experiences? Was there a culinary epiphany that triggered the realization? I've thought about these questions. I don't have a definitive answer. I have come to the understanding that the answer is not important. Whether I understand the underlying reasons or not, the fact remains that my obsession is embedded in the framework of the personality that is me. I like the result. I'm content with who I am.

After my father returned home from World War II in 1946, we resided in a second-floor apartment above the neighborhood grocery store owned and operated by my grandfather and grandmother DiLoreto. At the age of three years old, I have a vivid memory of greeting my father at the train station in Erie, Pennsylvania, upon his return from Europe. He picked me up to hug me, and I recall feeling the scratchy beard stubble on his cheek and the musky scent of the woolen uniform he had been wearing on the train trip from New York. This intense memory of texture and scent, permanently stamped in my brain, provides me a temporal benchmark from which I can order other palpable memories from this event onward in my early youth.

We lived in a primarily Italian neighborhood. My father's parents lived in a two-family home about a half block from our apartment, my paternal grandparents on the ground floor and my father's brother, Uncle Will, and his wife, Aunt Ann, on the second floor. My mother's parents lived in a two-family home about one block away, my maternal grandparents on the ground floor and at any given time the family of one of their sons or daughters on the second floor. Numerous aunts, uncles, and cousins lived close by. It was an easy walk or tricycle ride to visit many of them. One thing in common with all the visits was the offering of food and drink. As a formative child, I considered the ubiquitous availability of good food and drink as a normal aspect of visiting. It was always a sumptuous treat. When family or friends came to our apartment, the first words after "Hello" were "What do you want to drink?" or "Have you eaten yet?" Coffee, wine, sandwiches, finger food, and sweet desserts appeared almost magically and instantaneously. I became so accustomed to this norm that I didn't realize until I branched out in later years many other friends and families did not have the same emphasis on food and drink as an integral part of their social interaction. In the broader society at large, I missed the nuance of how good food enhanced the spirit in even the most routine of social gatherings.

I remember the humor I found in a recurring event regarding my Uncle Will and his coffee. Uncle Will was my father's younger brother who conveniently lived about a half block away from our apartment. He and his wife had no children, and Uncle Will was a frequent visitor to our apartment. I liked Uncle Will, and he seemed to favor me as a nephew. In retrospect, my fuzzy early childhood memory conveys the image that he treated me as a son he never had. Coffee was ubiquitous in our home, and the scent of freshly brewed coffee was the equivalent of aromatherapy in our home. Fresh coffee was available around the clock, and Uncle Will liked his coffee. Whenever he visited our home, Mom offered him a cup of espresso immediately after the greeting at the front door. In those days, a small container of sugar cubes was on the table for those who wanted to sweeten their coffee. Uncle Will would drop three sugar cubes in his espresso, but he never stirred. After the espresso cooled a bit, he would drink it in one tip of the demitasse cup. When he finished his drink, I would look into the bottom of his cup from my standing position on the chair next to him. I was fascinated with childhood curiosity by the unctuous black syrup remaining in the bottom of the cup. I recall a number of times when adults would ask Uncle Will why he did not stir the sugar in his espresso, and I would wait with a knowing grin for his response. His straight-faced answer was always, "I don't like it too sweet." He had his routine, and it was perfect for him.

CHAPTER 2

The Aroma of the Neighborhood

Within our immediate two-block neighborhood in my preschool years, there were three grocery stores. My DiLoreto grandparents owned and operated two of those. I was intimately familiar with the store we lived above. Although the store was small by today's standards, it stocked a modest supply of fresh fruits and vegetables, cheese, deli-style meat, canned goods, and baking items. Playing in the side yard or on the sidewalk in front of the store, the air carried the aroma of fresh produce in open bins, hard cheeses, and cured meats hanging behind the service counter. I became accustomed to those captivating scents. The store also carried some specialty items like bulk candy. I remember the bulk candy well. As you walked in the front door of the store, there was a series of small bins with glass doors to the left of the entrance containing hard candy, licorice, jelly beans, and other delicacies that tempted all children, especially me. I would walk up to the bins and press my nose against the glass until Grandma DiLoreto would come over to serve me a free piece of sweet, fruity, juicy candy. What a thrill!

Most of the people in the neighborhood were day shoppers. People came into the store with their own bag or box to buy the items they needed for a day or two of meals. In our case, my mother would just take my hand and walk down the stairs from our apartment and into the store to buy what was seasonally available in stock.

There was also a bakery in the neighborhood, and the smell of fresh, warm bread was pervasive. My dad loved his daily ration of fresh, crusty bread, and so did I. Occasionally, my dad would drive to a larger public market to buy items not available in the neighborhood markets, such as frozen food and fresh meat, and I really enjoyed going with him to see and smell the cornucopia of products. I also recall milk and cream were delivered to our doorstep by the milkman on a daily or as-needed basis. Fresh milk, cool and sweet, poured from glass bottles was my drink of preference. We never lacked fresh food; and we were blessed with breakfast, lunch, and dinner every day that was satisfying in quality and quantity.

CHAPTER 3

Supper at Home

I have to admit, my mother and father were not gourmet cooks. I would classify them in the eat-to-live category, and not the live-to-eat category. Although my mother had a bachelor's degree in education, she was a stay-at-home mom during my preschool years caring for me, my younger sister, and my younger brother. She was the youngest female of ten siblings, probably the smartest of all, and her emphasis was education and learning. Her mother and four older sisters were all excellent cooks. They were also physically substantial women, while my mother was a small and lithe hundred-pound package of energy. Mom had the intelligence gene, and her sisters had the cooking gene. Who can understand the idiosyncrasies of DNA? My mom didn't need to be a gourmet cook because she catered to my dad's unpretentious food preferences.

When my father returned home from work at about 5:30 p.m. every weekday, he was ready for dinner. Mom would have dinner prepared, although she called it supper, and we would sit as a family at the kitchen table to eat. My dad was a meat-and-potatoes guy, so dinners such as pot roast, Swiss steak, and pan-fried sirloin were the norm, with variations of potato preparations: mashed, fried, baked, or boiled. Mom always made a green salad, but it was always the same salad: iceberg lettuce, tomatoes, celery, cucumber, radishes, and an Italian-style vinaigrette dressing. Dad wasn't much of a salad guy, but he ate the radishes. Mom also always prepared a green vegetable with dinners, such as broccoli, Swiss chard, green beans, or zucchini.

18

Dad also wasn't much of a green vegetable guy, but he picked at the vegetables to set an example for us kids. More often than not, Dad cooked dinner on weekends. He liked to make pasta dishes, lightly dressed with a red sauce in Italian fashion. Ground beef, diced chicken, and pork chops often augmented the tomato-based pasta sauce.

To honor my father, I have inserted a recipe of his at the end of this chapter. Sorry, Mom, I love you, but I don't recall any of your "special" recipes, and sometimes you even seemed challenged by box-cake instructions.

This soup was my father's favorite. He used the Italian nickname for this dish, pasta fazool. I used to watch him make it, and I never saw him refer to a recipe. I've tried to replicate his alchemy with the following recipe, although I know I am taking some liberties with the original family recipe. Enjoy my father's favorite!

Pasta e Fagioli
(Pasta and Bean Soup)

Preparation: 45 minutes
Cooking: 60 minutes
Serves: 6–8

Step 1: Aromatics

> 2 oz. pancetta, 1/4 in. dice (option: bacon, blanched in boiling water)
> 2 tbsp. EVOO
> 2 small Calabrian pepper, minced, seeds and membranes
>   removed (option: 1/2 tsp. of dried red pepper flakes)
> 1 c. yellow onion, finely chopped
> 1/2 c. fennel bulb, finely chopped, and reserve some of the
>   leafy tops for use in step 2 (option: celery)
> 1 medium carrot, peeled and grated
> 2 cloves garlic, minced or pressed
> 1 c. *Roma tomato concassé (option: canned diced tomatoes)
> 1 tsp. kosher salt
> 1/4 tsp. fresh ground black pepper

Put the pancetta in a 3 1/2 quart soup pot and cook for about 5 minutes over medium-high heat to render the fat. Drain and discard the excess fat, leaving only the rendered pancetta and a thin film in the pot for flavor. Add the olive oil, pepper, onion, fennel, and carrot. Sauté over medium-high heat for 5 minutes until the vegetables are soft. Add the garlic, tomatoes, salt, and pepper. Sauté for another 3 minutes.

Step 2: Beans, Pasta, and Herbs

> 4 c. **veal stock (option: chicken stock, vegetable stock, beef stock)
> 1 1/2 c. dried cannellini beans, soaked overnight in water (option: 3 c. canned cannellini beans, drained and rinsed)
> 2 oz. dried porcini mushrooms, soaked overnight in water (option: 4 oz. fresh cremini mushrooms, sliced)
> 1 c. Swiss chard, washed, stemmed, and chopped
> 2 bay leaves
> 1 1/2 c. parcooked and drained orecchiette (option: small shells, small elbow macaroni, or any small pasta)
> 2 qt. ***salted water, to cook the pasta
> 2 tbsp. fresh flat-leaf parsley, chopped (or 1 tsp. dried)
> 1 tbsp. fresh fennel leaves, chopped (or 1 tsp. dried)
> 1 tbsp. fresh marjoram, chopped (or 1 tsp. dried)
> 1 tbsp. fresh oregano, chopped (or 1 tsp. dried)
> 2 tbsp. white wine
> 1 tsp. white balsamic vinegar (optional)

Add the veal stock to the pot. Drain the beans and add them to the pot. Drain the mushrooms, coarsely chop, and add them to the pot. Add the Swiss chard and bay leaf. Bring to a boil, then reduce the heat, cover, and simmer for about 15 minutes until the beans are soft.

While the soup is simmering, parcook the orecchiette in salted water for about 8 minutes, a few minutes short of being al dente. Drain.

Remove the bay leaf from the pot. Use a hand blender in the pot to partially puree the soup mixture. Leave at least half the beans intact. Add water or stock as necessary for desired consistency. Add the drained orecchiette, parsley, fennel leaves, marjoram, oregano, and wine. Cover and simmer for about 15 minutes. Test the whole beans for softness and the orecchiette for al dente texture. Do not overcook. When the soup is ready, stir in the vinegar.

Step 3: Finish

> 8 thin slices of crusty Italian bread
> 1 tbsp. EVOO
> 1/2 c. grated Pecorino Romano cheese

Preheat the broiler. Brush the bread slices with olive oil, and sprinkle some of the grated cheese on the slices. Broil 1 to 2 minutes until the cheese is golden.

Place a piece of the cheese toast in the center of each bowl. Ladle the soup into the bowls, and sprinkle the remainder of the grated cheese on the surface.

*Tomato Concassé

Cut an X in the bottom of each tomato. Blanch the tomatoes in a pot of boiling water for 30 seconds. Using a slotted spoon, transfer the tomatoes to an ice water bath to cool. When cool, drain. Remove the stems and peel off the skin starting from the X. Cut tomatoes in half lengthwise. Remove and discard the core and the seeds. Coarsely chop the tomato.

**Stock

Master Chef Auguste Escoffier says in his epic treatise *The Escoffier* on the fine art of French cuisine: "Stock is everything in cooking. Without it, nothing can be done. The cook mindful of success, therefore, will naturally direct his attention to the faultless preparation of his stock."

A great stock is judged by five criteria: flavor, clarity, color, body, and aroma. An excellent modern reference for preparing stock can be found in chapter 1 of *The Elements of Cooking* by Michael Ruhlman.

If you prefer to use a commercially available stock product, the boxed Swanson brand or Kitchen Basics brand are good choices but not as good as homemade stock.

***Salted Water

For cooking any type of pasta or vegetable, salted water translates to a 1 percent salt solution: 1 1/2 teaspoons of salt in one quart of water.

CHAPTER 4

Extended Family Contributions

At this point, the reader may ask, how could these plebian, nongourmet dinners at home with my parents drive an appreciation of fine dining? I alluded to the answer earlier. My mother's four sisters and her mother, my Grandma Verga, were excellent cooks. Their food was not just acceptable in quality and quantity; it was over the top. My Aunt Fannie prepared eye-popping entrées I never ate at home, such as roast duck, suckling pig, and cioppino. Aunt Mary had a cellar pantry stocked with items she dried or canned, and she had a large chest freezer filled with seasonal delicacies that she stored. One of my pleasant memories is eating her delicious, fresh-tasting strawberry shortcake in the middle of the cold, snowy winter in Pennsylvania.

Family gatherings brought out the best in these amateur chefs. The competition among the contributing family chefs was not explicit, but it surely was implicit, and self-pride resulted in great food. There were the major holidays, of course: Thanksgiving, Christmas, New Year, Easter, Memorial Day, the Fourth of July. Then there were nearly countless birthdays, weddings, anniversaries, births, christenings, confirmations, and other excuses for a celebration. In my mind's eye, I can still see and smell the mounds of tempting dishes. I remember the taste and textures of some of my favorites. I may not have realized it at the time, but my preschool and elementary school years were refining my senses and forming a framework for my obsession.

In retrospect, I am amazed how even a commonplace experience could be elevated to one of my sensory augmented memories. I recall an apple pie made by one of my aunts for a Thanksgiving dinner. I am sure I had previously eaten apple pie, but this memory is the first time I can vividly recall eating apple pie. The generously mounded pie was hot and fresh from the oven, with its tantalizing aroma filling the air. The lattice crust on top was interlaced with precision and browned to perfection. The apples used were the Northern Spy variety from a local orchard, and the baked apple slices in the filling had a creamy texture with a perfect balance of sweet and tart taste. Cinnamon, nutmeg, vanilla, and butter were proportioned to augment but not overwhelm the apple flavor. The flaky pie crust was so light it almost dissolved on the tongue. Of course, a dollop of cold vanilla ice cream complemented the warm slice of pie. For the rest of my life, all apple pies would be judged in comparison to this one.

At this point in my development, I looked forward with anticipation to the marvelous food I was blessed to experience on a regular basis. Although I enjoyed consuming the finished products, I was not the least bit concerned about the source of ingredients, techniques, and tools used to create the finished products. We are all born needing to eat but not knowing how to make food. I never thought about how the creation process could be as equally satisfying as the pleasure of consumption. That realization would come much later in my life.

To honor my mother's sisters, I have inserted a recipe at the end of this chapter. All the sisters made pizzelles, but they gave credit to the eldest sister, Aunt Angie. Pizzelles were the most important of all the Christmas cookies. I credit them for my love of anise flavor in other food besides pizzelles. I still have and use my Aunt Angie's pizzelle iron.

Pizzelles are a traditional Italian treat prepared at Christmas; however, they are appreciated throughout the year. The designs imparted into the cookie by the pizzelle iron mold and the anise flavor are the principal attractions to this delicacy. The following recipe is attributed to my mother's sister, my Aunt Angie. Buon appetito!

Pizzelles

Preparation: 15 minutes
Cooking: 30 minutes
Serves: About 40 pieces

Step 1: Wet ingredients

6 large eggs
1 c. granulated white sugar
1/2 tsp. vanilla extract
1/2 tsp. almond extract
1 tsp. anise oil (or 1 tbsp. anise extract)
1/2 c. clarified unsalted butter, room temperature
1/2 c. vegetable oil, neutral flavor

Whisk the eggs in a stand mixer using the whisk attachment. Add the sugar and whisk until smooth. Add the vanilla extract, almond extract, and anise oil, and continue to whisk. Slowly add the butter and oil, and whisk until thoroughly blended.

Step 2: The batter

4 1/2 c. all-purpose flour, sifted
2 tsp. baking powder

Replace the whisk attachment with the batter attachment. Slowly add the flour and baking powder, and beat until the batter is smooth. The batter should be slightly sticky.

Step 3: Bake in an electric pizzelle iron

1 can nonstick unflavored cooking spray

Heat the pizzelle iron according to directions. Many irons have an indicator light to indicate when the iron is ready. My iron has two molds to make two pizzelles at a time.

Spray each mold, top and bottom, with the cooking spray. Place one mounded tablespoon of batter into the center of each mold. Bake for about 30–40 seconds, depending on the temperature of the iron. It is normal for the first pair of pizzelles to be overcooked, undercooked, or improperly sized. Adjust the quantity of batter and the timing as necessary to bake a round, blond pizzelle. Immediately transfer the baked pizzelles to a cooling rack and continue to the next batch.

CHAPTER 5

The Matriarch

I would be remiss if I didn't give some praise to Grandma Verga. She raised ten children to adulthood, so it should be obvious she had inexhaustible domestic skills. Foremost, I recall her cooking and gardening prowess. In the backyard of her home, she kept an extensive garden that seemed to produce endless quantities of tomatoes, bell peppers, eggplant, zucchini, beans, and greens, to name a few. There was a long trellis run that supported prolific grape vines producing red grapes for Grandpa Verga's wine making. There was also a huge green Anjou pear tree, at least two stories tall, with copious fruit. Since we lived only a block away from the maternal grandparents, Mom walked me there very frequently, and I have fond memories of eating a warm, ripe tomato plucked directly from the vine and sampling a plump grape or two from the bunches on the vines and crunching a fresh pear when they were ripened. Grandma Verga also had a large cellar pantry she stocked with items she dried or canned. One of my periodic chores was helping Grandma Verga with her canning operations, which I didn't mind a bit because the aromas were almost euphoric, and the basement temperature was cool.

The most impressive activity I observed was Grandma Verga making pasta. I believe she made pasta every day. There was a large Formica-topped round table in her kitchen. She would empty a bag or two of flour on the table. Then she would make a deep well in the center of the flour and add eggs, salt, and a small amount of olive oil into the well. I referred to this as a volcano. With strong flashing hands, she would mix and knead the dough into a smooth ball. With similar efficiency, she would roll and spread the dough ball into a uniformly flat, thin layer on the tabletop, and she did not use a pasta machine of any kind. Flour dusted her apron and arms and my face too if I was watching too closely at the edge of the table. This whole process seemed like a magical transformation occurring in almost the blink of an eye. But there was more impressive magic yet to come. She would take a knife and cut the pasta into whatever shape was going to be cooked that day. The speed of the flashing knife blade and the precise uniformity of her cuts were a sight to behold. She had some small wooden hand tools to make special pasta shapes, such as tortellini, ravioli, agnolotti, gnocchi, farfalle, orecchiette, and cappelletti. All were made with assembly-line speed and precision. I doubt that it would be possible for anyone to make homemade pasta without sophisticated equipment as well as Grandma Verga. She dressed her pasta with a number of homemade sauces, including classic red marinara, stout meaty Bolognese, creamy carbonara, and piquant tuna with anchovies, to name a few. You haven't eaten authentic Italian food until you try homemade al dente pasta dressed with a homemade garden-fresh sauce.

To honor my Grandma Verga, I have inserted a recipe of hers at the end of this chapter. It's one she made for me in autumn, and I still make it to this day.

PREFACE

This was a favorite dish of my Grandma Verga, my mother's mother. She had a large pear tree in her backyard, and this recipe is one of the many uses for her prolific crop of fruit. It is a simple yet elegant dessert versatile enough to follow just about any cuisine as a delicious, sweet final course. Try it when fresh, crisp pears are in season. For a variation in fruit, try crisp nectarines, peaches, or figs too. Buon appetito!

Pears Poached in Spiced Wine

Preparation: 20 minutes
Cooking: 45 minutes
Serves: 4

Step 1: Prepare the fruit

4 Bosc, Anjou, or Bartlett pears (option: nectarines, peaches, figs)
2 tbsp. fresh squeezed lemon juice

Use firm fruit. Peel, core, and halve the pears. Place them in a shallow bowl, and pour the lemon juice over the pears. Turn the pears to be certain that the lemon juice coats the entire surface. This not only adds citrus flavor but prevents oxidation and discoloration of the pear halves. Set aside until poaching time, step 3.

Step 2: Prepare the poaching liquid

3 c. light-bodied red wine, Dolcetto or Barbera
1/2 c. sweet marsala, Ambra Dolce
1/4 c. sugar
1 3 in. cinnamon stick
4 whole cloves
2 pieces crystallized ginger
4 pods cardamom seed
1 pod star anise
4 strips lemon peel, 1/4 in. wide by 2 in. long

Pour the wine into a saucepan large enough to hold all the pear halves in one layer. Add the sugar. Tie the cinnamon stick, cloves, ginger, cardamom, and lemon peel together in a cheesecloth packet. Place the spice packet in the pan. Over medium heat, reduce the wine mixture by one-half to yield about one and one-half cups of liquid in the pan. Remove and discard the spice packet.

Step 3: Poach

Drain the lemon juice from the pears in step 1, and discard the liquid. Add the pears to the pan from step 2, hollow side down. Reduce the heat to low, and poach for about 10–20 minutes until tender. Carefully turn the pears halfway through the poaching.

Step 4: Finish

1 tbsp. unsalted butter
4 sprigs fresh mint

To serve, place two pear halves on each of four dessert plates, hollow side down. Set aside, and allow to rest at room temperature. The remaining poaching liquid should be syrupy and sweet. If necessary, continue to reduce the liquid over medium heat, and adjust the sweetness to taste with additional sugar or light corn syrup and/or ground cardamom. The reduced poaching liquid should yield at least one-half cup of syrupy liquid. Remove from the heat, and stir in the butter. Let the poaching liquid cool, and pour over the pear halves. Serve at room temperature. Garnish each plate with a sprig of mint.

PART 2

Coming of Age

CHAPTER 6

The New Neighborhood

When I was ten or eleven years old, my family moved from the urban apartment above my grandparents' store to a suburban single-family home. Life, as I had known it, changed almost beyond recognition. I recall that I was excited and thrilled with the change. A new adventure had begun. I have one poignant memory that underscored the perceived importance of this change. I overheard one of my mother's brothers make a comment to her in a wise-guy accent, "So now you're leaving the ghetto. Are you too good for the rest of us?" Although I'm sure he meant it as sibling teasing, it stung. However, our departure from the old neighborhood never stopped any of the relatives from visiting us in the new neighborhood.

Our new abode was a two-story, ten-room, four-bedroom brick house with a partially finished basement and a stand-up attic with staircase access. There were both front and rear staircases to the second floor, the front staircase from the living room being the more formal of the two. The living room was equipped with a tile fireplace, but the living room was rarely used except for social events. The windowed three-sided sunroom was the equivalent of a modern-day family room, with the television and comfortable seating for the entire family, and it was the most used room in the house. There were French doors between the living room and the dining room and between the dining room and the sunroom. The covered front porch was the place to relax and watch the leisurely ebb and flow of neighborhood activity. The detached two-car garage was convenient

35

for a number of reasons: my parents didn't have to search for a parking space on the curb as they did in the previous urban setting, there was space for yard equipment, my dad set up a modest workshop with power tools, and the garage apron provided a basketball half-court for the backboard and rim attached to the front of the garage. The lawn surrounding the home was small, but there were a number of tall two-story evergreen fir trees to add some character to the grounds. The slate roof also added some curb appeal.

Our home was located on a street one block long. There were probably ten homes on each side of the street, and each home had its own style. No two were alike. There were mature maple trees in the strip of grass between the sidewalk and the street on both sides. One end of the street was a T with a two-lane suburban thoroughfare, and at the other end was a large wooded expanse with a creek running through it. One block south of us was a parallel street on the perimeter of a huge park. The park was a flat expanse of wide-open areas of grass with a random scattering of mature maple trees throughout. The park served neighborhood families for entertaining children from toddlers to teens, and it was ideal for pickup games of baseball or football, and tree climbing was always on the agenda.

The two adjacent blocks of this new neighborhood were populated with six or more boys my age and a similar number of girls two years younger than I. We were never at a loss for preteen activities. From summer games in the park to winter snowball fights to exploring the woods to catching crawfish or tadpoles in the creek, the neighborhood was nearly a paradise for adolescents. However, one of the things lacking in this neighborhood was frequent contact with my relatives from the old neighborhood. On one hand, it expanded my horizons, but on the other hand, it reduced my access to family social gatherings and the associated great food. The memories of the invisible ribbons of aroma from busy kitchens, the sounds of sizzling oils and meats, the sampling of savory soups, the sight of pans filled with the promise of redolent sautéing vegetables or simmering sauces, and the buzz of happy people bonding over a table of delicious food were gradually preempted by the new environment. My early obsession with food had been overcome by the tsunami of social change.

CHAPTER 7

The New Standard for Dinner at Home

My younger sister and brother at this time were all in elementary school. My father was still employed at the General Electric Company in the development and production of the next generation of diesel-electric locomotives. My mother decided to apply her education to a full-time teaching position. She took a job teaching first grade at a public school only a couple of miles from our home.

Mom was still a hundred-pound package of energy. She was the first one up in the morning, already dressed for school, when she woke us three kids. While we were getting dressed for school, she made breakfast, and her breakfasts were not just a Pop-Tart. She mostly made hot breakfasts with eggs, bacon, and toast, or for variety on some days, she made hot oatmeal with fruit. To this day, I still rate a big, hot breakfast as one of my favorite meals. Mom was a firm believer that a good breakfast filled the tank to ensure good performance at school. Her experience as an elementary school teacher probably reinforced this belief. She also prepared our school lunch boxes. Lunch was usually a ham and cheese or a peanut butter and jelly sandwich, accompanied by an apple or orange, and a can of juice. During the weekdays, she returned home from school about three thirty or four o'clock in the afternoon, and then she started preparing for dinner.

My father still returned home from work at about 5:30 p.m. every weekday, and he was ready for dinner. Dad was still a meat-and-potatoes guy. In the new environment, Mom's weapon of choice in the kitchen was the pressure cooker. She could have dinner prepared when Dad arrived home, and she still called the meal supper. We would sit as a family at the kitchen table to eat. The pressure cooker made quick work of dinners such as pot roast, Swiss steak, stews, and chili. Potatoes with gravy, steamed vegetables, and Mom's standard green salad finished the menu. Pasta dishes prepared by Dad were still part of the weekend menu. We kids were old enough now to do routine tasks such as setting the table, mashing the potatoes, clearing the table, and washing the dishes. We took some of the load off our busy mom. The pace of life didn't lend itself to gourmet dining. In retrospect, I was satisfied and accustomed to this daily eat-to-live routine.

CHAPTER 8

An Uninspired Food Scene

As a family, we rarely went out for dinner at a restaurant. When we did, we went to small family-owned neighborhood Italian trattorias or small restaurants on the lake specializing in Lake Erie perch. In the late 1950s and early 1960s, I don't believe Erie had any ethnic Mexican, Chinese, Indian, or French restaurants. At least I don't recall ever seeing any as we drove around the city. The ethnic food I do remember could be found in family-owned Italian restaurants, family-owned eastern European restaurants, and Irish pubs. There were some chain restaurants like the Black Angus Steak House. There were a few fast-food places like McDonald's, which first came to Erie in the early 1960s. There were a number of hamburger and french fry places that catered to the tourists in the vicinity of Presque Isle state park. There were pizza shops and deli sandwich shops scattered around the city. However, there were probably fewer than a handful of fine dining restaurants because Erie was primarily a blue-collar city. The demographic didn't support upscale dining establishments. Chefs trained at the Culinary Institute of America or Le Cordon Bleu were not needed. Chefs competing for a James Beard award (started in the 1970s) were not important. Restaurants rated with a Michelin star (ratings started in the 1950s) were not a priority. My path to culinary appreciation was in the slow lane during this period, except for the microcosm of my new neighborhood.

CHAPTER 9

Expanded Horizons

After a casual glance at the residents of my new neighborhood, an observer would probably conclude that we were a waspish group. Not surprisingly, a search for the ethnicity of surnames would reveal a European diversity that included, in alphabetical order: Anglo-Saxon, Irish, German, Lithuanian, Russian, Scandinavian, Scottish, Slavic, and Welsh. My Italian surname rounded out the group. I recall that everyone was a naturally born American, and no one paid much attention to the ethnicity of prior generations. We were Norman Rockwell mid-twentieth-century Americans. On a humorous note, the only distinct differentiation among families occurred in the Christmas/Hanukah season: Christian families decorated their homes with colored lights, and Jewish families decorated their homes with white lights. Fortunately for me and my interest in good food, some ethnic influences still remained in the neighbor's family recipes.

The families of my new friends in the neighborhood introduced me to new culinary experiences. Some of the products and methods that were common to them were new to me. I would occasionally be treated to a lunch or a dinner at the home of a friend, where I would be served one of their commonplace dishes that I had never tasted before. Fortunately, I was not a picky eater, so I tried anything served. In many cases, I may have been curious or anxious, but I tried to maintain my cool to be appreciative in a nonchalant manner. A few of the new experiences are worth noting because they teased my palate and expanded the framework of my culinary obsession.

My best friend in the neighborhood had relocated to Erie from Natchez, Mississippi. His mother still prepared many dishes associated with the Deep South. Her Southern fried chicken was spectacular! The seasoned coating was crispy, and the meat was succulent. Compared to her SFC, KFC was cardboard. Although my family cooked greens (chard, spinach, and kale), she made delicious collard greens with ham hocks, which I had never eaten before. Although my family cooked polenta, she made creamy, buttery grits that gave a new perspective to cornmeal. Also, for the first time in my life, I was introduced to okra. I had never even seen or tasted okra. What a novelty! In my future employment careers, I would live in a number of locales in the Southern states. The introduction to Southern fare in my youth set a precedent for me to expand my culinary base to include many traditional dishes from south of the Mason-Dixon line.

I ate lunch one day in the home of my friend whose family had emigrated from Lithuania after World War II. The dish was a savory, sour soup made with eel and cabbage, served with black bread. Another novelty! I didn't know people actually ate unappealing eels. This was my first experience with eel and black bread, and I enjoyed the dish immensely.

The mother of one of my baseball buddies who lived next to the park I described earlier had some Asian ethnicity. She introduced me to pot stickers, among other things. Pot stickers may have been a ho-hum routine to many people, but they were exotic to me. Her pot stickers were a great snack after a spirited game of baseball. The perfectly fried pillows stuffed with pork, Chinese cabbage, and Asian spices satisfied the hungriest of adolescent boys. The Chinese cabbage (napa cabbage) she used was a surprise because I was only familiar with green cabbage I had seen in Irish and eastern European food. Also, prior to her pot stickers, I had never tasted Asian spices such as ginger, turmeric, and five-spice. My sense of flavor was maturing.

My mother taught a number of Jewish children in her elementary school. It seemed that conscientious teachers like my mother were revered by Jewish parents. As a result, she was often invited to events such as Bar Mitzvahs and Seder dinners. From her experiences and my experiences with my Jewish friends in the neighborhood, I was introduced to the concept of kosher food preparation, and dishes with a Russian or Eastern European flavor profile. On a humorous note, our Jewish friends often delivered chicken soup to our home if anyone was ill, and we respectfully referred to it as Jewish penicillin. To share a Jewish recipe I remember, I have attached one at the end of this chapter that was served and shared during the Passover season.

The aforementioned ethnic experiences awakened in me an awareness that the boundaries of the culinary genre were practically borderless, and I had only sampled the tip of the iceberg. I felt motivated to sample, experiment, and travel, and this motivation lay smoldering in me until I was old enough to spread my wings.

Brisket in this style is a Jewish tradition during Passover, which occurs in mid-April. The spring holiday commemorates the liberation of the Israelites from Egyptian slavery in about 1450 BC. Although this dish is not part of a traditional Seder dinner, it is commonly prepared during the Passover timeframe. The origin of this dish is generally accepted to be in the modern era from Eastern Europe. Enjoy!

Sweet-and-Sour Brisket, Jewish Style

Preparation: 20 minutes
Cooking: 4+ hours
Serves: 8

Step 1: Prepare the brisket

> 4 lbs. beef brisket
> 1 tbsp. unsalted butter

Trim the brisket to remove and discard excess surface fat. Melt the butter in a 12-inch skillet over medium-high heat. Brown the brisket, about 4–6 minutes on each side. Transfer the browned brisket to a platter.

Step 2: Sweet and sour sauce

> 2 c. yellow onion, chopped (about 2 medium onions)
> 1/2 c. celery, chopped
> 1/2 c. red bell pepper, chopped
> 1 clove garlic, minced

1 c. *beef stock (option: vegetable stock)
1 c. ketchup (option: 1/4 c. tomato paste, 1/2 c. diced toma-
    toes, 1/4 c. water, 1 tsp. honey)
1/2 c. brown sugar, packed
1/2 c. white wine vinegar (option: apple cider vinegar)
1 tsp. sweet paprika
1 tsp. hot paprika
1 tsp. ras el hanout
2 tsp. kosher salt (or to taste)
1 tsp. fresh ground black pepper (or to taste)

Add all the step 2 ingredients to a 6 1/2 quart Dutch oven (or a large Crock-Pot). Mix well, and bring the mixture to a boil. Place the brisket from step 1 on top of the sauce, fat side up. Cover, reduce the heat to low, and simmer for about 10 minutes. Baste the top of the brisket with the sauce while simmering.

Place a rack in the bottom position of the oven, and heat the oven to 275 degrees Fahrenheit. Transfer the Dutch oven to the oven, and cook for about 4 hours until the brisket is tender. About halfway through the cooking time, turn the brisket over in the sauce.

If you plan to use a Crock-Pot, start the cooking on high heat, then reduce the heat to low about halfway through the cooking time when you turn over the brisket. You may need more cooking time with a Crock-Pot at the low heat setting, so monitor the tenderness of the brisket and adjust accordingly.

Step 3: Finish

1/2 c. flat-leaf parsley, chopped
kosher salt, to taste
ground black pepper, to taste

When the brisket is cooked, transfer it to a cutting board, tent with foil, and let stand for about 15 minutes.

While the brisket is resting, skim any fat or scum from the surface of the sauce in the Dutch oven. If the sauce is too thin, reduce it over medium heat on the cooktop until it is the desired consistency. If the sauce is too thick, add additional beef stock or water until it is the desired consistency, and heat over medium-low heat on the cooktop.

Slice the brisket against the grain. To serve family-style, place the slices on a platter, ladle some of the sauce over the slices, and transfer the remainder of the sauce to a bowl for serving at the table. The brisket can be accompanied by Eastern European side dishes of vegetables for a traditional spring Passover season dinner.

*Stock

Master Chef Auguste Escoffier says in his epic treatise *The Escoffier* on the fine art of French cuisine: "Stock is everything in cooking. Without it, nothing can be done. The cook mindful of success, therefore, will naturally direct his attention to the faultless preparation of his stock."

A great stock is judged by five criteria: flavor, clarity, color, body, and aroma. An excellent modern reference for preparing stock can be found in chapter 1 of *The Elements of Cooking* by Michael Ruhlman. If you prefer to use a commercially available stock product, the boxed Swanson brand or Kitchen Basics brand are good choices, but not as good as homemade stock.

PART 3

The Evolving Adult

CHAPTER 10

Sharing the Thrill of Fine Dining

In my later teen years, a new obsession arose in me, the attraction to the fairer sex. In that regard, I assume I was no different from any other teenage boy. Also, the hometown dating scene was probably not much different than any other community in America. There were movies, weekend dances with a DJ in high school gymnasiums, see-and-be-seen venues, such as high school sporting events or amusement parks, the beach at Presque Isle State Park in the summer, and tobogganing in the winter. The dating format could be a committed couple going steady or two pairs double-dating or, more often, a larger group of friends with about equal numbers of boys and girls. In all cases, there were some common activities. First, there was usually some time allotted to food, such as pizza shops, sit-down hamburger and french-fry places, or drive-in locations where food was delivered to your car by waitresses on roller skates. Second, the more serious dating couples retired to serene spots overlooking Presque Isle Bay or Lake Erie for some window-fogging necking, which was euphemistically referred to as "watching the submarine races." For the most part, I went with the flow in the local dating scene. However, there were occasional dating activities that offered a more interesting twist. A round of golf at a public course appealed to some girls. There were some public stables where horse riding on rural trails was an option. I even recall going to a public target range to shoot .22 caliber rifles, which some girls found exciting. In my quest to impress my dates with a memorable event, I initiated another activity that was unique among my peer group: fine dining. The synergy of fine dining in the company of the fairer sex linked two of my passions into an almost overwhelming sensual delight. I found and repeatedly used a venue that satisfied my requirements for gourmet food, ambiance, and sophistication. This was a rare combination in my hometown.

The name of the restaurant was Antoun's Supper Club. Even the name evoked a feeling of class. The place was a large home that had been converted into a restaurant. It was set back an appropriate distance from a city street in a rectangular lot, with a short drive-way through manicured grounds to a small number of parking spots. Reservations were required. The girls wore dresses and pumps; and I usually wore an open-collar light-blue button-down shirt, a blue blazer, gray slacks, and Bass Weegun loafers. To enter the restaurant, you walked up a short flight of steps to the front door, where you were greeted by a hostess. She escorted you to your table, which was comfortably spaced with a few other tables in what used to be the living room, great room, or dining room of the home. The tables were dressed in linen, silver, crystal, and fresh flowers. The menu for the restaurant featured an interesting selection of continental cuisine and a wine list which I was unaccustomed to seeing on a menu in any other eating places I frequented as a teen. I remember a waiter (I'll call him Jacques) who was a very polite middle-aged man dressed in semiformal livery. Jacques was very helpful with menu selection, and he treated my dates with deference as if he were a coconspirator in my effort to impress. The multicourse meals (appetizer, salad or soup, entrée with sides, and dessert) were well-prepared, beautifully plated, and presented with élan by Jacques. They were the best dinners I had experienced up to this point in my life. With a couple of exceptions, my dates probably felt the same way. Let me expand on a couple of exceptions.

During one dinner, when my date was served the entrée of tournedos of beef, Jacques asked, "Will you be needing anything else?" He may have been expecting a request for a Béarnaise or a Bordelaise sauce, but I'm sure he wasn't expecting my date's response. She asked for ketchup! I was probably more surprised and embar-rassed than Jacques, but he kept a straight face and replied, "Of course, mademoiselle." I never asked the girl for another date. I don't think I was being a snob, but I concluded we didn't have enough in common.

Another time, my date ordered tagliatelle bolognese. The restaurant emphasized in the menu that this was an authentic recipe from Bologna, Italy, with Italian veal in the rich, creamy Bolognese sauce and the obligatory tagliatelle pasta made fresh in-house. I could tell by the look on her face when the dish was presented that she was confused. She tasted the dish, tried politely to push it around on her plate, but didn't eat much. I think she had expected spaghetti with ground beef in a red tomato sauce. The veal in the Bolognese sauce was too light for her, and the fresh tagliatelle pasta was too wide. In this case, the girl didn't want to go out with me again. I guess she concluded we didn't have enough in common.

Aside from these exceptions, fine dining at Antoun's Supper Club with a date was a thrill. Not only did the girls enjoy the unique experience but I also heard that they bragged to their friends about the adult aspect of the dinners. I wish I could have enjoyed the experience more often, but it was not something a teenager could afford on a regular basis. These fine dining events set a benchmark as my obsession with great food expanded later in my life.

CHAPTER 11

Dining with the Big Bands

The big band era is generally thought of as 1935 to 1945. However, vestiges of the big bands were still touring for another fifteen years. Some bands still carried their brand names from the earlier era, such as Artie Shaw, Benny Goodman, Jimmy Dorsey, Woody Herman, and Les Brown; but obviously, the band leaders and musicians were not the originals. Other bands such as Stan Kenton and Count Basie came on the scene later but still played big band music. Swing, jazz, standards, and dance music were the repertoire. I recall in the summers of my late teens these touring bands would come to Erie for a weekend gig. They played at a venue called Rainbow Gardens, which was a cavernous nondescript hall that was used for concerts, wedding receptions, and conventions. The demographics for these big band concerts were older couples who had lived as young couples in the primary big band era, and middle-aged couples who enjoyed socializing with friends while being entertained by the big band style of music. A much smaller group of attendees were people of my age. We considered the big band concerts at Rainbow Gardens primarily as another unusual dating opportunity and secondarily as training to be adults.

The hall was configured with the bandstand in the back, a dance floor in front of the band, and folding tables and chairs in the rest of the space. The tables were set up with a tablecloth, a bucket of ice, and plastic cups. Attendees brought their own beverages and food, like a fancy evening picnic. People arrived well before showtime with their picnic baskets to socialize, eat, and drink. For the most part, men wore ties and coats, and women wore party dresses and shoes suitable for dancing. Let me address some details regarding beverages and food.

The preparation of tables by the adults covered the spectrum from very simple (paper plates, plastic flatware, sandwiches, and mixed drinks) to elaborate (stoneware, metal flatware, an occasional candelabra, a catered menu, and wine). We youngsters generally tried to emulate the adults, but on the simpler side of the spectrum. Regarding beverages, our attempt to be grown-ups included the consumption of alcoholic beverages in moderation. At age eighteen, we were too young by law to purchase or consume alcoholic beverages in the state of Pennsylvania. However, New York state was just thirty miles to the east, and there the legal age to purchase or consume alcoholic beverages was eighteen years old. It may seem scandalous to some, but we used to drive to the New York state border, purchase alcoholic beverages, and return to consume them at Rainbow Gardens. No one of our age seemed to prefer wine, and beer did not seem suitable for the venue, so we brought spirits and mixers. The young girls cautiously sampled cocktails of Seagram's 7 and 7-Up or Southern Comfort and orange juice, but they mostly just drank Coca-Cola over ice. Regarding our food, there wasn't much interest in gourmet dishes, so we were satisfied with deli sandwiches, McDonald's burgers, or chilled shrimp with cocktail sauce. I may have been the exception with regard to food selection, and I experimented with bringing out-of-the-ordinary dishes. For one concert, I brought a pâté I had made, accompanied by a baguette. I recall that my friends were lukewarm to the dish, but some middle-aged adults at a nearby table were curious, bold enough to ask for a sample, and they devoured it. I have attached a recipe at the end of this chapter for a Pâté de Maison I enjoy.

The fine dining at Antoun's Supper Club and the big band concerts were life-changing events as I evolved into an adult. Like the quest of Don Quixote, I would continue to seek the company of an attractive woman, the aroma and taste of great food, and the beautiful sound of virtuoso music. I wanted more of these experiences to saturate my senses with sensual pleasure.

Pâtés are a versatile dish. They can be served as an elegant appetizer with croûtes, hard toasted French bread. They are also fine to have on hand for an impromptu meal since all you need to serve with them are a salad, French bread, and wine. There are nearly countless mixtures and techniques for pâté. In his encyclopedic book *The Escoffier Cookbook and Guide to the Fine Art of Cookery*, Chef Auguste Escoffier addresses hundreds of variations for pâtés, terrines, and galantines. In its most basic form, a pâté consists of a mixture of force meat (pureed meat), fat, and seasonings molded and slow-cooked in a bain-marie (hot water bath). The following recipe offers a basic, simple pâté of the house to satisfy both picnickers and epicures. If you like this, you may be motivated to delve into other variations for pâtés, terrines, and galantines. Bon appétit!

Pâté de Maison
(Pâté of the House)

Preparation: 12+ hours
Cooking: 1 1/4 hours
Serves: 6

Step 1: Marinate forcemeat

> 1 lb. chicken livers, sinews removed (option: duck liver, turkey liver, rabbit liver, other fowl/game livers, or a combination of these)
> 1/2 tsp. tinted curing mix, TCM (option: pink Himalayan salt)
> 1 pt. buttermilk (option: whole milk)

Remove any connective tissue from the livers, and rinse in cold water. Pat dry. Spread the livers in one layer in a casserole dish. Sprinkle the TCM or salt onto the livers. Add the buttermilk to cover the livers, using more buttermilk if required. Cover, refrigerate, and soak for at least 12 hours. Turn the livers occasionally to marinate uniformly. When ready, remove the livers, drain them on paper towels, and set them aside. Discard the marinade.

Step 2: Sauté aromatics

> 1/4 c. unsalted butter
> 1/2 c. brown onion, chopped
> 1/4 c. shallot, chopped
> 1 tbsp. garlic, chopped
> 1/4 c. brandy

Melt the butter in a 10-inch sauté pan over medium heat. Add the onion and cook for about 5 minutes until the onion is wilted. Add the shallot and garlic, and cook another 2 minutes until the garlic is fragrant. Add the brandy to deglaze the pan, and reduce until most of the liquid is evaporated, stirring to collect all the fond in the pan. Remove the pan from the heat and allow it to cool to room temperature.

Step 3: Blanch bacon

> 1 qt. water
> 10 slices thick-cut applewood smoked bacon

While the aromatics are cooling, bring the water to a boil over medium-high heat in a 12-inch sauté pan. Add the bacon to the pan. Blanch for about 5 minutes to eliminate the excessive salt and smoke flavor from the bacon. Remove the blanched bacon, and drain on paper towels. Chop four of the bacon slices into 1/4-inch pieces, and set them aside for use in step 4. Leave six bacon slices intact, and set aside for use in step 5.

Step 4: Mix

2 large eggs
2 tbsp. bread crumbs, finely ground
2 tbsp. all-purpose flour
2 tbsp. fresh flat-leaf parsley, minced (option: 2 tsp. dried)
1 tbsp. fresh tarragon, minced (option: 1 tsp. dried)
1 tbsp. fresh chervil, minced (option: 1 tsp. dried)
1 tbsp. fresh sage, minced (option: 1 tsp. dried)
1 tsp. kosher salt (or to taste)
1/2 tsp. fresh ground black pepper (or to taste)
1/4 tsp. ground allspice
1/4 tsp. ground nutmeg
1 tsp. Dijon mustard
1 tsp. truffle flavored oil
1 tbsp. fresh squeezed lemon juice
2 tbsp. dry sherry (fino or amontillado preferred)
1/4 c. heavy cream

Set up a food processor with a sharp blade attachment. Add the livers from step 1. Add the aromatics from step 2. Add the chopped bacon slices from step 3. Add all the ingredients listed above in step 4. Process the mixture until it is uniformly smooth. Use a spatula to scrape the sides of the food processor into the purée to assure a uniformly smooth mixture. If desired, you can press the mixture through a coarse wire-mesh strainer into a bowl, but this technique is not essential.

Step 5: Finish

2 mini loaf pans, 3 × 6 × 2 inches (about 10-oz. capacity)
1 roasting pan, 9 × 13 inches and at least 2 1/2 inches deep
        (option: 5-qt. soup pot)
Roasting rack to fit into the bottom of the roasting pan

Preheat the oven to 350 degrees Fahrenheit, and position a rack in the center portion of the oven.

Line the bottom and ends of the mini loaf pans with 2 whole bacon slices each from step 3. Spoon the mixture from step 4 into the loaf pans. Lightly compress the mixture with a spatula while filling to eliminate air pockets and to fill the loaf pans to within a 1/4 inch from the top. Cut the remaining bacon strips in half and cover the top of the mixture. Seal the top of the loaf pans tightly with a piece of aluminum foil.

Place the filled and sealed loaf pans on the rack in the roasting pan. Fill the pan with enough hot water to reach about 1/2 inch from the top of the loaf pans. If desired, you can place two other loaf pans filled about halfway with water on top of the loaf pans in the bath to further compress them and keep them from moving in the bath.

Place the water bath in the oven. Cook for about one hour or until the internal temperature of the pâté is 160 degrees Fahrenheit. When finished, remove the loaf pans from the water bath, and allow them to cool to room temperature for about 30 minutes.

Refrigerate overnight. To serve, remove the aluminum foil and the bacon from the top. Invert on a serving plate. Remove and discard the bacon that was lining the loaf pan. Slice and serve with crusty French bread or croûtes.

Pâtés will keep for up to two weeks refrigerated, but do not freeze as they will lose their smooth texture.

PART 4

Fine Dining
Put on Hold

CHAPTER 12

College Life

The focus in the next five years of my life, late teens, and early twenties were a college education and military training. I was on my own in the big world. They were exciting years with a number of noteworthy events, but they were sorely lacking in fine dining or gourmet food preparation. Family gatherings with a cornucopia of fine food were in the past. Neighborhood experiences with a sampling of interesting dishes from the families of my friends were just a memory. I was definitely in an eat-to-live phase of life.

As a freshman at Penn State University, I lived in a dormitory. Cooking was not allowed in the dorms. Not even immersion heaters were allowed, although nearly everyone used one to make a hot drink or a cup of soup. There were vending machines in the common rooms of the dorms, and it seemed that some students lived on chips, candy bars, and cans of soda. There was a cafeteria in the quad surrounded by the dorms of North Halls, but it was just standard cafeteria food. The protein served in the dinner meal was often called mystery meat. Nothing was memorable. Penn State was located in the center of the town of State College, Pennsylvania. Like many other college towns, State College provided the products and services that catered to the university and very little of anything else. Eating in the community consisted of fast-food places, pizza shops, takeout sandwiches, and bar food served with a beer at many local watering holes. I recall one venue that served fine food, and that was the restaurant at the Nittany Lion Inn. However, diner at the inn was an unusual event that occurred when parents made their occasional trips to the campus to visit their sons or daughters, or to attend a sporting event. I could probably count on one hand the number of times I dined at the Nittany Lion Inn.

In my sophomore year at Penn State, I joined the Kappa Sigma fraternity and moved into the off-campus fraternity house. The camaraderie with the brothers and the fraternity social life was a marked improvement over dormitory life, but there was no commensurate improvement in food quality. The chapter had a contract with a catering company that prepared meals for the house, which was a common practice for most other fraternity houses. It may have been a cut above the cafeteria food served to students in the dormitories. The meal service was a combination of buffet-style food and sit-down dinners served family-style. The food was sufficient in quantity and adequate in quality, but it was not noteworthy. As an example, we had a routine sit-down dinner on Friday that consisted of spaghetti with a tomato-based ground meat ragù, a salad, bread, and ice cream for dessert. We also tapped a keg of beer with the Friday meal that initiated the social activities for the weekend.

Later on, I moved into an apartment with one of the brothers from the fraternity, although we remained social members of Kappa Sigma. The reason for this change is beyond the scope of this story, but the change did result in the need for food preparation in the apartment kitchen. The meals we prepared were simple and repetitive. Breakfast was never much more than cereal with milk. Lunch, if we ate in the apartment, was cold-cut sandwiches with minimum garnish or canned soup. Dinner might have been an inexpensive slab of pan-fried beef, chicken, or pork, Rice-a-Roni, and a frozen vegetable if we felt ambitious. We probably ate dinner out at a fast-food venue, a pizza place, a takeout submarine sandwich shop, or on high stools at the counter at a bar as often as we ate in the apartment. My roommate was the antithesis of a foodie, and he probably would have been satisfied to wolf down canned and packaged processed food on a regular basis. So I did most of the market shopping and food preparation while we lived in the apartment, but I am not the least bit proud of my less-than-plebian culinary efforts. If my relatives from my youth could have seen my pathetic food preparation, I would have been disowned by the family! This period was no doubt the low point of my civilian culinary life.

CHAPTER 13

Start of a Career in the United States Marine Corps

I joined the United States Marine Corps in 1964, and I was designated a Naval Aviator in December 1966 after about two years of flight training. Needless to say, the focus during this period was intensive training and indoctrination into the culture of the Marine Corps. From a culinary perspective, this was a continuation of the eat-to-live status. Food at the mess halls was cafeteria-style, eaten from a metal tray. A common breakfast dish was ground beef in white gravy served on a piece of toast and known by all as "s——t on a shingle." Food at the Officers' Clubs was either bar food or from a short menu in the sit-down dining room. There was always a sufficient quantity of food, but the quality and service at the Officers' Clubs were better than the mess halls. However, even at the Officers' Clubs, I would rate the menus and food preparation as good but definitely not a fine dining experience.

While living in the Bachelor Officers' Quarters during flight training, the opportunities to drive into town for dining or entertainment were limited. Some of the air bases were located some distance from the nearest towns, such as Meridian, Mississippi, or Beeville, Texas, and these small towns did not offer a selection of fine dining venues. I recall an episode that was a new culinary experience for me, even if it wasn't fine dining. While in training at Pensacola, Florida, I went to a Mexican restaurant with a couple of my classmates. This was my first experience with Mexican food. Chips and salsa were a novelty. I was unfamiliar with the menu offerings such as chile rellenos or fajitas, so I relied on my friends to explain the menu selections. I enjoyed my first experience with Mexican cuisine, and it is still a frequent part of my culinary repertoire.

Many people consider Mexican food to be repetitive and average, but later in life, I was introduced to Chef Diana Kennedy and her expertise with interior Mexican cuisine, which is definitely not average. If there is a class of gourmet Mexican food, I would contend that it is some of the interior Mexican food described by Chef Kennedy in her book *The Essential Cuisines of Mexico*. Chef Kennedy has helped me to evolve beyond common tacos and enchiladas. I have attached a unique recipe at the end of this chapter that is my variation on one of Chef Kennedy's recipes.

The day my naval aviator wings were pinned on was the second most important day of my life. Earning my wings was a major milestone that marked the end of the development phase of my life and the beginning of the prime of life phase. What followed changed everything, including the reawakening of fine dining experiences. The culinary passion that had been lying dormant for a number of years was returning.

This entrée pairs turkey with mole, a picante sauce used in the cuisine of interior Mexico. The word *mole* comes from the Nahuatl Indian word *molli*, meaning "concoction," There are many stories attached to the origins of mole, but most agree that mole was born in the convents of Pueblo de los Ángeles. It is a savory sauce that goes well with flavorful meat such as turkey or wild game. Enjoy!

Turkey Mole
(Guajolote en Mole)

Preparation: 30 minutes
Cooking: 1 hour
Serves: 4

Step 1: Poach the turkey

> 4 turkey thighs, bone-in (option: pieces of duck, chicken, or
>   pork)
> 3 c. *salted water (or as required to poach the turkey)
> 1 small yellow onion, quartered with outer skin
> 1 stalk celery, coarsely chopped, with leaves
> 1 medium carrot, coarsely chopped
> 1 medium dried guajillo chili pepper
> 1 medium dried ancho chili pepper
> 1 bay leaf
> 6 whole black peppercorns

Place the turkey in a 5-quart pot or flameproof casserole with a lid. Add enough salted water to barely cover the meat. Add the onion, celery, carrot, dried peppers, bay leaf, and pepper corns to the casserole. Bring to a boil, then reduce heat to a simmer and poach covered for about one hour. Drain, reserving the strained liquid as turkey stock. Discard the solids. Skim the fat from the stock after it cools. The stock can be used in step 2 in a mole recipe that can be found in interior Mexican cookbooks or online. Dry the turkey thighs with paper towels, and set them aside.

Step 2: Brown and bake

    2 c. mole sauce, a quantity for 4 servings
    2 tbsp. vegetable oil (option: peanut oil)
    1 tsp. kosher salt (or to taste)
    1/2 tsp. ground black pepper (or to taste)

Preheat the oven to 275 degrees Fahrenheit.

Make the mole sauce using an authentic recipe of your choice and the turkey stock reserved from step 1. Set aside.

Heat the vegetable oil in the casserole over medium-high heat on the cooktop. Remove the skin and any remaining surface fat from the poached turkey. Salt and pepper the turkey to taste. Place the turkey thighs in the casserole and brown them, turning frequently for even color. Remove the casserole from heat.

Pour the mole sauce over the turkey. Turn the pieces to coat them with the sauce. Cover the casserole and place it in the oven. Cook for about 30 minutes, taking care not to let the sauce burn. If necessary, turn and arrange the turkey pieces for even coating and cooking.

Step 3: Finish

    2 tbsp. sesame seeds
    4 sprigs of fresh cilantro for garnish

When finished, serve the turkey covered with the mole sauce. Sprinkle with sesame seeds, and garnish with sprigs of cilantro.

*Salted Water

For cooking any type of pasta or vegetable, salted water translates to a 1 percent salt solution: about 1 1/2 teaspoons of salt in one quart of water.

PART 5

Raising the Bar

Newlyweds at Home

The most important day of my life followed one month after the second most important. The date was January 7, 1967. On that day, Donna Lee Pyle and I wed.

In quick sequence, I pinned on my naval aviator wings, married Donna Lee (whom I will henceforth refer to as DL), honeymooned in New York City, and traveled to Marine Corps Air Station Cherry Point, North Carolina, for duty. While we were waiting for a home to become available in government housing at Cherry Point, we temporarily rented a furnished apartment on the shore overlooking Bogue Sound in Morehead City, North Carolina. What a scenic setting for newlyweds! I could hardly believe my situation: I was a commissioned officer in the Marine Corps, living on the waterfront with a beautiful woman, driving a Corvette, and flying high-performance jet aircraft. Every evening when I returned home from work, we shared a romantic meal for two by candlelight and afterward cuddled in the warmth of the fireplace in the living room. DL did the cooking on weekdays, and I followed my father's protocol of cooking on weekends. Occasionally, we went into Morehead City for a seafood dinner at one of the many nice seafood restaurants that served both the local populace and the tourist trade. Seafood dinners here raised the bar from any of my previous seafood experiences.

DL's cooking style was based on her western Pennsylvania upbringing and her Irish, Scottish, and Eastern European ethnicity. She is a good cook. I recall an episode when she wanted to surprise me with spaghetti and tomato-based ground beef sugo dinner, which was outside her normal inventory of recipes. I arrived home from work, walked into the house, kissed her hello, and was overwhelmed by the aroma of garlic in the kitchen. I complemented her on making an Italian dinner for us, and I tactfully asked to see the recipe she was using. As I recall, DL was using the *Better Homes & Garden Cookbook*. The recipe called for three cloves of garlic, which could not account for the strong garlic aroma. I asked her, "Did you follow the recipe?" She replied, "Yes," but admitted she did not have enough garlic for the recipe. DL said that she only had two cloves, not the three cloves the recipe called for. When I looked in the pantry, I found that the two bulbs of garlic I had purchased at the market were gone. Upon further questioning, I discovered that DL was confused by the term "clove of garlic" and "garlic bulb." She had used two full bulbs, not three cloves of garlic! To avoid a newlywed confrontation, we ate the meal and accepted the aberration as a lesson learned. I probably pitted out my flight suit with garlic-scented sweat for the next two days! The recipe faux pas did not discourage DL, and I am so glad that she still cooks.

CHAPTER 15

Seafood Awakening

Our proximity to North Carolina's Outer Banks and Pamlico Sound provided an abundance of fresh seafood. Commercial fishing was a major business for Morehead City and nearby Beaufort. Additionally, the local restaurants and seafood markets seemed to have access to a profusion of briny products from Maine to Florida. We dined on some items that neither one of us had ever eaten, such as blue crab and varieties of eastern oysters, including Bluepoint, Wellfleet, and Pemaquid. Blue crabs were so prolific that we could catch a bucket of crabs in fewer than thirty minutes at the marina on the base at Cherry Point simply using chicken bones on strings and a long-handled fishnet. Fresh crabs made an unusual dinner feast. The crabs were boiled in a large stockpot. The table was covered with multiple layers of newspaper and set with shell cracking utensils, bowls of drawn butter, and a roll of paper towels. As the shell debris accumulated on the table, it was rolled up in a layer of newspaper, discarded, and we proceeded to the next batch of crabs on the next layer of newspaper. Oyster bars also abounded along the seashore drive from Atlantic Beach to Emerald Isle. DL was not too fond of raw oysters, so I ate my share and her share too whenever they were in season. In my hierarchy of favorite foods, seafood moved to the top of my list, and it is still a protein I favor with fine dining.

At this point in my culinary development, I recall having a conversation with a friend who was an aspiring foodie like me. He asked the theoretical question, "If someone put a gun to your head and said you could only eat one type of protein for the rest of your life, what would it be?" I responded, "Seafood." My pendulum of preferences had swung to an extreme. In my youth, the pendulum was on the opposite side of its arc, because I was served seafood irregularly, and what I was served was definitely not quality seafood. I was raised in a Catholic family, and the religious custom was to eat fish on Friday. In northwest Pennsylvania in the 1950s, the availability of fresh, high-quality seafood products was extremely limited. To make the situation worse, my father did not like seafood. As a result, our Friday seafood dinners were for the most part packaged, frozen, breaded fish sticks. They were tasteless and were served with ketchup or tartar sauce to make them marginally edible. After the Catholic Church changed the rules about fish on Friday, seafood all but disappeared from the family menu. The seafood awakening in my young adulthood in North Carolina was an epic change.

The techniques and ethnic variations for seafood dishes are nearly limitless. Bouillabaisse, Veracruz style red snapper, and smoked salmon are a few examples of my favorites. I also enjoy some simple comfort dishes, such as Southern-style fried catfish fillets, which are routinely accompanied with tartar sauce. I have attached a recipe at the end of this chapter that I believe elevates ubiquitous tartar sauce from mundane to gourmet.

Tartar sauce is a nice accompaniment to dishes such as Southern-style fried catfish fillets. However, commercial tartar sauce can be too Mayonnaise-forward, soupy, and bland. This tartar sauce recipe will not disappoint you. It can stand up to Southern-style fried catfish fillets and other similar dishes. My recipe is below. Enjoy!

Tartar Sauce (Enhanced)

Preparation: 10 minutes
Cooking: None
Serves: 2–4

2 tbsp. mayonnaise (Hellmann's brand preferred)
2 tbsp. sweet pickled cucumber relish
1 tsp. fresh squeezed lemon juice
1 tsp. prepared horseradish (Reese's brand preferred)
1 tsp. nonpareil capers, minced (Mezzetta brand preferred)
1 dash Tabasco pepper sauce (McIlhenny brand preferred)
1 pinch Chesapeake Bay seafood seasoning (McCormick brand preferred)
1 pinch kosher salt, or to taste

Combine all ingredients in a mixing bowl. Stir to mix thoroughly. Cover and refrigerate until ready to serve.

CHAPTER 16

Young Adults and the Social Scene

When a residence became available at Cherry Point, DL and I moved from our apartment in Morehead City to junior officer housing on base. We were now in a community occupied primarily by young couples like us. The men were physically fit, fire-breathing Marine Aviation warriors. New sports cars or high-performance autos lined the curbs. The wives were beautiful young women, and I recall one social event where three of the women present were former Miss America contestants: Miss Texas, Miss Pennsylvania, and Miss Ohio. The camaraderie and sense of identity were significantly more intense than the Kappa Sigma fraternity days at Penn State or at any other time in my life.

The entertainment facilities at Cherry Point revolved around the Officers' Club, the base movie theater, the base marina for boating and water sports, and some parks for family picnics or group functions. The small town of Havelock outside the main gate had limited facilities such as family restaurants, a movie theater, a department store, and a surprising number of furniture stores. Furniture production and sales were important businesses in North Carolina. Gourmet food or fine dining did not fit the demographics of Cherry Point or Havelock.

The junior officer community spawned its own social life. There were bridge clubs, poker groups, and occasional day trips to area attractions such as historic Revolutionary War residences in New Bern, beaches between Cape Lookout and Cape Hatteras, and Civil War forts. There were also frequent dinners for small groups in someone's home. In many cases, the dinners were interesting because the hosts who came from all parts of the country prepared their regional specialties. People from Southern California prepared their version of Mexican food, which differed from the Mexican food prepared by people from New Mexico or Texas. I found that the term *barbecue* took on a different meaning for both the type of meat and the type of sauce depending on the host's place of origin: Kansas, Texas, or South Carolina. The Cajun or Creole cuisine prepared by folks from Louisiana was a marked contrast to the classic clambake by folks from New England. In retrospect, I am still amazed at the variety and quality of meals prepared by the young adults in our social circle. I suspect that some of the fine-dining efforts were fostered by the inherent competitive spirit in the young Marine couples.

This period was the embryonic start of my efforts as a cook, or as I prefer to be described as, a culinarian. I purchased some fundamental kitchen equipment: a chef's knife, cutting board, high-quality pots and pans, and a small collection of good cookbooks. I experimented with a variety of cooking techniques from dry-hot grilling to slow-wet braising. I found that I was good with sauces, soups, and stews, but I was not very proficient with pastries and desserts. I also realized that I enjoyed preparing the food as much as I did consuming it. When everything came together for a dinner menu to share privately with DL or with a group of friends, I glowed from within.

CHAPTER 17

Let the Travel Begin

At the beginning of 1968, I received orders assigning me to a squadron in Vietnam. I would be gone for thirteen months. DL would remain in Cherry Point, and she took a job teaching Spanish at Havelock High School. We decided to celebrate with a one-week vacation prior to my departure. Mexico City was our destination. We stayed at the Continental Hilton Hotel in the heart of Mexico City on the Paseo de la Reforma. Although we filled our schedule with sightseeing and fine dining, the most memorable aspect of the trip was our arrival at the Mexico City airport. We collected our bags and exited the terminal to find transportation to our hotel. The moment we exited, a very distinguished-looking gentleman said "Hello" and asked where we were going. We told him we had reservations at the Continental Hilton, but we were cautious about dealing with the stranger. Fortunately, DL was fluent in Spanish, so there was no misunderstanding of his intent. He introduced himself as the minister for the 1968 Summer Olympics in Mexico City and offered us a ride to the hotel. We were still cautious. Soon, a black Mercedes limousine arrived at the curb, and the driver dressed in a black jacket and cap quickly opened the rear door for the minister. Our bags were loaded, and we climbed in beside the minister. On the drive to the hotel, he asked us if we planned to see the bullfights as part of our sightseeing. We said yes, and he said he would send his driver to the hotel later with complimentary tickets for us. The tickets were shady-side seats about four rows up from the arena railing. What a fortuitous surprise! It set the tone for the rest of the vacation. In addition to this unexpected social encounter, I recall two dining experiences that left their mark.

One night, we ordered a Caesar salad to be prepared tableside. The waiter wheeled out his cart with ingredients and equipment. With considerable showmanship, he prepared the salad while offering descriptive dialogue. He informed us with an aura of pride that the Caesar salad was invented in Mexico. If you thought it was an Italian recipe, you would be half right. Credit for the Caesar salad is given to Caesar Cardini, an Italian immigrant who was a restauranteur in Mexico. We have ordered tableside Caesar salad many times since then. On another night, we ordered soup as one of the dinner courses. We were intrigued by the soup's name, Caldo Tlalpeño. The version we ate that night was delicious, but a tad too spicy for our palate, even though DL and I like spicy food. At home after the vacation in Mexico City, I tried replicating the recipe with modifications, toning down the spice level to suit our taste. At the end of this chapter, I have attached my recipe for Caldo Tlalpeño for those who may want to try this flavorful soup with an unusual name.

About halfway through my thirteen-month tour of duty in Vietnam, I was authorized five days of rest and recuperation, known as R and R. DL and I arranged to meet in Hawaii. We decided to go first class, so we made reservations at the Royal Hawaiian Hotel on Waikiki Beach. The Royal Hawaiian was a classic prestigious hotel, sometimes referred to as the Pink Palace, and it was unlike any of the modern high-rise hotels on Waikiki. This was another precedent for us to travel with truly first-class accommodations, service, and dining. As an aside, while we were there, we literally bumped into two famous couples on the dance floor who were also staying at the Royal Hawaiian: General William Westmoreland and Admiral Ulysses S. Sharp. They looked at us, me with my Marine Corps haircut and Vietnam tan and DL glowing with youthful beauty, and probably deduced we were a couple on R and R. Westmoreland smiled at us and gave us a head nod. I felt proud to think that I was a lowly Marine first lieutenant hobnobbing at the Royal Hawaiian with the senior general from Vietnam.

The meals at the Royal Hawaiian were the best I had ever had up to this point in my life. Of course, my judgment was probably biased by the fact I had been eating mess hall food and canned rations for six months. Still, breakfast, lunch, and dinner were spectacular. Dinner in particular would almost bring tears to my eyes. The ambiance of the dining room, the linens, the multiple settings of stemware and silverware, the white-glove service, and the exquisitely plated presentations were world-class. This was the type of dining we both wanted to experience for the rest of our lives.

One afternoon, we were relaxing on chaise lounges on the private beach at the Royal Hawaiian. We looked at other Royal Hawaiian guests on the beach and concluded we were the youngest couple there. We were young, fit, and full of life and love. Without condescension or disrespect, most of the other couples seemed old (probably only middle-aged), fleshy, and pasty white. DL and I guessed that maybe they were people from mid-America who saved for years for a dream vacation to Hawaii. DL and I made a lovers' vow at that point. We agreed that we would take a vacation outside the continental USA every year. Jumping ahead to the present, we have kept that vow, with one or two exceptions such as the COVID-19 travel restrictions. We discovered that international travel also had the benefit of experiencing the different cuisines of the world.

I would be remiss if I did not mention a dinner we had on R and R in Hawaii. One night, we went to the highly-rated restaurant at the Kahala Hilton Hotel just north of Diamondhead. Although I do not remember all the details, we opted to have a French dinner. Two details still reside in my memory. I recall the assistance of our French-accented waiter in the description and selection of our courses for the meal. I recall the assistance of the sommelier for the selection of the wines to pair with the meal. The entrée was Chateaubriand for two, perfectly prepared medium rare, and presented with élan to the standard of a Michelin star restaurant. It was the first time we ordered Chateaubriand. The wine was a 1961 Bordeaux, and I vividly remember the vintage from the wine list because the wine cost as much as the dinner, although I do not recall the producer. It was the first time we drank a Bordeaux wine. This dinner went to the top of my list as the best dinner I ever had to this point in my life.

At the end of my R and R, I went back to the squadron in Vietnam. DL went back to Havelock. We would not see each other again for six months, but we set the precedent for travel and unique dining that have been key features of our life together since our first grand experience in Hawaii.

Caldo Tlalpeño is a traditional soup from interior Mexico. The name Caldo Tlalpeño indicates the soup originated in the Tlalpan area of Mexico City. Variations of this soup existed in Mesoamerica dating back to the fifteenth and sixteenth centuries. The most popular story for the origin of the name Caldo Tlalpeño dates back to the nineteenth century and the president of Mexico, Antonio López de Santa Ana. Santa Ana awoke in Tlalpan with a terrible hangover after a rambunctious celebration of the festival of San Agustín de las Cuevas. He asked his cook to prepare something to reinvigorate him, so she made a chicken soup with vegetables, epazote, and chipotle. Santa Ana asked the cook for the name of the soup, and she responded, "Caldo Tlalpeño." The dish is always made with chicken and chicken stock, but the vegetable selection is optional and may vary depending on the cook. However, epazote and chipotle peppers are key ingredients in this soup, so be sure to include them. Enjoy!

Caldo Tlalpeño
(Soup of the Tlalpan Area)

Preparation: 30 minutes
Cooking: 45 minutes
Serves: 6

Step 1: Chicken

1 lb. chicken meat: skinless, boneless, shredded

When making your Caldo, you can make preparation easier by cooking the chicken ahead of time. You can use roast chicken. Or you can use a slow cooker, pressure cooker, or stockpot to cook the chicken while simultaneously making chicken stock. In any case, shred the cooked light and dark chicken meat and set it aside.

Step 2: Aromatics

> 1 tbsp. vegetable oil
> 1 large yellow onion, chopped
> 1 large poblano pepper, seeded and chopped (option: Anaheim pepper)
> 1/2 c. celery, chopped (optional)
> 1/2 c. baby carrot, thinly sliced (optional)
> 2 medium garlic cloves, minced

Heat the oil in a 10-inch skillet over medium-high heat. Add the onion and pepper (and the optional celery and carrot, if using), and sauté for about 6 minutes until lightly browned, stirring frequently. Add the garlic, and sauté another minute until the garlic is fragrant. Remove from the heat, and set aside.

Step 3: Puree

> 1 c. *tomato concassé (option: canned diced tomatoes)
> 2 medium canned chipotle peppers in adobo sauce
> 1 tsp. ground cumin
> 1 tsp. ground coriander
> 1 tsp. achiote annatto condiment
> 1 tsp. salt
> 1/2 tsp. fresh ground black pepper
> 2 c. **chicken stock

Add all step 3 ingredients to a blender or food processor. Puree until smooth. Transfer the mixture to a 3 1/2 quart soup pot or Dutch oven.

Step 4: Soup base

  4 c. **chicken stock
  1 15.5 oz. can garbanzo beans, drained and rinsed (option:
        black beans)
  8 oz. corn kernels, cut off the cob (option: canned, drained,
        and rinsed)
  8 oz. green beans, chopped into bite-size pieces (optional)
  1/2 c. fresh epazote, chopped and loosely packed
  1/2 c. fresh cilantro, chopped and loosely packed
  1/2 c. fresh oregano, chopped and loosely packed
  1 tbsp. fresh squeezed lime juice
  salt, to taste
  fresh ground black pepper, to taste

Add all the step 4 ingredients to the pot from step 3. Add the aromatics set aside in step 2. Add the shredded chicken set aside in step 1. Bring the soup to a low boil over medium-high heat, then reduce the heat to medium-low and simmer for about 20 minutes until the beans are tender and the herbs are wilted. Adjust seasonings to taste. Stir occasionally.

Step 5: Finish

  1 medium avocado, cubed
  1/2 c. queso fresco, crumbled (option: shredded Mexican
        blend cheese)
  1/2 c. fresh cilantro, chopped (optional)
  1/2 c. corn tortilla chips, crumbled (optional)
  1/2 c. Crema Mexicana (optional)
  6 wedges fresh lime (optional)
  6 small radishes, sliced (optional)

Ladle the soup into six bowls. Serve the step 5 ingredients in separate small bowls at the table so that the soup can be individually garnished to taste.

*Tomato Concassé

Cut an X in the bottom of each tomato. Blanch the tomatoes in a pot of boiling water for 30 seconds. Using a slotted spoon, transfer the tomatoes to an ice water bath to cool. When cool, drain. Remove the stems and peel off the skin starting from the X. Cut tomatoes in half lengthwise. Remove and discard the core and the seeds. Coarsely chop the tomato.

**Stock

Master Chef Auguste Escoffier says in his epic treatise *The Escoffier* on the fine art of French cuisine: "Stock is everything in cooking. Without it, nothing can be done. The cook mindful of success, therefore, will naturally direct his attention to the faultless preparation of his stock."

A great stock is judged by five criteria: flavor, clarity, color, body, and aroma. An excellent modern reference for preparing stock can be found in chapter 1 of *The Elements of Cooking* by Michael Ruhlman. If you prefer to use a commercially available stock product, the boxed Swanson brand or Kitchen Basics brand are good choices but not as good as homemade stock.

CHAPTER 18

Second Honeymoon

I returned from Vietnam in early 1969, none the worse for wear. For various reasons, I was authorized about a one-month delay en route before I had to report to my new assignment at Cherry Point. DL and I arranged to meet at the Disneyland Hotel in California. Needless to say, we were both very excited about our reunion. We had only lived together for a year before I went to Vietnam for a year, so we were ready to restart married life. The restart was a monthlong second honeymoon.

Both of us had noticeably changed after one year of separation. My war experiences had put me in a constant state of yellow alert, with my head on a swivel. DL had become more independent after a year of managing the household, our finances, and some of the daily routine that had been my job. However, one thing that did not change was our mutual enjoyment of fine dining. In fact, we shared an elevated sense of pleasure dining together after a year of separation. The memory of our Hawaii R and R experience gave us a goal to replicate.

Starting at the Disneyland Hotel, we spent about five days exploring Southern California. Then we went to San Francisco for about five days. Las Vegas was next for about another five days. DL and I had never been to any of these destinations, so we covered the high points like tourists on a travelogue binge. We also dined as though the cost was not an issue. We were amazed at the number of great restaurants in San Francisco, and we were pleasantly surprised that Las Vegas hid some fine restaurants in the midst of countless eat-to-live buffets and fast-food venues catering to gamblers. We sought out gourmet dinners in Southern California, San Francisco, and Las Vegas, and for two weeks plus we had an uninterrupted nightly sequence of spectacular meals in beautiful venues with world-class service. We would not experience such a concentrated period of fine dining like this again until later in life when we traveled for two or three weeks at a time on luxury cruise ships.

We traveled from Las Vegas to my parents' home in Erie, where we planned to spend a week. When we arrived, my mother was nearly in tears thanking God that I had returned in one piece. She also had planned a backyard "Welcome Home" party with all my aunts, uncles, and cousins. From a food perspective, it was a flashback to my youth, where large family gatherings always brought out the best in the amateur chefs. My aunts with their customary expertise prepared mounds of tempting dishes. As Yogi Berra famously once said, "It's déjà vu all over again." We ate, drank, and conversed from noon to sunset. My father and most of my uncles were World War II veterans, so they were interested in the scope of my combat experience. The uncles who had fought the Japanese wanted to compare the Pacific island campaigns to the jungles of Vietnam. Of all the cousins, I was the only one who served in Vietnam, and they viewed me with a measure of awe and respect. I did not mind talking about Vietnam, but I have to admit I was more interested in reliving the family food of my youth. I had not eaten classic authentic Italian food in some time, so I relished every morsel.

Many of these family dishes were gourmet restaurant quality, and just as many more were delicious unpretentious comfort food. I have attached a recipe at the end of this chapter that is in the comfort food category. It is analogous to mac and cheese with an Italian flair.

The second course in a classic multi-course Italian meal is called the primo piatto, literally the first plate main dish which is the starch course of the meal. It is traditionally pasta or risotto, depending on the theme of the dinner. The following recipe could be used as a primo piatto in a classic Italian dinner, or as an individual gratin dish for lunch. In either case, it is ultimate comfort food, head-and-shoulders above ordinary mac and cheese. The baked combination of cream and five Italian cheeses give an authentic Florentine character to the dish. Buon appetito!

Baked Penne with Five Cheeses
(Penne e Cinque Formaggi al Forno)

Preparation: 15 minutes
Cooking: 20 minutes
Serves: 4–6

Step 1: Penne

> 4 qt. *salted water
> 12 oz. penne (about 2 oz. per person)

Bring the salted water to boil in a 5-quart pot over medium-high heat. Add the pasta, return to a full boil, and cook for about 10 minutes until just shy of al dente. Drain the pasta, and set it aside.

Step 2:

> 1 c. **panna da cucina
> 1 c. ***tomato concassé
> 1/4 c. freshly grated Pecorino Romano, loosely packed
> 1/4 c. coarsely shredded Fontina, loosely packed
> 1/4 c. crumbled gorgonzola, loosely packed
> 1/4 c. fresh mozzarella, shredded, loosely packed
> 1/4 c. ricotta
> 1/4 c. fresh basil leaves, chopped, loosely packed
> Kosher salt, to taste
> Fresh ground black pepper, to taste

In a large bowl, mix together all the step 2 ingredients until thoroughly combined. Take care in adding salt and pepper because the cheeses are naturally salty. Taste the mixture, stir, and taste again to season properly to taste. Add the pasta to the bowl, and toss until the pasta is coated and the cheese mixture is evenly distributed.

Step 3: Finish

> 4 tbsp. unsalted butter
> 2 tbsp. finely grated Parmesan

Preheat the oven to 425 degrees Fahrenheit with a rack in the middle of the oven.

I offer two serving options to finish the dish. For family-style dining, use a 1 1/2-quart baking dish that holds all the pasta and cheese. Or you can divide the pasta and cheese into 4–6 individual gratin dishes. In either case, gently pack the mixture into the dish or dishes, then dot with butter on top, and sprinkle the top with Parmesan.

Bake in the oven until the cheese is bubbling and the top starts to brown, about 10 minutes. Serve immediately.

*Salted Water

For cooking any type of pasta or vegetable, salted water translates to a 1 percent salt solution: about 1 1/2 teaspoons of salt in one quart of water, or 10 grams in one liter.

**Panna da Cucina

This is Italian cream for cooking. It's less fatty than heavy cream and is not as sweet as heavy cream. It does not whip well, but it is an essential ingredient in cream sauces. If you can't find authentic Italian commercial panna da cucina, use this substitute: by volume, 1/2 half-and-half, and 1/2 low-fat sour cream (or low-fat Greek yogurt).

***Tomato Concassé

Cut an X in the bottom of each tomato. Blanch the tomatoes in a pot of boiling water for 30 seconds. Using a slotted spoon, transfer the tomatoes to an ice water bath to cool. When cool, drain. Remove the stems and peel off the skin starting from the X. Cut tomatoes in half lengthwise. Remove and discard the core and the seeds. Coarsely chop the tomato.

CHAPTER 19

Return to Cherry Point

After a month of delay en route, DL and I finally arrived at Cherry Point. I was back in the cockpit again, only this time I was not a rookie. I was a combat veteran training the rookies. At the rank of captain, I had a billet in the squadron with more responsibility than before. However, DL and I were still assigned to junior officer government housing. In fact, the home we were assigned was on the same street about eight houses from the home we occupied in 1967. The environment seemed unchanged from our previous tour of duty at Cherry Point. The base was still the same. The town outside the gate was the same. The neighborhood looked the same: physically fit men, attractive wives, and hot cars. Fortunately, the quality of seafood in the local area was also the same, which was most welcome to me. I easily reverted to a higher frequency of seafood products in our dinner menus. How could I resist blue crab, oysters, and mixed seafood grill?

Besides my combat experience, there was another major difference between this tour of duty at Cherry Point and the previous. I was much more attuned to food preparation as an art. My sensory bank was filled with the sight, aroma, and taste of exquisitely prepared, and sometimes novel fine dining that I had experienced over the last few years. I was driven to replicate some of the experiences, and I learned some important introductory lessons. Probably the most important lesson was that you have to start with the best ingredients at the peak of freshness and flavor and never settle for the second best. "You can't make a silk purse out of a sow's ear." Another lesson was that recipes are simply guidelines, and the preparation of fine food requires instinct and taste rather than exact measurements. It is crucial to continually taste as you proceed. I also learned the three principles of French presentation for a dish: variety in color, volume (i.e., height), and mixes of texture. A lesson that was more difficult to quantify is conveyed in a quote from James Beard: "The secret of good cooking is first, having a love of it. If you are convinced cooking is drudgery, you're never going to be good at it." Over time, countless other lessons have been etched into my gray matter as I evolved to higher levels of amateur expertise.

As I became more ambitious in either replicating past meals or experimenting with ideas of my own, I added more tools to my kitchen. Tools do not have any magic to cook fine food, but they make it easier to prepare fine food. Some of the tools I added were a food processor, stand mixer, blender and, one of my favorites, the hand immersion blender. Other useful hand tools were brought into the fray, such as chinois, tongs, fish spatula, rolling pin, and others. As a novice culinarian, I felt I had enough kitchen equipment to tackle just about any food preparation task.

There was one dining event at Cherry Point that I recall because of its unique aspects. There was a civilian contractor technical representative assigned to the squadron to assist with any unusual technical issues arising in the maintenance of the aircraft. The tech rep was from the Long Island, New York, facility of the aircraft manufacturer. He was a first-generation Italian American. He was stereotypically Neapolitan—short, stocky, swarthy, animated, and gregarious. He invited about twelve of us junior-grade officers to his home for a Sunday dinner. It was a classic Italian family four-hour Sunday feast. We started with cold antipasti then hot antipasti. Soup was next. The pasta dish that followed was the dish I remember. It was a tomato-based ragù, simmered for hours with whole pork chops until the meat was fork-tender and seasoned with a balanced dose of traditional Italian herbs. It was served on a bed of linguine. There were also other courses of grilled chicken, salad, and dessert, but the memorable course was the pork chop ragù. As we were consuming this feast, the tech rep's wife was busy in the kitchen preparing each course and delivering it family-style to our group of appreciative young Marine pilots; and of course, the wine was flowing freely. At one point, I asked the tech rep when his wife would join us, and he said, "Oh, she doesn't eat with the men. She'll eat on her own in the kitchen." It reminded me of the scene in the movie *The Godfather Part II*, where the youthful Vito, Clemenza, and Tessio were eating spaghetti in Vito's apartment while they plotted against the neighborhood mobster, Don Fanucci. Vito's wife stayed in the kitchen preparing the food. The quality of the tech rep's feast rivaled my childhood memories of the weekend family meal, but the isolation of the women was not the case in my father's or mother's families, although this custom may have been normal in some Neapolitan or Sicilian families.

CHAPTER 20

Wine Is Food

From my earliest memories up to my young adulthood, I was captivated by the sensual pleasure of fine food. Although wine may have been served with meals, the wine was in the shadows from my youthful perspective as I focused on the characteristics of the food itself: presentation, aroma, taste, and texture. When I became old enough to order wine with a meal, my appreciation of wine peeked out of the shadows and gradually became equally important to the food. The milestone event that shifted my appreciation of wine into high gear was probably the 1961 Bordeaux that DL and I shared on R and R in Hawaii. From that point on, I started paying attention to wine selection as an integral part of fine dining.

Wine, tea, and coffee are beverages ubiquitous to mankind throughout history, culture, and geography. But of these, wine is unique. We may think of wine as only a beverage to please the senses, but wine transcends the attributes of tea, coffee, and all other beverages. I believe wine is food, and I contend that many experts of culinary Western culture would agree with me. Think of all the encyclopedic documentation on pairing wine with various foods and menu items. The concept of ideal wine and food pairings has evolved into both an art and science for professional chefs and sommeliers. Why? Because wine is food. Chefs strive for balance in the preparation of gourmet food, which is akin to the complex characteristics by which wine is judged: fruit, acid, sugar, floral, alcohol, tannins, color, and viscosity, to name a few. Let me offer a simple example: you probably would prefer a Bordelaise sauce instead of ketchup to enhance a filet mignon, and you would probably prefer a Bordeaux wine instead of a glass of water with the steak. The steak, the sauce, and the wine are complementary foods that create a superb culinary experience. The French, Italians, and Spanish have recognized this concept for centuries, where wine is an integral ingredient with the same status as all the other ingredients in the dish and not just an ancillary liquid to "wet the whistle." To consider wine as food can elevate eating to dining.

In my formative years living at home with my parents, I recall the standard greeting when family or friends came to visit. After the hugs or handshakes, the first question asked was, "Would you like a cup of coffee?" But if the visit also included dinner, no one asked, "Would you like wine?" The guests may be asked, "Would you like water with dinner?" It was understood that wine was always served with the dinner, but water was optional. In my youth, I never thought about this dinner format. It was just the normal routine. Later in life, in retrospect, I realized that wine was food. Now, more than ever, I realize that fine wine is gourmet food.

Humans have made wine for about eight thousand years, although scholarly wine experts may pontificate about the details. Don't obsess with the details. The fact is we have been enjoying wine unabated for centuries. The biblical record in Psalms 104:15 states, "Wine maketh glad the heart of man." During the reign of the first Roman emperor, Augustus, the famous poet Horace wrote, "Wine is life" and "Wine brings to light the hidden secrets of the soul." Regardless of your religious beliefs, let's not forget the first miracle attributed to Jesus Christ in the Gospel of John 2:1–2, changing water to wine at a marriage celebration in Cana. In the Renaissance era, the astronomer Galileo theorized, "Wine is sunlight, held together by water." Michael Broadbent, English master of wine, opined, "Drinking good wine with good food in good company is one of life's most civilized pleasures." As a final reference on the topic of wine as food, I offer an excerpt from an article by Gael Greene, restaurant critic for *New York* magazine: "I had to cook a dinner glorious enough to complement the Lafite-Rothschild Bordeaux wine. It took four days."

On a personal note, I recall my young adult daughter once ask me, "Dad, when did you become so interested in wine?" I thought about her question and dredged from my memory a story my mother told. I was her firstborn. Upon release from the hospital after my birth, my mother took me to her parents to show them their new grandson. My grandfather, who made his own wine, dipped his finger in a tumbler of wine he was drinking and offered it to me to suckle. My mother said I liked it. So at three days old, I started a lifetime of enjoyment of fine wine. Over time, that sensory pleasure augmented the enjoyment of gourmet food. Today, my passion for gourmet food, including wine as food, has evolved into one of life's greatest pleasures.

PART 6

Highlights of the First Career

CHAPTER 21

Formal Events

The military profession is noted for its discipline, ritual, and tradition. Of all the services in the United States military, the Marine Corps is arguably the most steeped in these characteristics. There are numerous clichés and expressions used by Marines to demonstrate their camaraderie and esprit de corps. Whenever two Marines meet, the standard greeting is, "Semper Fi," a commitment to be always faithful. Another dogmatic belief is, "Once a Marine, always a Marine." One of my favorites is heard at the birthday celebration for the Marine Corps every November 10 commemorating the birth of the Marine Corps in 1775, "Two hundred forty-five years of tradition [insert the current age] unhampered by progress." The annual celebration of the Marine Corps' birthday is the most important formal ceremony for Marines. Second only to the Marine Corps birthday, a periodic formal event called mess night is another ceremony for members of a specific unit—for example, a battalion or a squadron. Attendees wear their most formal dress uniforms with appropriate accessories. A rigid protocol is followed in accordance with chapter 24 of Marine Corps Drill and Ceremonies Manual MCO P5060.20. The entrée is always prime rib, paraded through the dining room and presented to the presiding officer, known as the President of the Mess. Port wine and cigars are enjoyed after dessert at the conclusion of the formalities. A variation of mess night is called Dining-Out. Dining-Out follows all the protocols of a mess night, but spouses and guests are authorized to attend. DL loved Dining Out events.

They gave her the infrequent opportunity to wear a long formal gown, her finest jewelry, and a salon coiffure. They also gave the Officers' Club kitchen staff the grand opportunity to procure the highest quality food products, demonstrate their culinary expertise, and prepare a multicourse meal served by white-jacketed attendants. For meat lovers, the large slices of FDA Prime grade prime rib were a tasty sight to behold. The formality and ritual of a Dining-Out event were difficult to replicate in any other life experience.

CHAPTER 22

Living in Japan

In the mid-1970s, I received orders for a tour of duty in Okinawa, Japan. The orders were designated as "unaccompanied," which meant that the orders did not cover expenses for bringing my wife and six-year-old daughter with me. The orders did not restrict my family from accompanying me, but I would have to bear all expenses for their travel, housing, and subsistence. We did not want another extended family separation, so we decided to incur the costs. I traveled to Okinawa as ordered, and as soon as I arrived there, I started looking for an apartment. I leased a place in the indigenous community of Yamzato, on Jagaru Road, about three miles from where I would be working at Marine Corps Air Station Futenma. I also bought a used car from a Marine who was departing Okinawa as I was arriving. It was an old Toyota that had who knows how many previous owners, and we named it Rusty Red. DL and Alison followed me to Okinawa shortly thereafter.

For those not familiar with the living accommodations of the Japanese middle class, I will give a brief description of our apartment. It was small. Everything seemed proportionately smaller than what a Westerner may consider normal. There were two bedrooms, and they were no bigger than eight feet by ten feet. The floors of the bedrooms were about three-inch-thick tatami fiber mats. There were no beds; we would be sleeping Japanese-style with futons and contoured pillows on the tatami. There were no walk-in closets, just a clothes hanging bar and some shelves along one wall. The interior walls of the bedrooms were sliding wood and paper screens that opened the bedrooms to the living area. The bathroom was literally a bathing room: walls fully covered with ceramic tile, the floor was also ceramic tile sloping to a drain in the center of the room, a hand-held shower head on a hose on one wall, a sink on the opposite wall, and a one-person sit tub on the back wall. The toilet was in a separate closet-size room, about three feet by five feet, and thankfully equipped with a western-type toilet, not a slit trench in the floor you squatted over like in some public areas. I came to accept the bathroom and toilet room concept as clean, efficient, and civilized. The living area and the kitchen were open spaces, separated only by a waist-high counter. The kitchen had a half-size refrigerator, probably no more than ten or twelve cubic feet capacity. The stove had four small burners and an oven sized for one chicken, an oven powered by propane. The sink was small with one well. Propane also powered the tankless on-demand hot water system. The Japanese were ahead of the time with tankless hot water. There was limited shelf space in the kitchen for storage, but no cabinets or pantry. I was concerned that the kitchen was going to be a challenge for meal preparation, but I reasoned that if Japanese families could do it so could we.

The family in one of the houses next door to our apartment had a girl about our daughter's age. Her name was Yumi Chan. Alison and Yumi Chan struck up a friendship, and when they were not in school, they would play together in front of our homes. Neither one spoke the other's language, but that did not stop the play. They jumped rope and mimicked each other's rope jumping chants without understanding the words of the chants. They also played a game that we call rock paper scissors, but in Japan, it is called Janken. The hand gestures and rules were the same. The origin of the game was in the Han Dynasty in China in about 200 BCE.

An interesting dining event occurred with Yumi Chan. The girls were playing in our apartment while I was preparing a simple dinner of Irish stew: beef, potatoes, onions, and carrots in a thickened sauce. DL had set three place settings of bowls, napkins, forks, and spoons on the kitchen counter where we normally sat on three barstools to eat our dinner. DL tried to interrupt the girls' play to send Yumi

Chan home, so DL got her English-Japanese dictionary and found the word for "dinnertime," which she spoke to Yumi Chan. The young girl answered DL with "Hai" (yes), and then she went into our bathroom to wash her feet, hands, and face. After cleaning herself, she climbed up on one of the barstools, DL's barstool, and waited to be served dinner. This series of events took us by surprise, so Alison and I sat with Yumi Chan, and DL was forced with good humor to stand and watch the dinner. We saw that the spoon and the fork were a puzzle to Yumi Chan, but she adapted and held them in one hand like chopsticks. She also seemed curious about the contents of the Irish stew as she picked up and examined the pieces. Still holding the English-Japanese dictionary, DL tried to describe the pieces. In one instance, Yumi Chan lifted a slice of carrot, and DL said, "Ninjin."

Yumi Chan looked at DL and said "Hai, hai," which I am sure was her polite way to say, "Yes, yes, of course, it's a carrot."

As we were finishing our dinner, we heard a loud call from her mother next door: "Yumi Chan! Yumi Chan!" Our impromptu guest climbed down from the barstool, bowed, and ran home. I suspect she had an interesting story to tell her mother.

My duties at Futenma included flying a two-engine transport aircraft, the C-117. We carried Marines and supplies to units deployed in the Pacific Rim from the Philippines to northern Japan. On return trips to Futenma after our cargo had been unloaded, we often brought back personal items that we had purchased. Although not entirely legal, the authorities turned a blind eye to these activities, so I used the opportunity to furnish our apartment. In the Philippines, I bought some rattan furniture: a papa-san chair, a princess chair, four barstools, and a coffee table. In Korea, I bought futons for the bedrooms, a number of large pillows for the living area, and for the kitchen: aluminum pots and pans, reusable plastic place settings, and stamped flatware. Probably the most useful appliance I acquired was an automatic rice cooker. We did not have a television in the apartment, but I purchased some good quality audio equipment in Japan: tuner/amplifier, open reel tape deck, turntable, and speakers. In no time at all, we were comfortable in the apartment.

Food shopping was an adventure. There was a large commissary (military supermarket) at Kadena Air Base, where we shopped about once a week. Supplying the market with off-shore Western food products caused some peculiarities, for example, all the meat was frozen. The selection of fresh vegetables and fruit was limited. Frozen and canned foods were readily available. In addition to the commissary, there was an indigenous farmers market with open stalls of locally grown produce within walking distance of our apartment. Like the shopping habits of the local Japanese, we shopped there almost daily. However, we were warned to wash all local produce in a light solution of bleach for health reasons. Health concerns aside, the produce was fresh and flavorful. We tried some items from the farmers market that were new to us, including crosnes (Japanese artichoke), black radish, daikon radish, kabocha squash, pointed cabbage, and some leafy greens that were a mystery. We also shopped at small seafood markets and roadside seafood stands. The variety and abundance of fresh seafood were incredible, as you would expect from a small island nation. One of the issues that upset DL was the lack of dairy products. The Japanese do not eat milk, cream, butter, or cheese, so although we could buy frozen dairy products from the commissary at Kadena, none was available in the local economy. DL shed a tear or two after she first arrived when she did not have a dollop of cream to put in her coffee. She finally settled for evaporated canned milk.

We frequently ate out. There were a few small family-style restaurants on Jagaru Road in Yamzato. One of our favorites was close-by, and we called it the Green Awning because it did not have an English name on the marquee, and there was a green awning over the entrance. You entered, took off your shoes, placed them in a shoe hive just inside the entrance, and were then taken to a table. The tabletop was fifteen inches above the floor, but there was a deep step in the floor below the edge of the table. There were no chairs, so you sat on the floor with your legs below the table and made yourself comfortable with cushions. The menu did not have any English translations, but fortunately, there were photos of the menu offerings. We would point to the photos, the waitress would say, "Hai" (yes), and we would respond, "Arigato" (thanks). Of course, there was no flatware, so we used hashi (chopsticks). The food was consistently good and surprisingly inexpensive. My six-year-old daughter, Alison, instantly fell in love with all types of Japanese food and became very proficient with hashi. She frequently ordered Sukiyaki, which is ubiquitous throughout Japan, and I have included a recipe at the end of this chapter which is my version of this common comfort food.

There were other local family restaurants we frequented. Some specialized in teppanyaki (meat and vegetables grilled on a metal plate) and shabu-shabu (meat and vegetables self-cooked piece-by-piece at the table in boiling water surrounding a brazier). We also developed a habit of eating at the Kadena Officers' Club on Friday. The format we enjoyed was a buffet-style happy hour with a prolific selection of Japanese delicacies. The tempura vegetables and the variety of sushi were our favorites.

We occasionally made the short drive to Naja, the largest city in Okinawa. I recall two memorable meals, although I do not recall the names of the restaurants. The first was a restaurant that specialized in Kobe beef. The meat was a relatively rare delicacy valued for its flavor and tenderness and governed by some strict production rules. It was very expensive, and it seemed that only the upper-class Japanese and Westerners frequented the restaurant. This was my first experience with Kobe beef. The second experience was a restaurant with the reputation for employing the best certified chef of sashimi, bite-sized pieces of raw fish eaten with dipping sauces. I was served a platter of sashimi that rivaled in beauty the stained-glass Rose Window of Notre Dame de Paris. The different colors of the fish, the intricate cuts, and the precise symmetry were a work of art. Oriented around the top of the platter were five small bowls of dipping sauces. In addition to the beautifully plated sashimi, the waitress placed a centerpiece on the table in traditional Japanese minimalist style: a single stemless rose in a clear shallow bowl with a couple of drops of water sprinkled on the petals simulating dew. I probably sat and stared at the presentation for minutes before I finally had the courage to desecrate the beauty of the platter. This dish was the most spectacular presentation I had ever been served in my life.

PREFACE

When we lived in Japan, our family was introduced to a savory soup dish. The term comfort food might have been coined for this ubiquitous bowl of rich, home-style broth filled with thinly cut beef, noodles, and a selection of Japanese vegetables. The traditional accompaniment of beaten egg makes a silky dipping sauce. Enjoy!

Sukiyaki

Preparation: 30 minutes
Cooking: 45 minutes
Serves: 4

Step 1: Prepare the beef

1 lb. beef top sirloin
2 tbsp. canola oil (option: vegetable oil)

Wrap beef in plastic wrap and freeze until firm but not frozen solid, about 30 minutes. This will assist with thinly slicing the beef. Remove and discard the plastic wrap. Slice beef across the grain with a sharp knife into very thin slices, less than 1/8-inch thick. Place the slices in one layer on a platter, cover with plastic wrap, and allow to warm to room temperature for about 15 minutes.

Heat the oil in a deep 3 1/2 quart pot over medium-high heat. Add the beef and cook for about four minutes, stirring frequently, until the beef strips are medium rare. Transfer the beef to paper towels to drain, and set aside.

Step 2: Prepare the noodles

> 2 qt. water
> 4 oz. rice vermicelli noodles (option: cellophane mung-bean
>   vermicelli)

Clean the 3 1/2 quart pot from step 1. Bring the water to a boil over high heat. Add the noodles, and cook for about three minutes. Using a slotted spoon or a spider, transfer the noodles to a colander. Rinse with cold water, and set aside. Remove the pot from the heat, and retain the water for use in step 3.

Step 3: Prepare the greens

> 2 oz. kombu (dried Japanese seaweed), cut with scissors into
>   1/2 × 2-in. strips
> 4 oz. napa cabbage, cored and cut crosswise into 2-in. strips
> 4 oz. mizuna (Japanese mustard greens), cut into 2-in. pieces,
>   or watercress

Kombu can be purchased at Asian markets. Soak the kombu in the water in the 3 1/2 quart pot from step 2 for about 15 minutes. Then bring the pot to a simmer over low heat, and cook covered for another 15 minutes.

Add the cabbage and mizuna to the pot, cover, bring to a low boil over medium heat, and cook for about 5 minutes. Drain the greens in a colander, and set them aside.

Step 4: Sauté vegetables

> 1 tbsp. canola oil (option: vegetable oil)
> 4 oz. ninjin (Japanese carrots), thinly sliced diagonally
> 4 oz. negi (Japanese leeks), cut diagonally in 1-in. pieces
>   (option: 1 bunch scallions, white and pale green parts
>   only)
> 2 stalks celery, cut into thin crescents

2 oz. fresh enoki mushrooms, spongy root ends trimmed
2 oz. fresh shitake mushrooms: discard stems, cut caps in 1/4
   inch slices

Heat the oil in a 12-inch sauté pan over medium-high heat. Add the step 4 vegetables. Cook for 4 to 6 minutes until the vegetables have softened, stirring frequently. Remove from the heat and set aside.

Step 5: Finish

4 cups dashi (option: miso/mushroom broth or vegetable
   stock)
1/2 c. soy sauce, or to taste
1/2 c. mirin, or to taste
1 tsp. sugar, or to taste
4 oz. firm tofu, halved lengthwise and cut into 1/4-inch slices
4 large eggs

Clean the 3 1/2 quart pot used in steps 1, 2, and 3. Combine the dashi, soy sauce, mirin, and sugar in the pot. Dashi with various flavor profiles can be purchased at Asian markets. Bring the mixture to a low boil over medium heat, then reduce the heat to low. Add the tofu slices. Then add the vegetables from step 4, and allow the pot to return to a simmer. Then add the greens from step 3, and allow the pot to return to a simmer. Then add the noodles from step 2, and allow the pot to return to a simmer. Then add the beef from step 1. Add additional dashi or water to achieve the desired soup consistency. Cover, and simmer for about 5 minutes.

While the sukiyaki is simmering, beat the eggs, one egg for each person being served, and transfer the beaten eggs into individual dipping bowls. If desired, other optional dipping sauces can be offered in individual bowls, such as wasabi, sweet and sour, and sticky plum.

Ladle the hot sukiyaki into four shallow soup bowls, and serve immediately.

Caution: eating raw eggs could be a health hazard.

CHAPTER 23

Environs of Monterey Bay

I was fortunate to be assigned a tour of duty at the Naval Postgraduate School in Monterey, California, for advanced degree studies. This was definitely an enviable duty assignment. The Monterey area was idyllically beautiful, and people visit there as tourists, honeymooners, golfers, wine aficionados, and maritime enthusiasts. Although I was a full-time postgraduate student in the Aerospace Engineering Department, DL and I found extracurricular time to enjoy the coast from Paso Robles to San Francisco.

The Naval Postgraduate School was, and still is, a beautiful campus. The headquarters building on the campus is the old Hotel Del Monte. In its heyday from 1880 to 1942, the Hotel Del Monte was one of the finest luxury hotels in North America. It had a colorful history with notable guests who were business moguls, movie stars, and foreign dignitaries. Jean Harlow is reputed to have scandalized the clientele by swimming naked in the hotel's outdoor pool. The building and grounds were leased to the United States Navy in 1942. The building was renamed Herrmann Hall, and it was reconfigured with administrative offices, living quarters, restaurants, bars, shops providing various services, a chapel, and the glamorous Barbara McNitt Ballroom. The ballroom was an ornate architectural masterpiece with ten thousand square feet of floor space, which was the venue for many social events such as the annual formal Sea Service Ball and an annual variety show where students from twenty-six countries who were attending the Naval Postgraduate School put on acts that showcased their individual cultures.

With daily classes, evening study, and working in the laboratory on my experimental thesis, I was too busy to perform daily meal preparation at home. Fortunately, DL is a good cook, and we have very similar tastes and preferences. DL is also the queen of table setup to match with the meal: tablecloth, napkins, table runner, table centerpiece, seasonal decorations, china, crystal, silverware, and candles. So DL handled most of the weekday cooking, and I contributed on weekends. Even with my busy student schedule, I still had to have my valued time in the kitchen or I would have gone into culinary withdrawal. To say that we ate well in our home would be an understatement. We had access to fresh seafood and produce because of Monterey's geographic location. Monterey Bay supported the commercial fishing industry, and one of the principal products was squid. I frequently went to Fisherman's Wharf with an empty two-gallon bucket in the evening when the ships docked, and I would fill the bucket with freshly caught squid at a ridiculously low price. We made squid steaks by splitting the larger squid bodies, squid rings for Genovese-style fried calamari or seafood stews, and we used the tentacles in either the fried calamari or in a red tomato sauce with pasta. Another geographic advantage was the proximity to Salinas, California, which is one of the most prolific agricultural areas in the state. We would periodically make the short drive to Salinas, visit the farmers market, and bring home a crate filled with fresh seasonal produce that cost about $5. Salinas also offered a number of unpretentious but excellent family-owned Mexican restaurants that catered to the Mexican field workers and also to the tourists and locals looking for authentic Mexican comfort food.

We infrequently dined at the restaurant in Herrmann Hall. It was a good restaurant, but it was not a competitive dining experience with the number of great restaurants in Big Sur, Carmel, Pacific Grove, Monterey, and Seaside.

The Nepenthe restaurant in Big Sur has been described as "a view with a restaurant." Perched on the cliff eight hundred feet above the Pacific Ocean, the restaurant arguably has one of the best views of any restaurant in the world. The menu features California, Greek, and Mediterranean dishes prepared from locally grown food. I will admit that no matter how much you try to focus on the beautifully presented excellent food, your attention is inevitably drawn away from the meal to the view. I suggest that Nepenthe is a bucket list experience.

Carmel is a quaint town. There are no buildings higher than two stories. The residents tend to be affluent and private. Clint Eastwood was once the mayor. Carmel is the gateway to the exclusive seventeen-mile drive and to the famous golf courses of Pebble Beach, Spyglass Hill, and Spanish Bay. Carmel's charming ambiance appeals to tourists and honeymooners looking for a relaxing, laid-back destination. I offer without proof my contention that Carmel probably has more fine dining boutique restaurants per capita than any other town in the United States. During busy times when DL and I wanted to decompress, to feel prosperous and pampered, we dined at any cozy, chic bistro in Carmel, and we were never disappointed. I recall one night we went to dinner with a couple to one of those cozy, upscale restaurants in Carmel. I do not recall the specifics of the dinner except for one event. After the entrée was delivered to the table, the waiter asked if the lady would like some shaved truffles to top her dish. She said yes, and the waiter shaved a few small slices of black winter truffle on her dish. He paused, looked at her, and she nodded that she would like a few more shavings. The waiter obliged. When we finished the dinner, and the waiter presented the bill, our friend was flabbergasted at the additional charge for the truffles. Winter black truffles cost over $500 per pound, and her few shavings of truffle cost more than her dinner entrée! It was a good lesson for me on the rare and luxurious nature of truffles. If money was no object, an overnight stay or at least a spectacular dinner at the Highlands Inn on Highland Drive in Carmel offered the luxury of a secluded hotel with a stunning view of the Pacific Ocean, but be judicious when you ask for truffle shavings!

Pacific Grove is a community west of Monterey and north of Carmel, at the south end of the crescent-shaped Monterey Bay. The city is famous for the annual migration of monarch butterflies and its

Victorian homes. It is endowed with more Victorian homes per capita than anywhere else in the United States, and some of them have been turned into stately bed-and-breakfast inns. I recall one that had been transformed into a Michelin star fine dining restaurant called Maison Bergerac. The family Bergerac visually and gastronomically transported their guests to France for an evening. Madame Bergerac managed the front of the house, and Chef Monsieur Bergerac performed his magic in the kitchen. Their adult son and daughter served the tables. Reservations were required and needed to be made six months in advance. The venue seemed popular with gourmet clientele from San Francisco, about two hours north. DL called in November to schedule a reservation for my birthday celebration in April. There was no ostentatious signage to identify Maison Bergerac as a restaurant, just a discreet plaque above the front door of the classic Victorian building. To enter Maison Bergerac, you rang the doorbell at the entrance. Madame Bergerac greeted you and escorted you to your table, where she presented you a scroll wrapped in a ribbon describing the menu for the evening, a prix fixe dinner consisting of seven courses in the French banquet sequence. I do not recall the entire menu, but I do remember some unforgettable items. The third course, which was seafood, was Coquilles Saint-Jacques au Brouilly (scallops with a red wine sauce), and I had never before had scallops in a red wine sauce. The fourth course was a palate cleanser, and I was served a grapefruit sorbet for this intermède. I had never before had a palate cleanser between courses. The fifth course was a meat entrée, and I was served sliced medium-rare tenderloin of wild boar with a silky-smooth Bordelaise demi-glace. The boar was accompanied by fondante potatoes. I had never before had wild boar or fondante potatoes. The wine served with the entrée was Châteauneuf-du-Pape, a Southern Rhone blend. The sixth course was a salad, céleri-rave rémoulade (celery root with remoulade dressing). I had never before had a celery root salad. All these items were new to my dining experience and fomented an intense memory. The food, ambiance, and service rank this meal in my all-time top three dining experiences. Also, the Châteauneuf-du-Pape vaulted to the top of my list of favorite wines. After my birthday celebration at Maison Bergerac in April,

DL called to schedule another meal there, but unfortunately, they were booked beyond September, when I was scheduled to graduate from the Naval Postgraduate School.

Monterey held its own with quality restaurants in comparison with its neighboring communities. The area around Fisherman's Wharf and the marina offered a number of good choices. The area around the Sardine Factory, made famous in John Steinbeck's novel, was equally good. The only issue I had with those venues was the tourist crowd, where the hustle and bustle detracted from the overall dining experience. However, DL and I were never at a loss to find a nice, more private spur-of-the-moment restaurant nearby our home.

With a modicum of humility, let me address a cooking competition I entered. The Monterey Fairgrounds advertised a Chili Cook-Off one year. I decided to compete. I practiced at home with various ingredients and techniques until I developed a recipe that I thought would be competitive. To my surprise, I won! I have attached my winning recipe, Chili del Rey, at the end of this chapter. I still make this recipe every year in January when we invite friends to our home to watch the college football bowl games. Be forewarned, it is a labor of love.

Monterey County started to emerge as a successful wine region in the 1960s. DL and I enjoyed visiting some of the new, aspiring wineries. Three, in particular, were frequent destinations for us, and two of them were in Carmel Valley. Chateau Julien was a beautiful facility modeled after a generic French chateau. The place was so idyllic that it was a popular venue for wedding receptions. The lodge at Bernardus Winery was a modern-rustic building with an open-beamed ceiling and a huge fireplace where DL and I would relax by the hearth with a glass of Bernardus Cabernet Sauvignon. Heller Winery was also an up-and-coming winery at the time. The vineyards in the area were planted on warm, east-facing hilly benches and ridges, which were prime locations for Cabernet Sauvignon and Merlot grapes. If you want to try a California wine from other than Napa or Sonoma, look to Monterey County's Santa Lucia Highlands. It is a small but mighty winegrowing appellation that cultivates arguably California's best Pinot Noir and Chardonnay.

DL and I have fond memories of the years we spent in the Monterey environs. We have occasionally returned for a weekend vacation and to visit friends who decided to retire there. It is one of the most beautiful and hospitable parts of California. Find out for yourself.

I entered a chili cook-off held at the Fairgrounds in Monterey, California, in 1979. I was fortunate to have my submission, Chili del Rey, judged the winner of the competition. It's not a recipe for anyone who wants instant gratification. This recipe is a labor of love. It has become a tradition for Donna Lee and me to serve this to neighbors on New Year's Day as we watch the college bowl games. My recipe is below. Enjoy!

Chili del Rey

Preparation: 24 hours
Cooking: 2–3 hours
Serves: 12

Step 1: Marinate and cook beef and peppers

3 lbs. sirloin steak, cubed
3 cloves garlic, pressed
1 bunch green onions, chopped (about 6–12 onions depending on size)
3 large jalapeño peppers, seeded and diced (or to taste)
3 large serrano peppers, seeded and diced (or to taste)
3 large hatch peppers, seeded and diced (or to taste)
1 large poblano pepper, seeded and diced (or to taste)
1 tbsp. chili powder
1 tbsp. molasses
1 tbsp. Worcestershire sauce (Lea & Perrins recommended)
1 tbsp. Steak sauce (Lea & Perrins recommended)
1 medium lime, juiced

1 tsp. kosher salt

1/2 tsp. Tabasco sauce (McIlhenny recommended)

1/2 tsp. Liquid smoke, mesquite flavor (option: hickory flavor)

1/2 tsp. Kitchen Bouquet browning sauce

1/4 tsp. ground black pepper

2 cans Bock beer (24 oz.)

Combine all ingredients in an 8-quart pot. Marinate in the refrigerator for at least 24 hours. Stir occasionally. After marinating, bring to a boil over medium-high heat, then simmer for 30–45 minutes until the contents are tenderized and the liquid is reduced by about one-half. Stir frequently, and skim any fat from the surface. Set the pot aside.

Step 2: Sauté sausage and onions

1 lb. Mexican chorizo sausage, casing removed (not Spanish chorizo; option: spicy pork sausage)

2 tbsp. corn oil

1 medium sweet onion, chopped

1 medium yellow onion, chopped

1 medium red onion, chopped

3 stalks celery, chopped

1 large carrot, peeled and grated

Lightly brown the chorizo over medium heat in a 12-inch sauté pan for about 15 minutes to render its fat, breaking it into coarse pieces as it cooks. Drain the fat from the pan and discard. Add the corn oil and the vegetables. Sauté over medium heat until the vegetables are tender, about 12 minutes. Drain any remaining oil and discard. Transfer the mixture into the large pot with the mixture from step 1.

Step 3: Cook tomatoes and seasonings

> 2 cans diced tomatoes with juices (28 oz.)
> 2 cans tomato sauce (28 oz.)
> Dried spicy-hot seasonings:
> 1 tbsp. chipotle chili powder
> 1 tsp. ground cumin
> 1/4 tsp. curry powder
> 1/4 tsp. cayenne pepper
> 1/4 tsp. red pepper flakes
> Dried spicy-pungent seasonings:
> 1/2 tsp. dried basil
> 1/2 tsp. ground coriander
> 1/2 tsp. ground savory
> 1/4 tsp. ground cloves
> 3 large bay leaves
> Dried seasonings for color:
> 1/2 tsp. paprika
> 1/4 tsp. mustard powder
> 1/4 tsp. turmeric
> 1 oz. unsweetened chocolate, grated
> Fresh herbs for herbaceous complexity:
> 1/2 c. fresh cilantro, chopped (option: 4 tsp. dried)
> 1/2 c. fresh parsley, chopped (option: 4 tsp. dried)
> 1/2 c. fresh oregano, chopped (option: 4 tsp. dried)
> 1/4 c. fresh Mexican marigold, chopped (option: 2 tsp. dried
>   tarragon)
> 2 tbsp. fresh sage, chopped (option: 1 tsp. dried)
> 2 tbsp. fresh thyme, chopped (option: 1 tsp. dried)

Add the tomatoes, tomato sauce, and all the dried seasonings to the large pot but not the fresh herbs. The quantities of dried seasonings can be adjusted to suit your taste. Bring to a boil over medium-high heat, and then reduce heat to simmer for about 30–45 minutes until the liquid is reduced. I use an aluminum simmer pad on the burner so the heat is more evenly distributed to the pot without burning the mixture on the bottom. Stir frequently, and skim excess oil from the surface. In the last 15 minutes of simmer, add the fresh herbs to the pot and stir.

Step 4: Finish

1/4 c. masa harina (option: cornmeal)

Garnish:
    1 bunch green onions, chopped (about 12 onions)
    1 c. Mexican cheese, grated

Add the masa harina, and continue to simmer for an additional 5 minutes until the chili has thickened to the desired consistency. The spiciness of the chili is primarily dependent on the spiciness of the peppers used in step 1, which can vary significantly. Taste the chili while it simmers and add chili powder, cayenne pepper, and salt to taste.

Serve with steamed white rice and cornbread. Garnish with green onions and grated Mexican cheese.

CHAPTER 24

Southern California Food and Music

The last tour of duty in my Marine Corps career was at Marine Corps Air Station El Toro in Southern California. I was a lieutenant colonel, and I was fortunate to be selected for squadron command. It was an honor, a challenge, and a thrill all at the same time. The squadron did all the things all squadrons did, such as readiness training and deployments, but our squadron probably conducted more off-duty social functions than most. DL was the quintessential commanding officer's wife. She was a mother hen to the wives of the junior officers in the unit. She was also a creative force who drove me to host social functions for the officers and wives. We organized holiday dinners, cookouts, brunches, excursions to local sporting events, and any other excuse for a party DL could conjure. Although the menu planning might not have been up to gourmet standards, the food and drink were a catalyst for the development of brotherhood, pride in the unit, and esprit de corps. As a reprise to the Chili del Rey recipe I mentioned in a previous chapter, my squadron officers ate buckets of that chili and drank cases of beer during the New Year college football bowl games.

My tenure as a squadron commander was two years. After relinquishing command, I transferred to a staff position at a higher headquarters. This was the twilight of my twenty-year Marine Corps career. The new position was more of an eight-to-five assignment, so

DL and I had an abundance of time to enjoy the southern California coast from San Diego to Los Angeles. It seemed natural to seek out new restaurants, but we also discovered a music scene to explore. Music had a similar appeal that good food offered. Both stimulated the senses. Whereas the aroma and sight of a good dish filled the space between the plate and your head and teased your brain with the anticipation of taste, the sound and the sight of live music struck a harmonic chord in your brain that resonated with pleasure. We had a regular weekend routine of dining out in one of the many beach communities and then attending a concert. Our menu preference was usually fresh Pacific seafood. Our music preference was jazz presented in small, intimate venues. We saw so many small bands, quartets, and solo performers that it would be mind-numbing to name them. Suffice it to say that we could fill a multipage list of notable performers. Let me name three for emphasis: Cannonball Adderley, Chick Corea, and Kenny Burrell.

There was a period when I went on an unexplainable quest to find the best bouillabaisse on the Southern California coast. From the time decades prior when I was first drawn to seafood, stews and soups from the sea attracted me. I would peruse a restaurant menu for this type of fare, such as cioppino, zuppa di pesce, shrimp or lobster bisque, she-crab soup, clam or conch chowder, shrimp/crab/oyster gumbo, Breton stew, Thai tom kha gai, matelote, bouillabaisse, etc. For reasons unknown, I considered bouillabaisse the pinnacle of this genre, probably because my taste preferences tilt toward French cuisine and flavor profiles. I sampled too many bouillabaisse dishes to recall, and although there were many great offerings, none stood out as a clear winner. In retrospect, I was Don Quixote chasing the impossible dream and jousting with a series of windmills that were the equivalent to bowls of bouillabaisse. I have attached a simple, quick bouillabaisse recipe at the end of this chapter. It may not be a bouillabaisse you would be served in Marseille, France, but it is a version you would be proud to serve at a summer brunch.

This is a light French seafood stew perfect for a summer brunch. The recipe is a simple, quick version of the classic French Mediterranean dish. It does not include potatoes like some bouillabaisse recipes, and the vegetables are cut into thin, spoon-sized julienne strips. It works well with a variety of firm fish, so use what looks best at the market. Bon appétit!

Bouillabaisse d' Eté
(French Seafood Stew for Summer)

Preparation: 45 minutes
Cooking: 30 minutes
Serves: 6

Step 1: Aromatic vegetables

    2 tbsp. EVOO
    1 medium fennel bulb, white part only, cored and thinly sliced
    1 medium yellow onion, thinly sliced pole-to-pole
    1 medium leek, white part only split lengthwise and thinly
        sliced
    1 medium red bell pepper, cored, seeded, and thinly sliced
    1 stalk celery, thinly sliced half-moons
    2 cloves garlic, thinly sliced

Heat the oil in a 3 1/2-quart soup pot over medium-high heat. Add the fennel, onion, leek, bell pepper, and celery. Sauté for about 5 minutes until the vegetables are slightly tender. Add the garlic and sauté another minute until the garlic is fragrant. Stir occasionally.

Step 2: Seafood

> 1 c. dry white wine (unoaked Burgundian Chardonnay
>   preferred)
> 2 c. *tomato concassé (option: canned petite diced tomatoes)
> 4 c. **fish stock (option: water)
> 1 ***sachet d'épices
> 1/4 tsp Saffron threads
> 1 lb. cod fillet, skin and bone removed, cut into 2-in. pieces
>   (option: sea bass, halibut, grouper)
> 1 lb. jumbo shrimp, 21–25 count, peeled and deveined
> 1 lb. mussels, scrubbed and debearded (option: clams)
> 1/2 tsp. kosher salt (or to taste)
> 1/4 tsp. ground white pepper (or to taste)

Add the wine to the pot and bring to a boil over medium-high heat. Stir to deglaze any browned bits of vegetables on the bottom or sides of the pot. Add the tomatoes, and simmer for 5 minutes or until most of the liquid has been reduced. Add the fish stock, sachet d'épices, and saffron. Reduce the heat to medium low, cover, and cook at a low boil for about 15 minutes. Add the cod, shrimp, and mussels. Cover, and simmer about 6 minutes until the shrimp is pink and the mussels have opened. Do not overcook or the fish will start to break apart. Discard any mussels that do not open.

Step 3: Finish

> 1 tsp. red wine vinegar
> 1 tsp. fresh squeezed lemon juice
> Kosher salt (to taste)
> Ground white pepper (to taste)
> 2 tbsp. fresh tarragon, chopped (option: fresh chives, snipped)

Stir in the vinegar and lemon. Adjust salt and pepper to taste. Remove and discard the sachet d'épices. Ladle into soup bowls. Sprinkle with the tarragon. Serve with crusty French bread.

*Tomato Concassé

Cut an X in the bottom of each tomato. Blanch the tomatoes in a pot of boiling water for 30 seconds. Using a slotted spoon, transfer the tomatoes to an ice water bath to cool. When cool, drain. Remove the stems and peel off the skin starting from the X. Cut tomatoes in half lengthwise. Remove and discard the core and the seeds. Coarsely chop the tomato.

**Stock

Master Chef Auguste Escoffier says in his epic treatise *The Escoffier* on the fine art of French cuisine: "Stock is everything in cooking. Without it, nothing can be done. The cook mindful of success, therefore, will naturally direct his attention to the faultless preparation of his stock."

A great stock is judged by five criteria: flavor, clarity, color, body, and aroma. An excellent modern reference for preparing stock can be found in chapter 1 of *The Elements of Cooking* by Michael Ruhlman. If you prefer to use a commercially available stock product, the boxed Swanson brand or Kitchen Basics brand are good choices but not as good as homemade stock.

***Sachet d'épices

Place two sprigs each of parsley and thyme in a piece of cheesecloth. Add two bay leaves, six cracked Tellicherry black peppercorns, and a whole clove. In addition, for this sachet, add 1/2 teaspoon of fennel seeds and two 1/4-inch strips of lemon peel. Fold opposite edges of the cheesecloth over the herbs, roll the cheesecloth from an open edge, and bind the roll with kitchen twine.

P ART 7

A Second
Career Starts

CHAPTER 25

Transition from Marine Corps Uniform to Coat and Tie

I retired from the Marine Corps after twenty years of active duty plus four more years of active reserve duty. In anticipation of retirement from the military, I enrolled in a course at American University titled Strategy of Career Transition. It was a very worthwhile endeavor. We studied topics such as business management theories, business organizational structures, business marketing concepts, creating department budgets, price estimating, how salary scales are set, résumé preparation, interview techniques, and other subjects that differentiate the private sector from the public sector. Six months prior to my military retirement date, I was sending résumés to numerous companies, and I was networking with friends and acquaintances who were already employed in the private sector. This effort paid off as I was quickly called for a number of interviews, and I received a few offers of employment. I accepted an offer from the Marquardt Company in Van Nuys, California. Marquardt developed and produced rocket thrusters and ramjets. I was a fit because I had three degrees in engineering: a bachelor's degree in aeronautical engineering, a master's degree in aerospace engineering, and a professional aerospace engineer degree. My experimental thesis was the "Analysis of Two-Phase Flow in the Deflagration of Metalized Solid Rocket Propellant." DL affectionately called me her rocket scientist. I was also trained in program management at Fort Belvoir, and I was ultimately certified as a program management professional by the Program Management Institute.

We bought a home in Calabasas, California. It was a very comfortable home in a gate-guarded development around the small, man-made Lake Calabasas. Our new situation had both similarities and differences to what we had become accustomed to in the latter stages of my military career. In our leisure time, we still followed the weekend routine of dining out and then attending a concert. However, the options available to us in the San Fernando Valley and the Los Angeles areas were much more extensive than our previous beach communities. We added live theater, larger concert venues, and the Los Angeles Symphony to our playlist. We were entertained by some big-name stars, such as Dave Brubeck, Miles Davis, and Frank Sinatra. The dining experiences were similarly expanded. We dined at two of Wolfgang Puck's restaurants: Spago in Beverly Hills and Chinois in Santa Monica. I recall ordering one of the chef's specialties at Chinois for my entrée, which was a large whole sizzling Pacific Snapper, the skin scored on the side, herbs in the scores, finished with ginger and ponzu sauce. Someone once said, "You eat with your eyes first," and in the case of this entrée, you feasted with your eyes. At the other end of the spectrum, one of our favorite restaurants was Café Bellissimo, an unpretentious family-run Italian place in Woodland Hills, where the waiters took the stage and sang between services. Their voices were showbiz quality, and the food was great. The waiters were probably all aspiring stage actors. Dinner at Café Bellissimo made for both a tasty and entertaining evening.

With plentiful and easy access to fine dining, our new lifestyle was similar to the previous in that regard. However, other social aspects were profoundly different. Where the Marine Corps demographic was couples of similar ages, values, and interests, the new community covered the gamut from young couples entering the business world to established families to retirees. The concept of military unit identity and camaraderie did not translate to companies in the private sector or to civilian communities. The impact of these differences was many fewer social events. After the eight-to-five weekday, business associates diffused into their own personal, private worlds. Weekend group social activities were infrequent and seemed restricted to a smaller crowd of like-minded friends. DL and I did not judge this new normal as good or bad, and we accepted the challenge of adapting. Part of the adaptation was the decision to improve our culinary skills and our knowledge of wine.

CHAPTER 26

Informal Culinary Development

In the San Fernando Valley and the Los Angeles area, we were introduced to a number of culinary learning experiences. We signed up with some fine dining restaurants for their periodic private wine dinners. Typically, the restaurants would plan a multicourse menu paired with quality wines. The restaurant's event manager or chef or wine manager would explain the food preparation techniques and the logic behind the wine pairings. Many patrons simply stored the restaurant's information in their short-term memory while they enjoyed a gourmet meal. Others, like DL and me, recorded the restaurant's information in long-term memory or in written notes, while still enjoying the gourmet meal. I was particularly interested in the chef's explanation of both his classic techniques and personal tricks. These private wine dinners became a monthly event for us.

I will name a few restaurants that hosted memorable wine dinners, although I do not do so as an endorsement for the establishment. Naming the restaurants simply helps to clear the cobwebs of my memory to recall the enjoyable experiences. Geoffrey's Malibu has been in its present Malibu location since 1948, but obviously, it has been redesigned and renovated over the years. Special private dining events at Geoffrey's Malibu are truly special, and they catered to upper-tier Malibu residents and celebrities. Davenport's Restaurant in Woodland Hills specialized in customizing upscale dining events to the requirements of the group being served to ensure a unique dining experience. Pearl District restaurant in Westlake Village provided consistently high-quality menus with focused wine pairings at reasonable prices. As a point of reference, I will note that the average business life of a restaurant in the United States is about three years, so very few restaurants DL and I frequented thirty years ago are still operating. Those few that are still in business share some common traits, including a great location, a pedigree of superior executive chefs, the ability to adapt or pivot as social conditions change, and a lineage of owners with sound business acumen.

Cooking classes also became a favorite activity. Some classes were held in the classrooms of high-end markets. Others were held in restaurant meeting rooms. For most of the classes, you watched the instructor prepare a recipe while following along with a hardcopy handout. In a few others, the attendees were coached through a participative hands-on session, and these were definitely the most informative and enjoyable. Once again, these cooking classes became a monthly event for us. One cooking class, in particular, seemed to have more of an impact on my culinary development than others. It was offered at a local country club by the resident chef. The subject was the five classic French mother sauces (béchamel, velouté, espagnole, tomato, and hollandaise), as defined by the historically preeminent French chef Auguste Escoffier. Some culinarians, notably Jerald Chesser CEC, define only four mother sauces, by excluding hollandaise because it is essentially a stand-alone sauce without being the base for derivative sauces as are the other four. This was my first formal introduction to both the five mother sauces and to the culinary legend Auguste Escoffier. After this class, I went to a bookstore and bought the classic book *The Escoffier Cookbook and Guide to the Fine Art of Cookery* by Auguste Escoffier, first published in 1905. I contend that any aspiring chef, amateur or professional, should commit the first 135 pages of the book to memory. The book is the cornerstone in the structure of formal culinary training, and it ignited in me the burning desire to undertake formal culinary training in the future. As an aside, I started to frequently include hollandaise sauce in my meals because its rich, creamy lemon-butter flavor enhanced so many dishes. However, I found that making the sauce was time-consuming and unforgiving, so I experimented with making a faux hollandaise that was easier and foolproof. When dinner guests accepted my faux hollandaise as the real thing, I documented my process in the recipe included at the end of this chapter. It's not intended to be a deception, just simply delicious!

For DL and me, wine tasting events were analogous to cooking classes. A number of wine retailers in the greater Los Angeles area had classrooms on their premises for periodic wine tastings. The themes varied, such as a single varietal or a geographic area, but the format was usually six different wines offered in two-ounce tasting pours. In addition to the wines, the moderators provided as much detail as the guests wanted, such as residual sugar content, acid percentage, time aged in oak barrels, etc. I respected and envied these expert moderators and decided that I wanted to pursue certification as a sommelier in the future.

Over time, some of the neighborhood wine stores we frequented could not compete with big-box retailers such as Total Wine and BevMo. Fortunately, these large wine and spirit retailers continued the practice of weekly wine tasting events for customers interested in expanding their knowledge of wine. I found that these large retailers conducted wine tasting events with more variety and professionalism by trained sommeliers. DL and I still attend wine tastings not only for entertainment but also to assist in identifying wines we want to purchase. Recommendations and wine ratings by experts may be a starting point for selecting wine, but ultimately, we learned to buy and drink wines that we taste and enjoy. I agree with the wisdom a wine tasting moderator once espoused: "Never apologize for or be ashamed of your own taste in wine. Preferences for wines vary as much as those for art or music."

Another controversial benefit of wine tasting is stimulation and health of the brain. The respected Yale neuroscientist Gordon Sheperd explained this theory in his book *Neuroenology: How the Brain Creates the Taste of Wine*. His book and research conclude that tasting wine proved to stimulate the brain even more than solving a sophisticated logical puzzle. According to the book, the process of contemplative evaluation of wine sends a "flavor signal to the brain that triggers massive cognitive computation involving pattern recog-

nition, memory, value judgment, emotion and, of course, pleasure."
Regardless, I enjoy the variety, complexity, and of course the sensuality of wine, one of mankind's greatest discoveries.

In French cuisine, hollandaise is one of the five grand sauces, some-times referred to as the five mother sauces. Although most gourmets like hollandaise, many home chefs are reluctant to make the sauce. Many are intimidated by the process, and they fear the sauce will break, leaving them an unappealing mess. This recipe is a simplified foolproof version made quickly in a blender. Although professional chefs may look down their noses at this recipe, those of us who pre-pare fine food for family and friends may want to try this the next time we make eggs Benedict or asparagus with hollandaise or as a dipping sauce for artichokes. My recipe is below. Enjoy!

Faux Hollandaise Sauce

Preparation: 5 minutes
Cooking: 10 minutes
Serves: 8

Step 1: Vinegar reduction

> 2 tbsp. white wine vinegar (option: cider vinegar)
> 2 tbsp. water
> 12 whole black peppercorns, cracked

Place the vinegar, water, and cracked peppercorns in a small saucepan. Reduce by half over medium heat. Strain the remaining liquid through a fine strainer into a blender. Discard the solids.

Step 2: Blend

    3 large egg yolks
    4 oz. cream cheese (Philadelphia brand recommended)
    1/2 tsp. Dijon mustard

Add the yolks, room-temperature cream cheese, and mustard to the blender. Blend until smooth, about 15–30 seconds.

Step 3: Finish

    1/2 c. unsalted butter
    1 tbsp. fresh squeezed lemon juice
    1/4 tsp. kosher salt
    1 dash Tabasco sauce (McIlhenny brand preferred)

Place all step 3 ingredients in the small saucepan. Melt the butter over medium-low heat, stirring occasionally. Do not allow the mixture to boil or bubble. With the blender on, pour the butter mix slowly into the blender. Blend until smooth, about 30 seconds.

Transfer the finished sauce to a metal bowl, and place the bowl over a pot of simmering hot water. Stir occasionally to uniformly warm the sauce until ready to serve.

Chapter 27

Annual Travel Expands

DL and I continued to live up to the vow we made on Waikiki Beach regarding annual travel. In my full-time employment status, we were able to plan only one two-week trip per year for international travel. However, the scope of our travel planning expanded beyond trips outside the continental United States. We evolved into a routine of two types of travel: first, the annual international vacation still had priority, and second, we added occasional weekend trips to USA cities we had never visited or we wanted to revisit. One item both of these forms of travel shared in common was a variety of fine dining experiences we discovered. We had some experiences so noteworthy they are embedded in my memory. I would like to touch on three international trips and three weekend trips where there was an interesting dining experience.

CHAPTER 28

Noteworthy International Trips

We booked a two-week excursion to Italy called Italy by Train, which included five days in Milan, five days in Venice, and five days in Rome. It was such an exciting trip that it is probably worthy of its own extended travelogue, but I want to describe a specific dining experience in Rome. One night, DL and I went to a famous restaurant, Il Vero Alfredo, located on the Piazza Augusto Imperatore near the Mausoleum of Augustus. The restaurant is world-famous for its signature dish, Fettucine Alfredo, originally created by Alfredo di Lelio in 1908. Of course, DL ordered the Fettucine Alfredo, which was further described on the menu as *triplo burro* (triple butter). A mountain of dressed pasta was delivered to DL and looked to be enough for a family platter! DL ate a reasonable portion share, but it seemed that she had hardly trimmed the peak off the mountain. At this point, Alfredo came to the table. He was a rotund man, with black hair, a bushy black mustache, and a gracious smile. We were told he was Alfredo III in the di Lelio lineage. He looked at DL's dish and gestured, "Non le piace?" (Don't you like it?) DL answered with her hands spread, "Si, ma troppo!" (Yes, but too much!) He gave her a big toothy smile, a pat on the back, and he moved on to the next table to socialize with the customers. The food, venue, and hospitality were world-class.

Dinner in Rome at a famous restaurant among Imperial Roman landmarks was exciting, but DL and I wanted to sample a less ostentatious part of Rome. One evening, we decided to visit Trastevere, an area of Rome on the southwest side of the Tiber River. It is said that the commonplace Romans live in Trastevere. We walked into the heart of Trastevere over the Ponte Garibaldo. It was at dusk turning to darkness. We randomly strolled through the warren of dark, narrow, meandering streets where the only illumination was the muted glow of apartment lights through curtains. The buildings abutted the narrow streets and alleys, creating the impression we were walking through a maze, with almost no view of the night sky. At the end of one of the streets, we saw the glow of some brighter exterior lights. As we approached, we found that the lights were a small alfresco trattoria on one side of a minor piazza opposite a modest neighborhood church. We sat for dinner along with a few Trastevere couples who were probably regulars at the trattoria. I vaguely remember a dinner of arancini; bucatini all'Amatriciana; arugula and tomato salad with balsamic vinaigrette with whipped ricotta, honey, and figs for dessert; and a bottle of local Latio red table wine. The overall impression was a typical, home-style, flavorful Trastevere dinner in a very traditional setting. But the excellent food was only a small part of the lasting memory of that dinner. The cloth napkins at the table setting were embossed with the name Vincenzo, presumably the owner of the trattoria. When DL saw the name, she explained to the waiter in her broken Italian that my name was Vincenzo, and she asked if she could keep a napkin as a souvenir. The waiter furrowed his brow and waved his finger from side to side indicating no. Her disappointment was short-lived. When the waiter delivered the bill after the dinner, he delivered it on a clean, folded Vincenzo napkin. He smiled and explained in his broken English that he wanted us to have a fresh napkin as a souvenir. It was heartwarming, and we still have that napkin to keep alive that great memory of dinner in Trastevere. If the reader is inclined to share a piece of this memory with me, I have attached my version of bucatini all'Amatriciana at the end of this chapter.

Up to this point, DL and I had done our own detailed vacation planning: transportation, accommodations, excursions, and potential dining venues. We decided to try the format of an all-inclusive resort. A trip to Nassau in the Bahamas was our first experience with an all-inclusive resort. We stayed at a Grand Hyatt resort on Cable Beach. We were not disappointed. In fact, we were overwhelmed in a good sense with all the luxury amenities offered by the resort. The laid-back mood in the resort and in the Bahamas, in general, was a stark contrast to both my job and the social scene in the Los Angeles area. After the first day in the resort, I removed my wristwatch and left it in our room. One afternoon while we were lounging at one of the swimming pools, my mind abruptly woke to the realization that I was playing Bingo. I never play Bingo! It was just a function of the complete decompression that had insidiously enchanted me. Great food was everywhere: at bars on the beaches, buffets at the pools, breakfasts and brunches on verandas dispersed on the grounds, and the restaurants of course. This was the Bahamas, so seafood prevailed, to my pleasure. There was one dish that was ubiquitous in the various venues, Bahamian Conch Chowder. We had never eaten conch before, a large sea snail. They were harvested in the wild in their elaborate shells and were called Queen Conchs in the Bahamas. I probably ate scrumptious conch chowder every day at the resort. "Conched out" was an expression the locals used to describe both the laid-back mood and the availability of conch chowder. We were definitely conched out for the better part of a week. It took a day or two to recover our normal pace when we returned home.

We enjoyed the all-inclusive format of our Bahama vacation so much we booked a similar vacation a year later. We went to the Dorado Beach Resort on the north shore of Puerto Rico, about thirty miles west of San Juan. Once again, we were not disappointed. Our accommodations were a private suite on the beach, literally less than a hundred yards from the water. When we awoke on the first day, we went out on our veranda to observe that our private beach had been raked. Not one stone or a seaweed leaf was visible on the manicured beach. Two chaise lounges and an umbrella were in place. This was a daily activity by the resort staff. The resort grounds were tropically beautiful, an attentive compromise between landscaped and wild.

When walking the grounds after sunset, we were entertained by a symphony of untamed sounds, primarily the haunting mating call of a small frog called a coqui. We were told the frog was named for its call, "Co-keee." DL wanted to see a frog but never did. She asked a groundskeeper how she could find one.

He asked her, "How long will you be here?"

She responded, "Five days."

He politely chuckled and said, "I've been working here for five years, and I've never seen one!"

The quality and quantity of food at the Dorado Resort were comparable to the Grand Hyatt in Nassau, and I was pleased with the abundance of fresh seafood. We were served a number of dishes that were augmented by a savory, aromatic Puerto Rican vegetable salsa, sofrito, and I liked it enough to add it to my personal inventory of favorite salsas. The one feature of the Dorado Resort that stood out from all the rest was the restaurant called Mi Casa. Mi Casa was an old, authentic Spanish colonial building about one hundred yards from the seashore. It was a uniquely spectacular venue, and after dinner there on our first night, we decided to take dinner there every night. We were seated at a table for two on an open veranda. It was a moonless night with a crystal clear sky. The black dome of the heavens was pinpricked by countless stars, and the stars could be seen all the way to the horizon. At the water's edge, six-inch surf gently rolled up to kiss the sand with a soothing burble. From where we sat, we could see the blue-green bioluminescence flicker in the curl of the small waves. Mi Casa is well-known in the resort world for its remarkable food, but I have to admit I do not remember the gourmet meal I was served on that first night because it was trumped by the magnificent scene.

Considering the almost countless variations of modern Italian tomato-based pasta sauces, why would Amatriciana sauce deserve special attention in an Italian recipe file? I offer three primary reasons: first, it is one of the first tomato sauces with a written record found in the 1790 cookbook *L'Apicio Modern* by Roman chef Francesco Leonardi; second, Amatriciana is thought to have its origin as a sauce from Roman antiquity; and third, it uses guanciale, a unique Italian cured meat prepared from pork cheeks (the name is derived from *guancia*, Italian for "cheek").

In the late 1700s, a large percentage of Europeans feared the tomato. A nickname for the fruit was Poison Apple because it was thought that aristocrats got sick and died after eating tomatoes. The truth of the matter was that many Europeans used pewter plates which were high in lead content. When served on these plates, the high acidity of the tomato would leach lead from the pewter, resulting in many deaths from lead poisoning. No one made the connection at the time, and the tomato was thought to be the culprit. After the mid-1800s, with the invention of pizza in Naples, widespread acceptance of the tomato grew in Europe.

This tomato-based sauce is named for its traditional city of origin, Amatrice. The city is located in the northeast corner of Lazio province in central Italy, about seventy miles northeast of Rome, along the spine of the Apennine mountains. If you were to order this dish in Amatrice, it would most likely be served with bucatini pasta. Bucatini looks like thick spaghetti, but the strands are hollow, like a small drinking straw (in Italian, *buca* means "hole"). The sauce has been declared Lazio's Prodotto Agroalimentare Tradizionale. Although the traditional sauce uses tomatoes, guanciale, and Pecorino

Romano cheese, I will offer some variations that have evolved. Buon appetito!

Amatriciana Sauce with Bucatini

Preparation: 20 minutes
Cooking: 40 minutes
Serves: 6–8 as a primo piatto or 4 as a main dish

Classic Amatriciana
4 c. *concassé of Roma tomatoes (option: canned Italian tomatoes)
4 tbsp. EVOO, divided into two equal portions
8 oz. guanciale, 1/2 inch dice
3 medium garlic cloves, minced
1 tsp. red pepper flakes (or to taste)
1/2 tsp. kosher salt (or to taste)
1/4 tsp. fresh ground black pepper (or to taste)
1 lb. bucatini
4 qt. **Salted water
1/2 c. Pecorino Romano cheese, grated
2 tbsp. fresh flat-leaf parsley, chopped

Puree the tomatoes to a smooth consistency in a food processor or with an immersion blender in a bowl. Set aside.

In a 3-quart saucepan, heat two tablespoons of the oil over medium-high heat until the oil shimmers. Add the guanciale, and sauté for 6–8 minutes until the pieces are golden brown. Drain the guanciale on paper towels, but leave a film of oil and fat in the pan.

Return the pan to the cooktop over medium heat. Add the garlic and pepper flakes, and sauté 1–2 minutes until the garlic is fragrant. Return the guanciale to the pan. Add the pureed tomatoes, salt, and pepper. Stir to thoroughly mix the sauce, reduce the heat to a simmer, and cook uncovered for about 15–20 minutes until the sauce begins to darken and thicken.

While the sauce is cooking, add the bucatini to vigorously boiling salted water. Cook about 12 minutes until the pasta is al dente. Drain the pasta.

Combine the hot sauce and the hot pasta. Toss to thoroughly and evenly coat the pasta. Divide the dressed pasta on serving plates (6–8 plates for a primo piatto, or 4 main course plates). Sprinkle the Pecorino Romano and parsley on top, and drizzle the remaining EVOO on top. Serve immediately.

Variation with other than guanciale
8 oz. pancetta, 1/2 inch dice
or
8 oz. rindless slab bacon, 1/2 inch dice
or
8 oz. sliced smoked bacon, 1/2 inch dice

If guanciale is too difficult to find, try one of the meat options listed. Then follow the remainder of the classic Amatriciana recipe.

Thickly sliced pancetta is readily available from most markets' deli sections. However, pancetta is not as flavorful as guanciale, and it usually has more fat. You may need more than 8 ounces initially to yield a reasonable amount after rendering and draining.

Slab bacon is readily available from most markets. Because it is sold as a slab, you can cut pieces to whatever size you desire. Like pancetta, slab bacon is not as flavorful as guanciale, and it usually has more fat. You may need more than 8 ounces initially to yield a reasonable amount after rendering and draining.

Packaged sliced bacon is the least desirable option. Although readily available, its smoked flavor (hickory, mesquite, apple, etc.) will adversely affect the taste of the dish. If bacon is used instead of guanciale, blanch the bacon in boiling water for at least one minute to minimize the wood-smoked flavor of the bacon before use.

Variations with aromatics
1/4 c. yellow onion, minced
and/or

2 tbsp. red Pepperazzi sweet peppers, diced (DeLallo brand
    preferred)
and/or
1/4 c. dry white Italian wine (Cortese, Falanghina, Pinot
    Grigio, etc.)
and/or
1/4 c. fresh basil leaves, coarsely chopped (option: fresh
    oregano)

Although not part of the classic recipe, many people like the
additional flavor of onion, sweet peppers, and basil. If you choose to
use the onion and/or the Pepperazzi, sauté them for about 6 minutes
before you add the garlic and pepper flakes, then continue with the
recipe. If you choose to use the wine, add it to the saucepan after the
garlic and red pepper are sautéed, then reduce it by at least half. If
you choose to use the fresh herbs, add them to the recipe with the
pureed tomatoes.

Variation to the red pepper flakes
1 tbsp. chopped Calabrian peppers (or to taste)

If you choose to use Calabrian peppers, simply replace the red
pepper flakes with the Calabrian peppers, then continue with the recipe.

Variation to the bucatini
1 lb. spaghetti
or
1 lb. linguini

If bucatini is too difficult to find, try one of the pasta options
listed. Then follow the remainder of the recipe.

Variation to the Pecorino Romano cheese
1/2 c. Parmigiano-Reggiano cheese, grated
or
1/2 c. Asiago cheese, grated

If you choose to use optional cheese, simply replace the Pecorino Romano with the cheese of your choice.

*Tomato Concassé

Cut an X in the bottom of each tomato. Blanch the tomatoes in a pot of boiling water for 30 seconds. Using a slotted spoon, transfer the tomatoes to an ice water bath to cool. When cool, drain. Remove the stems and peel off the skin starting from the X. Cut tomatoes in half lengthwise. Remove and discard the core and the seeds. Coarsely chop the tomato.

**Salted Water

For cooking any type of pasta or vegetable, salted water translates to a 1 percent salt solution: about 1 1/2 teaspoons of salt in one quart of water.

CHAPTER 29

Noteworthy Weekend Trips

Two factors determined the destinations for our weekend trips. First was our curiosity and desire to visit cities we had never visited or we wanted to revisit. Second was the inexpensive nonstop round-trip flights advertised by airlines. We were enrolled in various airlines' email alerts that usually advertised promotions early in the week. If we saw a promotion to a city of interest and our weekend schedule permitted, we would book the trip. The measure of spontaneity in this approach to travel infused a bit of excitement into the trips.

One recurring weekend destination for us was New Orleans. We would fly into New Orleans, take the courtesy transportation to the Sheraton Hotel on Canal Street, and had no need for a rental car. The French Quarter was just across Canal Street, and numerous excellent restaurants were within walking distance. At the time, I felt that the three best cities in the USA for fine dining were New York, San Francisco, and New Orleans. I still feel New Orleans is a preeminent destination for those seeking the epitome of plated ecstasy. On a few occasions, when DL and I did not have firm lunch or dinner plans, we would just take a leisurely walk from the Sheraton Hotel and randomly stop at a restaurant. Our routine was to order the chef's special or the restaurant's signature dish. We were never disappointed. I can say with my hand over my heart, I've never had a mediocre meal in New Orleans, whether it was Cajun/Creole, Italian, French, or seafood. To describe in detail the fine dining experiences we have had in New Orleans would require a separate travelogue.

Suffice it to say we have some favorite restaurants that we like to visit. In no special order: Acme Oyster House, French Quarter; Antoine's, French Quarter; Calcasieu, Warehouse District; Commander's Palace, Garden District; Compére Lapin, Warehouse District; Galatoire's, French Quarter; Irene's, French Quarter. In addition to the superior fine dining, even the street food in the Crescent City is noteworthy, and I have attached a Po'Boy sandwich recipe at the end of this chapter as an example. New Orleans is to foodies what Disneyland is to children.

Prior to the year 2000, I would have ranked San Francisco at the top of my fine dining destinations. I loved the availability of classic French cuisine. I loved the European ambiance of the city. Of course, I also loved the fresh seafood. However, in my opinion, San Francisco's fine dining reputation has gradually deteriorated since 2000. There seem to be fewer Michelin star restaurants. The general quality of food has transitioned to mediocre. The city itself and its infrastructure have a worn-out, run-down visage. What a pity! Where are the notable executive chefs? What happened to the civic pride that made San Francisco one of the most beautiful cities in the USA? I have not given up on San Francisco dining. There is always the possibility of a revival. DL and I still visit there on weekends but infrequently compared to prior to 2000. We stay at the Marines' Memorial Hotel, a private members-only facility conveniently located on Sutter Street, just a couple of blocks from Union Square, Chinatown, and the Powell Street cable car line. On one occasion, we took our three grandsons to San Francisco for a long weekend. We ate at one of our favorite restaurants, Scoma's on Pier 39. The boys loved the experience because they had their first ride on a cable car, and they were fascinated by the seals who feasted on the offal thrown overboard by the fishermen cleaning their catch pier-side. At Scoma's, our ten-year-old grandson Mitch saw that one of the restaurant's specialties was Dungeness crab, but he had never had it before. He decided to try it, but he was confused that the menu said, "Market Price." He asked, "Grandpa, what does 'Market Price' mean?" I told him Dungeness crabs were a delicacy in short supply but to go ahead and order the entrée, and we would know the price when we were given the bill. I also ordered the Dungeness crab entrée. Scoma's exceeded our expectations with a creamy, rich crab bisque to awaken our taste buds, the Dungeness crab platter to tease our eyes, and a garnish of buttered early summer vegetables to add color and texture. I felt very gratified watching my grandson roll his eyes, hum a frequent throaty "Ummm," and enjoy probably the best dinner of his young life. The issue of market price faded away as we indulged.

On other weekend trips to San Francisco, we decided to dine outside the city environs. A short drive across the Golden Gate Bridge brought us to Sausalito. Ondine restaurant faces east with an expansive view over the Sausalito marina to the San Francisco skyline across the bay. The restaurant has been in business for decades and has maintained a record of four-star reviews. Ondine's menu carried an interesting collection of New American, Italian, and seafood cuisine. From my experience, it has not degraded over time as many fine-dining restaurants in San Francisco have. Its consistent performance is the reason I return there when I'm in the San Francisco area. Other restaurants may offer a similar high-class culinary experience, but very few can compete with the view.

An hour's drive north of San Francisco, one can find the pinnacle of fine dining at Thomas Keller's French Laundry in Yountville, if one makes a reservation well in advance. It is well worth a weekend drive. The French Laundry has been named the number one restaurant in the USA numerous times by many critics and gourmet publications. A parade of renowned chefs has worked at the French Laundry before moving on to successful careers in their own restaurants. The restaurant is housed in a beautiful building that dates from 1900 and is in the National Register of Historic Places. Thomas Keller's staff are vetted preeminent professionals who provide a level of service second to none and make the customers feel like royalty. Entrées are expensive, more than $100, and prix fixe dinners over $200, but one might argue that the total experience is worth the price. I enjoyed a prix fixe dinner of which I can only recall the oyster appetizer and herb-roasted lamb with an assortment of garnishes, sauces, and desserts prepared with unique culinary techniques. Marie

Antoinette and Louis XVI probably feasted no better at Versailles. DL and I have had the opportunity to dine at great restaurants throughout the world, but the thrill of plated ecstasy at the French Laundry is the experience of a lifetime. The food, ambiance, and service rank this meal in my all-time top three dining experiences.

Rather than enumerating other weekend adventures that have delighted DL and me, let me tease the readers with a few destinations they may want to consider. Try the gourmet dining in Park City, Utah; Santa Fe, New Mexico; Savannah, Georgia; and Charleston, South Carolina. Other weekend destinations that may seem more ordinary but can offer fine dining experiences include Austin, Texas; Memphis, Tennessee; Kansas City, Missouri; and Portland, Oregon. I encourage you to unleash your spirit of adventure, look for inexpensive airfare, pack a small travel bag, seek out great restaurants, and treat yourself to your own version of plated ecstasy.

Credit for this recipe comes from, of all places, a mystery novel by prolific bestselling author James Patterson. Throughout his story, Patterson includes "recipes from the Killer Chef food truck." The story is set in New Orleans, and the following recipe is a classic French Quarter po'boy sandwich. I was skeptical of a recipe in a mystery novel, but I tried it. It was great! I'm sure Patterson won't mind that I added this excellent po'boy recipe to my personal recipe file. Bon appétit!

Blackened Catfish Po'Boy

Preparation: 15 minutes
Cooking: 20 minutes
Serves: 2

Step 1: Prepare the catfish

> 2 6 oz. catfish fillets, about 8-in. long (option: tilapia, cod, or other)
> 1 tbsp. honey
> 1/2 tsp. kosher salt
> 1/4 tsp. fresh ground black pepper
> 1/4 tsp. cayenne pepper
> 1/2 tsp. paprika
> 1/4 tsp. ground cardamom

Pat dry the fillets with a paper towel. Coat both sides with honey, and then season all over with salt, pepper, cayenne, paprika, and cardamom. Don't scrimp! Set aside.

Step 2: Aromatics (the Cajun Trinity)

> 1 tbsp. grape-seed oil (option: vegetable oil)
> 1/2 c. yellow onion, thinly sliced
> 1/4 c. green bell pepper, quartered lengthwise and sliced into
>   thin strips
> 1/4 c. celery stalk, sliced into thin crescents

Place the oil into a 12-inch cast-iron skillet over medium heat. When the oil is shimmering, add the onion, green pepper, and celery, then stir to coat. Sauté for about 10 minutes, stirring occasionally, until the onion, pepper, and celery are soft and beginning to brown. Remove the vegetables from the pan and set them aside.

Step 3: Prepare the baguette

> 1 small baguette, about 16 in. long
> 1 tbsp. unsalted butter
> 1 tbsp. prepared horseradish (Reese's preferred)
> 2 tbsp. mayonnaise (Hellmann's preferred)
> 1 tsp. fresh squeezed lemon juice
> 1/2 tsp. Creole seasoning (Tony Chachere's preferred)

Cut the baguette in half crosswise to make two 8-inch lengths. This length should match the length of the fish fillets. Then split the baguette portions down the middle lengthwise. Melt the butter in the cast-iron skillet from step 2 over medium-high heat. When the butter is bubbling, place the baguette pieces facedown in the pan. Make sure the cut surface is in contact with the pan and toast until golden brown, about 2–3 minutes.

While the baguette is browning, mix together the horseradish, mayonnaise, lemon juice, and creole seasoning in a small bowl. Transfer the toasted baguettes to a plate, and spread the creamy mixture generously on the toasted surfaces.

Step 4: Blacken the fillets

1 tbsp. grape-seed oil (option: vegetable oil)

Add the oil to the cast-iron skillet used in steps 2 and 3. Heat the oil over medium-high heat until the oil is shimmering. Add the fillets and cook until the spice coating is blackened, about 2–3 minutes. Turn the fillets and blacken the other side, about 2–3 minutes. Depending on the thickness of the fillets, more or less time may be required to cook the fillets through. Remove from the heat.

Step 5: Finish

Place the blackened fillets from step 4 on the bottom half of the toasted baguettes pieces from step 3. Top the fillets with the vegetables from step 2. Gently press the top half of the baguettes on top of the vegetables. Serve hot.

PART 8

Moving up the Corporate Ladder

CHAPTER 30

Antennas Up

I enjoyed my high-tech job at the Marquardt Company. I worked with a bright group of engineers and scientists on leading-edge space propulsion programs. DL and I were also happy with the nearly boundless food, wine, and music entertainment opportunities in the San Fernando Valley and Los Angeles areas. However, I observed business conditions in the company that raised concerns about my career path. I had been promoted to a level in the organization where it appeared I could advance no further because of the status quo of the organization above me and stagnant company growth. In addition, there was the specter of the company being acquired by a competitor or splitting into two smaller business lines. These conditions compelled me to start a search for a new job in a healthier business environment. My search antennas were up as I networked with business associates, researched companies with growth potential, and assessed the quality of life in various geographic areas.

In my new job search, I planned to emphasize my general management experience and success, with less emphasis on my technical qualifications in aerospace engineering. I was targeting high-level management positions or opportunities with a potential path to executive management. Over a few months, I was called for a couple of telephone interviews and a couple of face-to-face interviews. The opportunity I found most promising was with a company called GEC Marconi Avionics in Atlanta, Georgia. The company was part of a large global aerospace and defense corporation called GEC Marconi

PLC with its corporate headquarters in England. The company in Atlanta met some of my search criteria. It was a midsized company with a robust business backlog. The business plan envisioned growth into a new business line with the associated requirement for new management. For the most part, the executive staff of the company was composed of senior individuals, many probably nearing the end of their careers. The location of the company on the north side of Atlanta seemed vibrant and new. I was very happy to be called to Atlanta for an interview, and I had done meticulous preparation for the interview.

The interview went very well. I thought the chemistry with the staff was excellent, and I was impressed with the efficient operation of the business. When I returned home, DL and I cautiously celebrated what I thought was a positive step on the path to a new position. I received a phone call within a week inviting me for a second interview. Great news! But then came a surprise. I was told I would be interviewing in Washington, DC, at the GEC Marconi PLC corporate marketing office, not in the Atlanta facility. Although I would meet with a few people in the corporate office, my main point of contact would be a man named Lloyd Pointe. I was unprepared for this turn of events. I diligently spent the better part of a few days on the phone and researching business journals to gather information on the GEC Marconi PLC Washington, DC, office and Mr. Pointe. As it turned out, the intelligence on Mr. Pointe was most valuable.

CHAPTER 31

Food and Wine in the
Interview Process

Mr. Pointe was not a direct employee of GEC Marconi PLC. He owned his own marketing company, and he was under exclusive contract with GEC Marconi PLC. Most importantly, I learned he collected fine wine, mostly Bordeaux, and he was reputed to enjoy gourmet food. I immediately started a crash reading exercise in *The Sotheby's Wine Encyclopedia* by Tom Stevenson to enhance my understanding of Bordeaux wine, and I scanned *The Classic French Cookbook* by Le Cordon Bleu to refresh my memory of classic French fare. I am glad I did.

The exposure to the GEC Marconi PLC Washington, DC, office and its staff was uneventful. Afterward, Mr. Pointe took me to a nice bistro in old-town Alexandria for a late lunch. It must have been one of his regular dining locations because everyone called him by name and seated us at "his regular table." We chatted about potential employment with GEC Marconi while we perused the menu. After a polite period of time, I announced my selection, which I recall was a lunch portion of entrecôte béarnaise (a small boneless rib eye with sauce béarnaise and shoestring fried potatoes). Mr. Pointe nodded, which I interpreted as "Good selection," and then he handed me the wine list. At this point, two thoughts entered my mind. First, was this a test to see if I drank wine at midday with lunch? Or second, was this a test to see if I knew anything about wine? I did not want to go over the top on a wine selection, but I still wanted to show a level of sophistication. I studied the wine list, and I asked what he had ordered, then I ordered a 1990 Chateau Giscours from the Bordeaux Margaux appellation which is classified as a third tier in the 1855 classification system. He smiled and said, "Good choice, great vintage year," and then we chatted a bit about Bordeaux wines, although he did most of the talking. It was difficult for me to contain my excitement when the episode with Mr. Pointe was over. When I returned home, DL and I opened a bottle of Bordeaux wine and celebrated what I thought was the final step on the path to a new position with GEC Marconi Avionics. After a short wait of a day or two, I received another phone call with an offer of employment as a senior program manager for a new product line with a generous compensation package, and I would be reporting directly to the president. I was also offered a generous relocation package, including a furnished apartment, real estate services, shipment/storage of our personal property, an automobile allowance, and monthly round-trip transportation between Atlanta and Calabasas. Mr. Pointe's stamp of approval sealed the deal. We were on our way to Atlanta.

PART 9

Moving to Dixie

CHAPTER 32

My Temporary Domicile

I had mixed emotions about departing Calabasas for my new job in Atlanta. I was excited about the new position, but I was stressed about leaving my wife and daughter in Calabasas. I made all the financial and administrative preparations I could think of before departing. This was not the first time for DL and me to endure a family separation, so I was confident she could manage the household tasks while continuing in her full-time high school teaching position. During two previous periods of family separation, DL had successfully demonstrated her independence and good judgment by both selling one of our homes and renting another. However, I was equally concerned about the welfare of my daughter. She was a recent college graduate, and I would not be close at hand to offer fatherly assistance and advice as she transitioned to the next stage of her life. I packed my car for the cross-country drive to a new opportunity, but as I drove away looking at DL and Alison in the rearview mirror waving goodbye, my stomach was churning, and my eyes were damp.

The drive cross-country was uneventful, with the standard availability of motels and restaurants along the interstate highways. In midafternoon on the final leg of the drive, I approached the outskirts of Atlanta heading east on Interstate 20. As I crested a ridge, the skyline of downtown Atlanta seemed to visually pop out of the earth, beautifully illuminated by the western sun at my back. I interpreted the view as a sign that Atlanta was welcoming me with its finest spectacle. I was instantly transformed from the boring monotony of driving into a state of euphoria.

I found my way to my leased apartment. It was in a modest-sized building with good curb appeal in a nice quiet area. The location was a short commute from my new company. I checked in at the leasing office and was escorted to the furnished apartment, which was to be my residence for the better part of a year. It was a spacious one-bedroom apartment, and the interior was sparkling clean. The matching furniture was upscale with no ticky-tacky pressed wood laminate or vinyl. The appliances throughout were brand-new, including a television and stereo tuner. The kitchen was well equipped with quality cooking and dining necessities, so I would not be constrained to fast food, frozen dinners, or Hamburger Helper. The amenities at the facility included an exercise room, swimming pool with hot tub, and a concierge-type lounge serving hot and cold drinks with pastries, and maid service. The overall setup exceeded my expectations. The only downside was that I would not be sharing my bed with DL.

I unloaded my car, cleaned up, changed clothes, and then I asked the front desk about nearby restaurants. There were several within walking or short driving distance. I selected one at random and headed out for my first true sit-down meal after a few days on the road. The restaurant was a cozy family-type neighborhood restaurant, not a chain restaurant, and it was doing a brisk business. As I entered, I sensed the aroma of food frying in the kitchen and the undercurrent of subdued banter as patrons enjoyed their dinners. The scene could have been a movie set depicting home-style comfort dining in a typical Southern restaurant. I was seated in a padded booth. My waitress was right out of central casting: thirtyish with a big smile and a soft Southern accent. I wanted to follow the script, so I ordered a typical Southern dinner. I was very pleased to have well-prepared and nicely presented Southern fried chicken, collard greens with bacon, fried green tomatoes, cornbread, Georgia peach cobbler for dessert, and iced tea. Of course, the default in the south for iced tea is sweetened. If you want it unsweetened, you have to specifically ask. I was content.

I had arrived on a weekend, so I slept in on my first full day in Atlanta. It helped with the time zone adjustment. I had no food in the apartment, so eating breakfast out was on the agenda. While driving to the restaurant on the previous night, I had seen a busy, well-lit diner. It was called the Waffle House, and I subsequently discovered that there seemed to be a Waffle House at just about every major intersection. I was introduced to the unique Waffle House breakfast experience. The small place was crowded, so I had a short wait for a seat. While waiting, fresh hot coffee was available. I soon found a seat with a menu at the table, and I was immediately approached by a waitress. She was friendly and ready to take my order. What speedy service! To stay in character, I ordered eggs over easy, hash brown potatoes, country ham, creamy grits, and biscuits with sausage gravy. I was surprised at what happened next. The waitress turned toward the short-order cooks feverously working on the line behind the counter and yelled out my order, which I learned was the Waffle House process. There was no need to order coffee because the waitress continuously topped off my mug with fresh hot coffee on her rounds. Although a foodie may scoff at Waffle House food, I thought it was good diner food, especially the hash brown potatoes. The fact that so many Waffle Houses have had business success over such a long period of time speaks well for their business model. Years later, I still occasionally visit a Waffle House for breakfast, and I always order the hash brown potatoes.

After breakfast, I decided to do some food shopping. I did not plan to eat breakfast, lunch, and dinner out every day, so I needed to stock my refrigerator and pantry. I went to a nearby supermarket called Publix. It was large, clean, and well-stocked. At the time, the Publix chain of markets was the largest chain in Georgia. For the period of time we lived in Georgia, Publix was the market we primarily used. It provided 95 percent of our food shopping needs. The other 5 percent were unusual items, infrequently used, that we obtained at specialty markets, such as bison tenderloin, goat chops, salsify, sea beans, cherimoya, lychee, or hard-to-find ethnic ingredients. I would not be entertaining in my apartment, so I did not need to stock any exotic items. However, I was not going to compromise on preparing fine dining meals for myself in my apartment, and Publix provided everything I would need. I also found a small wine shop near my apartment, and I purchased a mixed case to pair with various meals I intended to prepare. With my larder filled, I was settled into my new temporary domicile.

CHAPTER 33

The New Work Environment

On Monday morning, I arrived for my first official day at GEC Marconi Avionics. It was a two-story building on fifteen wooded acres in an industrial complex with other similar business buildings. I was dressed for success in a tailored navy-blue suit, white shirt, red silk tie, and cap toe cordovan Oxford shoes with a matching belt. I checked in at the security desk in the lobby. I was expected, and the security officer called Human Resources to escort me. The better part of the day was filled with administrative requirements such as issuance of a photo ID security badge, an introduction to the company's policies and procedures, security clearance application, computer system access, and a myriad of other forms and disclosures. Then I was taken to my office. It was an appropriately sized private office equipped with the standard-issue company furniture and a view of the grounds from a window behind the desk. I shared an administrative assistant with three other peers in adjacent offices. It was a busy humdrum day except for lunch. A few of my new associates drove me a short distance to the renovated Historic Train Depot in Norcross. We had reservations at a fine dining restaurant called The Crossing. The restaurant served contemporary American cuisine in an upscale setting. I do not recall what I ordered for lunch because in this case, the food was trumped by the getting-to-know-you dialogue with my new associates. I do recall I requested unsweetened ice tea, and no one had wine with lunch. Between the office environment and lunch at The Crossing, it was a good start. I would return to The Crossing frequently in the future.

The pace of work picked up quickly. The effort to plan, organize, staff, direct, and control the new product line was considerable. But I had an abundance of time to apply to my responsibilities. Living alone, with no family or household obligations, I could work twelve hours a day and often six days a week. I found the level of activity exciting and invigorating. My only leisure time activities were a strenuous daily workout at the exercise facility, preparing a good evening dinner, and watching a movie on television. I can assure you, I did not skimp in the preparation of delicious French, Italian, Asian, and seafood dinners. And I did not drink cheap wine either. An occasional night out for dinner provided some variation to the routine, and it allowed me to explore the fine dining scene in the area. This minimal leisure time activity and eight hours of sleep were all I needed to maintain a good attitude and good health.

CHAPTER 34

Walkin' in Tall Cotton

Although I was busy on the job, I made time after hours and on weekends to exercise the real estate services provided to me in the terms of my employment. The agent was a superb professional. She asked me polite but detailed questions about my housing requirements, family, financial situation, social priorities, and leisure activities. Then she started with a high-level familiarization of the communities in North Atlanta. As we explored the area, she took into account my likes and dislikes, eliminated options that did not fit, and introduced options that fit. After a relatively intense search effort, we narrowed the options to the suburban bedroom community of Alpharetta.

There were a number of impressive communities in Alpharetta, but the one that struck a harmonic chord in me was Nesbit Lakes. It was an exclusive gate-guarded community of about four hundred beautiful homes that were on spacious lots along meandering streets around a couple of small lakes. The grounds were meticulously landscaped, with stands of mature hardwood trees and Loblolly pine trees throughout. By my standards, it was an idyllic setting.

The realtor set up a meeting with the Nesbit Lakes developer, and he in turn set up a meeting with a custom builder. We met at the Nesbit Lakes clubhouse. The developer showed me undeveloped lots that were available, and the builder showed me plans and photos of custom homes he had built in Nesbit Lakes, St. Ives Country Club, and Country Club of the South. Just as I was ardently touched by the ambiance of Nesbit Lakes, I was equally enthused about one of his floor plans and elevations. I was given copies of both the lot locations and the house plans, which I sent to DL for her review and comment.

DL and I bought, sold, or rented about ten residences up to this point in our married life, so we were well-versed in each other's requirements in a home. We trusted each other's judgment. We decided that I would take the lead on the building of the new Alpharetta home, and DL would have the lead on selling our current Calabasas home. I contracted the custom builder to start on the home in Nesbit Lakes, and DL put the Calabasas home on the market. At this time, the national real estate market was heavily in our favor. We would be able to buy twice the home in Nesbit Lakes compared to the value of our Calabasas home. I monitored the construction progress in Nesbit Lakes every weekend and sometimes on a weekday. DL sold the home in Calabasas in a matter of weeks. She would remain in the home until the end of the school year, then she would put our household goods in storage and join me in Atlanta.

When she arrived, my sterile apartment immediately came alive with her vibrant spirit. I adjusted my work routine to a more normal schedule so we could share my free time exploring our new environment. I introduced DL to our builder and to the builder's interior design consultant. DL took the lead working with the consultant on the details of the interior design. Progress on the new home moved at a fast pace during the summer. As if by time-lapse magic, the home quickly materialized from an undeveloped lot into a beautiful 5,600-square-foot home. It was two stories and included a partially finished daylight basement (windows along the rear wall). Palladian windows fifteen feet tall were in the entry foyer, the living room, and the great room. The master bedroom suite was on the main floor, so the second floor would get little use except for visiting friends and relatives. There was not one flat ceiling in the home. All the ceilings were barrel vaults, domes, or tray ceilings. What relevance does this narrative about the home have with my culinary interests? I will cite three key points: first, the kitchen—with all associated appliances, countertops, cabinets, and pantry space—was upgraded to gourmet kitchen standards; second, there was a wine cellar with a total capacity for 1,200 bottles; and third, the home was an impressive show-place for entertaining. DL and I planned to use the home extensively for social events, and we did.

As we neared completion of the home, the interior design consultant told us in her best *Gone with the Wind* accent, "With this custom home, in this Nesbit Lakes community, you'll be walkin' in tall cotton!" DL and I had found the epitome of the good life in the heart of Dixie.

CHAPTER 35

Welcome to Nesbit Lakes

The closing of our new home was on time and uneventful. There were only a few items on the punch list that required attention, and the home exceeded our expectations. The builder's construction techniques and attention to detail were peerless. We have all heard horror stories about antagonistic relationships between home builders and their clients. Not so in our case. In fact, we became social friends with the builder and his wife.

When our personal property arrived, DL and I wasted no time in setting up our household. Even after everything was unpacked and arranged, the home had some unfurnished spaces because this home was twice as large as the Calabasas home. Fortunately, we had lists of suggestions from the interior design consultant, so we methodically shopped for appropriate furniture and accessories to tastefully finish outfitting our home.

While we were personalizing our new home, we started to establish relationships with our neighbors. The first contacts were next-door neighbors who took the initiative to bring us the ubiquitous "welcome to the neighborhood" casseroles. In addition to being thankful for a prepared meal in the midst of unpacking chaos, we paid attention to the quality of the casseroles to estimate the culinary skills of the neighbors. The normal dialogue of introductions, questions, and answers followed. One humorous interchange was with neighbors who asked where we previously lived. When we said California, there was a sigh and a response with a chuckle, "At least you're not Yankees from New York or Boston!" I mentioned that I had previously lived in South Carolina, Mississippi, Florida, and Virginia and that my daughter was born in North Carolina while DL and I were living there. They seemed soothed by the history of our previous domiciles south of the Mason-Dixon line. On another occasion, DL and I were taking a walk to a nearby boardwalk and gazebo on the lake when we met a stylish woman carrying a crystal goblet of wine while walking her dog. We said hello, introduced ourselves, and then the conversation turned to wine. We immediately bonded. She became a social friend with a similar interest in food and wine. In general, the Nesbit Lakes population was gregarious and always willing to share their Southern hospitality.

I was pleased with two other rather trivial aspects of our new situation in Nesbit Lakes. First, we were relatively close to a toll road, Route 400, that ran south from Alpharetta into Atlanta. It gave us easy access to the fine dining and shopping in the Buckhead area and to the fine dining and Woodruff Arts Center in downtown Atlanta. Second, there was a nice neighborhood restaurant minutes away from the entrance to Nesbit Lakes that gave us a venue for impromptu dinners whenever the spirit moved us. It was our go-to place for dining out on short notice. The chef there was innovative and consistently good. I have attached an uncommon recipe at the end of this chapter that is my interpretation of one of his signature dishes.

PREFACE

This is a simple recipe that can be prepared in minutes. It is difficult to find a listing for Checca in Italian cookbooks, and I was first introduced to it in a small neighborhood Italian trattoria in Alpharetta, Georgia. The version described below is now one of our family favorites, and this version can be a light dinner or a midday lunch. It can also be prepared without the shrimp as a primo piatto in a classic Italian dinner sequence. Fresh grape tomatoes, fresh basil, and high-quality robust olive oil are essential for the sauce. Buon appetito!

Checca with Shrimp

Preparation: 15 minutes
Cooking: 30 minutes
Serves: 4

Step 1a: Prepare the grape tomatoes

> 2 qt. water
> 1 lb. grape tomatoes
> 1 qt. ice water

Step 1a is the preferred method to prepare the tomatoes. Bring the water to a rolling boil in a 3-quart pot. Add the tomatoes, and return to a boil for one minute. Drain the tomatoes and immediately plunge them into the ice water. When the tomatoes have cooled after a few minutes, drain, and transfer the tomatoes to a cutting board.

Cut about 1/16 inch off the stem end of a tomato, and discard. Pinch the opposite end, and the tomato will slide out of the skin. Discard the skin. Cut the skinned tomato in half lengthwise. Repeat with the remainder of the tomatoes. Set aside in a bowl.

Step 1b: Prepare Roma tomatoes

    5 medium *Roma tomato concassé

Step 1b is an option if you choose to use Roma tomatoes and not grape tomatoes. Use either step 1a or step 1b.

Step 2: Pasta

    4 qt. **salted water
    8 oz. spaghetti (4 servings, at 2 oz. dried pasta per person;
           option: capellini, vermicelli, linguine, fettucine)

Bring the water to boil in a 5-quart pot. Cook the pasta according to directions until al dente. Drain the pasta, and then return it to the pot. Cover and keep warm.

Step 3: Base sauce

    1/2 cup EVOO
    4 medium garlic cloves, minced
    2 c. fresh basil leaves, chiffonade and loosely packed

While the pasta is cooking, heat the oil in a 12-inch sauté pan over medium heat. Add the garlic, and sauté until fragrant, about one minute. Add the tomatoes from step 1, and sauté for about three minutes. Lightly crush the tomatoes as they cook with the back of a spoon. Add the basil, stir, and immediately remove from the pan from the heat.

Step 4: Shrimp

> 1 lb. jumbo shrimp, 26–30 per pound: peeled, deveined,
>   tailless
> 1 tsp. salt (or to taste)
> 1/2 tsp. fresh ground black pepper (or to taste)

Add the shrimp to the sauté pan with the base sauce from step 3. Return the pan to the cooktop over medium heat, and cook until the shrimp are pink. Stir frequently. Add salt and pepper to taste.

Step 5: Finish

> 2 tbsp. Parmesan cheese, grated (optional, and not
>   recommended)

Add the finished sauce from step 4 to the pasta in the pot from step 2. Stir to thoroughly dress the pasta with the sauce. Distribute the Checca onto four serving plates. Garnish with Parmesan cheese, if desired, keeping in mind that "authentic" Italians frown on using cheese with seafood.

*Tomato Concassé

Cut an X in the bottom of each tomato. Blanch the tomatoes in a pot of boiling water for 30 seconds. Using a slotted spoon, transfer the tomatoes to an ice water bath to cool. When cool, drain. Remove the stems, and peel off the skin starting from the X. Cut tomatoes in half lengthwise. Remove and discard the core and the seeds. Coarsely chop the tomato.

**Salted Water

For cooking any type of pasta or vegetable, salted water translates to a 1 percent salt solution: about 1 1/2 teaspoons of salt in one quart of water.

PART 10

Fine Dining and Wine in Atlanta

CHAPTER 36

Nesbit Lakes Dining Club

As we met more neighbors, and we attended social functions at the Nesbit Lakes Clubhouse, we developed friendships with people who had similar interests to ours. We paid particular attention to those who were culinarians and those who appreciated fine wine. These friendships evolved into reciprocal dining invitations to our home and theirs. In most cases, I was impressed with the culinary skills and the knowledge of wine demonstrated by our growing circle of friends. Although the format of dinners covered the spectrum of ethnic cuisines and levels of formality, I was surprised at the recurring theme of Low Country cuisine. I assumed that our proximity to Savannah, Georgia, and Charleston, South Carolina, had some influence on this proclivity. I learned that Low Country cuisine shares features with traditional Southern cooking. Its geography, economics, demographics, and culture pushed its culinary identity in a different direction from the style of the Deep South. With its rich diversity of seafood from the coast, its concentration of wealth in Charleston and Savannah, and a vibrant African cuisine influence, Low Country cooking has strong parallels with Creole and Cajun cuisine. I thoroughly enjoyed dishes like Brunswick stew, shrimp kedgeree, Charleston red rice, and Hoppin' John. I was also introduced to the vinegar and mustard-based Low Country barbecue sauce, which is significantly different from more common red tomato-based barbecue sauces. Low Country barbecue sauce is the customary accompaniment with pulled pork in the coastal regions of South Carolina and Georgia. I became a devotee of this combination.

It was not long before DL and I were invited to join the Nesbit Lakes Dining Club, a small group of couples who met monthly to enjoy an upscale meal prepared by one of the couples on a rotating basis. Apparently, we had been privately vetted by the club as a result of our social activity to date. The club had loose dining guidelines that gave couples the opportunity for variety and initiative. At this point, I had compiled a substantial list of personal recipes that I had tested and enjoyed, so DL and I were delighted with the opportunity to entertain our guests with creative dinner themes and menus. Additionally, the inventory of fine wine in our cellar was expanding with both new-world and old-world varieties. We were on a par with the best of our associates regarding the pairing of wine and food. The competition among Club members was not explicit, but it surely was implicit, and the couples' self-pride brought out the best in these amateur chefs.

There was a humorous event I recall from one of our club dinners. A side dish planned by one of the couples was going to be sautéed greens, shallot, and bacon. They had selected spinach as the greens. It seems they had never made this dish for a party of eight. They grossly underestimated the amount of spinach they would need. When they added the spinach to the sautéed shallot and bacon, the leaves immediately wilted to a small volume, as they normally do. This resulted in about one tablespoon of greens per person with a disproportional amount of shallot and bacon. The embarrassed lady of the house exclaimed, "I bought three bags of spinach. I thought that would be more than enough for eight people. I didn't know it would cook down so much! I'm so sorry!" We all accepted the apology with a good laugh and treated the situation as a lesson learned for sautéing greens.

While living in Georgia, I developed a taste for Brunswick stew. There are dozens of recipes in Low Country and colonial Virginia cookbooks for Brunswick stew, and from these, I developed a blend of ingredients and techniques that suited my taste. DL and I favor the use of rabbit and chicken in the dish. I have attached my version of Brunswick stew at the end of this chapter.

Residents of Brunswick County, Virginia, and Brunswick, Georgia, are rivals for the provenance of this dish. Thomas Jefferson listed Brunswick Stew in his collection of favorite recipes. Early colonialists traditionally made the dish, at least in part, with rabbit or squirrel, which they regularly hunted. Although originating in Virginia, the dish has evolved as a Southern specialty in many regional variations. I was first introduced to the stew while living in Atlanta, so my preference runs to the variation from Brunswick, Georgia. This version uses equal parts of rabbit and chicken as the protein. Domestic rabbit can be purchased in the frozen meat section of major supermarkets. It is usually in a three-pound package of ready-to-cook tender young rabbit cut into eight pieces. If you balk at using rabbit, or you cannot find it at your market, substitute pork shoulder, a.k.a. Boston Butt, trimmed into large pieces equal to the amount of chicken. Personally, I prefer to use rabbit. My recipe below attempts to replicate the version of Brunswick Stew served in southeast Georgia. Enjoy!

Brunswick Stew

Preparation: 30 minutes
Cooking: 1 1/2 hours
Serves: 8

Step 1: Brown the meat

    1/4 c. bacon drippings, divided
    2 tsp. salt, divided
    1/2 tsp. cayenne pepper, divided

3 lbs. rabbit, cut into 8 pieces
3 lbs. chicken thighs, skinless with bone in

Heat two tablespoons of the bacon drippings in a 3 1/2-quart Dutch oven over medium-high heat.

Pat dry the rabbit. Season the rabbit with one teaspoon of salt and 1/4 teaspoon of cayenne pepper, or to taste. Place the rabbit in the Dutch oven and brown the pieces, turning frequently until uniformly golden, about 10 minutes. Do not cook through because it will be stewed in steps 3 and 4. Transfer the rabbit to a holding platter.

Heat the remaining bacon drippings in the Dutch oven over medium-high heat. Pat dry the chicken. Season the chicken with one teaspoon of salt and 1/4 teaspoon of cayenne pepper, or to taste. Place the chicken in the Dutch oven and brown the pieces, turning frequently until uniformly golden, about 10 minutes. Do not cook through because it will be stewed in steps 3 and 4. Transfer the chicken to a holding platter. Retain any residual bacon drippings and fat in the Dutch oven.

Step 2: Aromatics

1 c. yellow onion, halved and thinly sliced
1 c. green bell pepper, chopped
1 c. celery, chopped
2 medium garlic cloves, minced

Add the onion, bell pepper, and celery to the Dutch oven. Cook over medium-high heat until the onion wilts, about 6 minutes. Then add the garlic and cook for about another minute until the garlic is fragrant.

Step 3: Liquid base

1 qt. *chicken stock
2 bay leaves

Add the chicken stock and bay leaves to the Dutch oven. While the stock and aromatics are heating over medium heat, scrape the bottom and sides of the Dutch oven to loosen any fond from the browned meat in step 1 and the browned aromatics in step 2.

Return the rabbit and chicken from step 1 to the Dutch oven, including any juices on the platter. Bring to a low boil, then cover, reduce the heat to low, and simmer about 30 minutes until the rabbit and chicken are starting to separate from the bone.

At this point, you have two options for handling the meat. The first is to leave the meat as is, on the bone, in the liquid base for a more rustic stew. The second is to transfer the meat with a slotted spoon to a platter, allow it to cool enough to handle, then remove the meat from the bones. Cut the meat into bite-sized pieces, then return the meat and any juices to the Dutch oven, and discard the bones.

Step 4: Vegetables

> 2 c. **tomato concassé (option: two 14.5-oz. cans of diced tomatoes, drained)
> 2 c. corn kernels, steamed and cut from the cob (option: 16 oz. frozen corn)
> 1 14.5 oz. can lima beans, drained (option: 8 oz. frozen lima beans)
> 1 c. fresh okra, sliced into 1/2-in. coins (option: frozen okra)
> 1 tbsp. fresh marjoram, chopped (option: one teaspoon dried marjoram)
> 2 tsp. Worcestershire sauce
> 1 tsp. sugar
> 1/2 tsp. Tabasco sauce
> Salt, to taste
> Fresh ground black pepper, to taste
> 1 tbsp. apple cider vinegar (optional)

Add all the step 4 ingredients to the Dutch oven. Bring to a low boil, then cover, reduce the heat to low, and simmer about 15 minutes until the vegetables are tender.

Sample the stew, and adjust the seasonings as desired. Add the optional vinegar, if desired. Remove and discard the bay leaves.

Step 5: Finish

1 10.5 oz. can cream corn (optional, to thicken)
Chicken stock (optional, to thin)

After the stew is cooked, the flavors will have thoroughly blended, but you may want to adjust the consistency to suit your preference. If the stew is too thin, add some of the optional cream corn to thicken it as desired. If the stew is too thick, add additional chicken stock to thin it as desired. If any of these optional ingredients are added, simmer for an additional 5 minutes.

Serve the stew in shallow soup bowls, especially if you have left the bones in the rabbit and chicken. A shallow bowl provides easier access for a knife to trim the meat into bite-sized pieces. Accompany the stew with hot biscuits.

*Stock

Master Chef Auguste Escoffier says in his epic treatise *The Escoffier* on the fine art of French cuisine: "Stock is everything in cooking. Without it, nothing can be done. The cook mindful of success, therefore, will naturally direct his attention to the faultless preparation of his stock."

A great stock is judged by five criteria: flavor, clarity, color, body, and aroma. An excellent modern reference for preparing stock can be found in chapter 1 of *The Elements of Cooking* by Michael Ruhlman. If you prefer to use a commercially available stock product, the boxed Swanson brand or Kitchen Basics brand are good choices, but not as good as homemade stock.

**Tomato Concassé

Cut an X in the bottom of each tomato. Blanch the tomatoes in a pot of boiling water for 30 seconds. Using a slotted spoon, transfer the tomatoes to an ice water bath to cool. When cool, drain. Remove the stems and peel off the skin starting from the X. Cut tomatoes in half lengthwise. Remove and discard the core and the seeds. Coarsely chop the tomato.

CHAPTER 37

Fantastic Neighbors

As the construction of my home in Nesbit Lakes was underway, new construction started on the lot next to ours. On one of my routine visits to check the progress of our home, I saw a gentleman also checking the progress on his construction next door. We introduced each other and went through the ritual of getting acquainted as new neighbors. John was a tall man about my age with a substantial but well-groomed blond mustache. I found that he was the sales representative in the southeast United States for the Seagram Company. He had a very friendly, assertive personality that you would expect in a man of his position. When I mentioned my interest in wine and spirits, he motioned me to his car. He opened the trunk to expose bottles of Seagram products and other marketing paraphernalia. He asked what I liked and then handed me bottles of Chateau Greysac Bordeaux wine, Absolut vodka, and a single-malt scotch of a brand I do not recall. I was floored! I had just met the man, but I had the feeling this was going to be a great friendship.

When his home was completed and he moved in, we met his wife, Lynn. She had as much vibrant personality as John. She was also an excellent cook. We reciprocated countless times with dinners at our homes. Lynn was indeed a good cook, and John was very generous with wines and spirits. DL and I made our best efforts to match the high social standards they set, but Lynn and John were in a class by themselves. Not only were their dinners first-class events, an invitation to one of their frequent seasonal house parties was a prized ticket. Of all the good friends we had made in Nesbit Lakes, they were the cream of the crop. I would like to believe they had similar feelings about us.

In the realm of restaurants and clubs, John was well-connected. He seemed to know all the players, and they knew him. When we would go out on the town together, I sometimes felt a twinge of guilt thinking that I was taking advantage of John's friendship. I would bet that thought never crossed John's mind. He was a generous, self-confident extrovert. As a result of our socializing, I was introduced to many of the fine dining restaurants in the Atlanta area that may have taken me years to discover on my own.

I give John credit for one of the major milestones in my life, my certification as a sommelier. Through the course of our friendship over a few years, John became familiar with my intense interest in fine wine. Our dining experiences always included an analysis and discussion of the wines we would select to pair with our menu. He also knew I had a decent-sized library of reference books on wine, and I had a wine cellar with a global selection of quality wine. One day, he approached me to say that he was coordinating a training session for Seagram employees in the wine sector of the business at a convention site in Hilton Head, South Carolina. Seagram had contracted the Court of Master Sommeliers to conduct two phases of training: the introductory course and examination and the deductive tasting method workshop. He asked me if I would like to attend because he had more space available than he had planned for Seagram employees. I was surprised and a little intimidated by the idea. I told John that although I had a good informal knowledge of wine, I did not think I knew enough to be successful in a formal training setting. He gave me a succinct piece of advice to be successful. With a bit of friendly condescendence, he said, "Just read and memorize *The Wine Bible* by Karen MacNeil." So I bought the book and read it cover to cover. I must have remembered enough of the book because I passed the introductory course and examination. I also successfully completed the deductive tasting method workshop, probably because of my practical experience drinking wine with dinner daily for years. I had no interest in higher levels of training in the Court of Master

Sommeliers because I had no intention to ever work as a master sommelier, but I was proud to have achieved the certificate for successfully completing the first level. I credit both John's generosity and sage advice for this accomplishment.

Even after we both left Nesbit Lakes as we moved on in our careers, DL and I maintain contact with Lynn and John to this day. We have visited each other in later residences. They invited us to their daughter's wedding. We receive his annual Christmas letter, and a compilation of these very humorous missives could probably be published. DL and I have resided in numerous places, and from the perspective of food and wine, Lynn and John rank as our number one neighbors of all time.

CHAPTER 38

Buckhead and Downtown

I have already expressed my opinion that New Orleans, New York, and San Francisco are the best cities in the United States for fine dining. The Atlanta area is not in the same tier, but I discovered that the area offers fine dining venues comparable with any other metropolitan area in the next tier. For those who have never visited Atlanta, you may have the stereotypical notion that the cuisine is one-dimensional fried chicken, grits, and greens. You would be sadly mistaken. Atlanta still carries some of the sophistication that was its character over 150 years ago. As a transportation hub, state capital, host to professional sports, center for manufacturing business, and host to the 1996 summer Olympics, Atlanta attracts a clientele who value fine dining. I was pleasantly surprised by the variety and refinement of Atlanta's restaurants.

Buckhead is an upscale area about five miles north of the center of Atlanta. The 30320 zip code in Buckhead is listed as the second wealthiest zip code in the South. Due to this wealth, Buckhead is promoted as the Beverly Hills of the South. It contains the highest concentration of ritzy boutiques in the United States. It is also home to exclusive condos, bars, clubs, the Waldorf Astoria, and a number of foreign consulates. It should not be surprising that this demographic supports a plethora of the finest restaurants in the southeastern United States.

DL and I had easy access to Buckhead from Alpharetta via the route 400 toll road. We frequented Buckhead for fine dining, upscale shopping, and evening entertainment. Our outings were not just on special occasions, and we viewed the area as the epicenter for a night out on the town, either by ourselves or with like-minded friends. We had many spectacular meals in Buckhead, and I would be hard-pressed to single out one event over countless others. I do remember a few courses because they were distinctive dishes. Although DL and I considered ourselves sophisticated consumers, there were a few products that I fancied but DL did not. DL did not share my enthusiasm for oysters, mussels, lamb, veal, and beef carpaccio. So I looked for these items on menus, knowing that I would not be preparing them at home. The Atlanta Fish Market, an unpretentious name for a great Buckhead seafood restaurant, served an inimitable appetizer of PEI Mussels Fra Diavolo in a steaming pot with chili marinara. Another one of my Atlanta Fish Market entrées was Gulf Grouper Francese. Chops in Buckhead is consistently ranked as one of the top ten steakhouses in the country. Their appetizer of Tenderloin Carpaccio with Vidalia onion aioli and flash-fried capers was one of my favorites. I also could not resist their large bone-in veal rib chop. Another one of the great Buckhead restaurants with an unpretentious name was the Capital Grill. They served an all-American variety of steaks and seafood. One of my go-to selections there was lamb rib chops with mint gremolata. I would love to revisit Buckhead to see if it still is the culinary mecca I remember, but until then I will find sensual pleasure in the memory of its sumptuous fare.

Downtown Atlanta offered a number of attractions we frequented. The Woodruff Arts Center was home to the Atlanta Symphony Orchestra, the Alliance Theater, and the High Museum of Art. DL and I were season ticket holders to the Atlanta Symphony Orchestra when Yoel Levi was the conductor, and we attended all the monthly classical concerts. We also bought tickets to the Alliance Theater for performances of interest to us, and we visited the High Museum of Art when new exhibitions were introduced. Whenever we traveled to Downtown Atlanta, we took the opportunity to sample the fine dining, and Atlanta's restaurants were formidable even compared to Buckhead. When we lived in the area, Pano and Paul's Restaurant was an icon, and chef Pano Karrassos was a celebrity. I recall one of his signature dishes, which I ordered more than once, his West Virginia Pheasant entrée. Another celebrity chef was Guenter Seeger, who had his flagship restaurant in Atlanta with another in New York. Veni Vidi Vici was a chic Italian trattoria near the Woodruff Arts Center in a perfect location for a pretheater dinner. The restaurant had a stellar reputation for an interesting menu of meticulously prepared and artfully presented dishes. They were noted for their handmade pasta and delectable desserts. One of their house specialties was Coniglio in Agrodolce, rabbit in sweet-and-sour wine sauce, and every time I ordered, it was even better than the previous. Another one of their dishes occasionally available was osso buco with Barolo braised veal shanks on a nest of handmade pappardelle. I ordered the osso buco whenever it was on the menu, and I considered it their best dish. Because we regularly attended the symphony, we regularly dined at Veni Vidi Vici. One night, as DL and I were leaving Veni Vidi Vici, we saw Tony Bennett standing in front waiting for his son to bring their car to the curb. After I overcame my initial surprise, I said hello and had a brief conversation with him where I told him I was a fan, and I had seen him recently live at the newly renovated Savannah College of Art and Design theater. After we both concurred that the food at Veni Vidi Vici was exceptional, we said goodbye and went on our way. What a friendly guy.

CHAPTER 39

The 1996 Summer Olympics

We were fortunate to be living in the Atlanta area during the 1996 summer Olympics. This was the second time for us to witness the Olympic spectacle as residents in the area where they were held. The first time was when we were living in Laguna Hills, California, during the 1984 summer Olympics in Los Angeles. Olympics always infuse an area with renovations to infrastructure, increase in tourism, expanded local entertainment activities, and emphasis on fine dining catering to the global audience. The 1996 summer Olympics in Atlanta followed this format. The preparation for the games, and the games themselves, made for exciting times.

My company had purchased blocks of tickets for our employees to attend a number of the Olympic events. DL and I saw our share; however, one episode stands out above the rest. To set the stage for this narrative, I need to digress for a moment to explain DL's interest in the Spanish language and culture. DL majored in college in the Spanish language, including sabbaticals at the universities of Valladolid and Salamanca in Spain. She speaks and writes in the Castilian form of the Spanish language, which is generally accepted as the purest form. She also chaperoned a number of summer excursions for high school Spanish students traveling to Spain. She has traveled the breadth of the country, and she is enamored with the people, culture, and cuisine. With the Olympics in Atlanta, she took the initiative to contact the Spanish Olympic Committee and invite them for an evening happy hour at our home. They graciously accepted.

To express her fondness for all things Spanish and to make our Spanish guests feel at home, DL planned a spread of typical Spanish tapas and a variety of Spanish wine. The tapas included Gambas al Ajillo (shrimp in garlic sauce), Membrillo y Manchego (quince paste with Manchego cheese), and Tortilla Española (Spanish potato and onion omelet). The wines included Tempranillo from Rioja, Tinto Fino from Ribera del Duero, and Monastrell from Jumilla. It was a lively evening with a large group of appreciative Spaniards enjoying the ambiance of our splendid home. Then a news announcement shattered the joy of the evening. A bomb had exploded in Olympic Park. Our guests frantically communicated with their associates, and they were relieved to learn that none of their contingents was injured. After a few deep breaths and prayers for those who were injured, we continued the tapas and wine well into the evening, although with a more reserved demeanor. The social aspect of the evening was a great success. At the end of this chapter, I have included a recipe for the Tortilla Española we served.

Variations of this recipe are found throughout Spain, and it is ubiquitous in tapas bars. Do not let the name mislead you. This is not a breakfast dish. This omelet is commonly referred to as a Tortilla Española. Gently cooked potato and onion bound with egg and browned in best-quality Spanish olive oil make an eye-pleasing and flavorful bite. Enjoy!

Spanish Potato and Onion Omelet
(Tortilla Española)

Preparation: 20 minutes
Cooking: 30 minutes
Serves: 16–24 appetizers

Step 1: Sauté the potatoes and onions

> 5 medium russet potatoes
> 1 medium yellow onion
> 1/4 c. EVOO (Spanish first press preferred)
> 1/2 tsp. kosher salt (or to taste)
> 1/4 tsp. ground black pepper (optional)

Peel the potatoes. Quarter them lengthwise, and then cut crosswise into fine slices. Use a mandolin for uniformly thick slices. Peel and chop the onion. Heat the olive oil in a 12-inch sauté pan over medium heat. Add the potatoes and onion to the pan, and sprinkle with salt and pepper. Sauté the vegetables for about 15 minutes, stirring frequently. The potatoes may break apart as they cook and are stirred; this is to be expected. Do not allow the potatoes and onion to brown. Remove the pan from the heat, and allow it to cool for at least

10 minutes. The potatoes and onions can be sautéed several hours in advance of the next step with equally good results.

Step 2: Finishing the omelet

> 1/4 cup EVOO, divided into 4 portions
> 4 large eggs
> 1 tbsp. milk
> 1/4 tsp. kosher salt (or to taste)

Lightly beat the eggs, milk, and salt. Divide the beaten eggs equally between two mixing bowls. Add equal portions of the cooled potato-onion mixture to the bowls. Sprinkle salt to taste. Thoroughly mix the eggs and the vegetables.

Heat one tablespoon of the oil in an 8-inch nonstick sauté pan until the oil ripples (about 350 degrees Fahrenheit). Pour the mixture from one of the bowls into the pan. While the omelet is cooking, shake the pan and slide a spatula around the edge of the omelet to keep it free and to form a high, rounded edge. Also, tilt the pan to allow the wet egg to flow over the edge of the omelet. When the omelet is almost firm, hold a plate upside down on top of the sauté pan. Invert both, sliding the omelet onto the plate as you do. Heat an additional one tablespoon of oil in the pan, then slip the omelet back into the pan, browned side up. This is easier to do if the plate you use fits nearly inside the pan. Shake the pan while the second side browns.

When the first omelet is finished, transfer it to a platter, and repeat the process with the contents of the second mixing bowl.

The omelet may be served hot as the first course to a meal or at room temperature as part of a selection of tapas or an appetizer. Presentation is enhanced if the omelet is cut into rhombus diamond shapes, about 1 1/2 inches long by 3/4 inch wide.

CHAPTER 40

My Fifteen Seconds of Fame

Without a conscious realization, I had been experiencing a culinary transition for a number of years. It was insidious, but I came to fully accept the concept once I was aware. My preparation of gourmet food was as satisfying and sensual as the consumption. My reading about culinary techniques, the various cooking classes I attended, the memory of epicurean meals I had been served, and the establishment of a gourmet kitchen in my home all contributed to more creativity, innovation, and ambition in my preparation of food. I developed a deeper understanding of a quote by Julia Child, "Some people like to paint pictures, or do gardening, or build a boat in the basement. Other people get a tremendous pleasure out of the kitchen because cooking is just as creative and imaginative an activity." I smile and nod my head in agreement.

I get great satisfaction preparing a multicourse meal for dinner parties with friends or relatives. The satisfaction is underscored when they are genuinely pleased with the scope of my effort. However, my greatest satisfaction derives from surprising DL with an intimate dinner for just the two of us. Actress celebrities are famous for their sensuality and their appreciation of the seductive nature of fine food, so it should not be a surprise that Sophia Loren philosophized, "The most indispensable ingredient of all good home cooking: love for those you are cooking for." I try to use a maximum dose of the love ingredient when I cook for DL. One year on Valentine's Day, I prepared a meal for DL focused on the panache of the holiday.

The entrée was an Italian-style dish using some of her favorite ingredients: shrimp, mushrooms, and artichoke hearts. She enjoyed the entrée so much that she sent a copy of my recipe and her laudatory comments to Betty Parham, staff writer for the food section of the *Atlanta Constitution* newspaper. Betty ran an article titled "Cupid in the Kitchen" on the front page of the food section in February 1991. She also sent a staff photographer to our home to take photos of us and our entrée to accompany the article. As an aside, we invited the photographer to dine with us, and he graciously accepted. Needless to say, when those who knew us saw our photos and recipe in the newspaper, they called to congratulate us. There were even some employees of my company who stopped me in the hallways to say they read the article. I remember one employee, who had obviously read too much between the lines in the article, asked the location of my restaurant so he could try the dish! The compliments continued for a while, and my reputation among my close friends as a good chef was enhanced. This event was my fifteen seconds of fame. As an example of a loving culinary effort, I have attached a copy of my published recipe at the end of this chapter.

Another surprising consequence of my fifteen seconds of fame was a letter I received from David Benefiel, the executive chef at the Hyatt Regency Atlanta. He had seen the article about my recipe in the *Atlanta Constitution*. He had tried my recipe, and he extended his compliments. He asked my permission to include my recipe on the menu of the Avanzare Restaurant at the Hyatt. In return for my permission, he offered us a complimentary dinner at Avanzare to sample his version of the recipe. Of course, DL and I accepted the invitation, and we were treated to a superb dinner. David took the time to briefly sit with us at our table and to share a glass of wine with us while we discussed the preparation techniques for the entrée. I felt honored to be participating in a culinary discussion with a certified executive chef. What a thrill!

A Memory of a Romantic Dinner by Vince DiLoreto

On Valentine's Day one year, I created a special dish for dinner for my wife and me. It contained some of Donna Lee's favorite food: shrimp, artichoke hearts, and mushrooms. The presentation made it a perfect dish to serve for a romantic dinner. The table was set with the best china, crystal, and silverware. Red candles and soft music added a glow to the ambiance. The meal was paired with a bottle of Vernaccia di San Gimignano, an excellent Tuscan white wine. Candles and a bubble bath were staged near the Jacuzzi for romantic relaxation after the meal. It was a memorable evening that you may want to replicate. My recipe is below. Buon appetito!

Gamberetti la Donna
(Shrimp for Donna)

Preparation: 1 hour 15 minutes
Cooking: 45 minutes
Serves: 2

Step 1: Aromatics

> 1/4 c. extra virgin olive oil
> 1/2 c. cippolini onions, quartered
> 1/2 c. fennel bulb, white part only, coarsely chopped
> 2 cloves garlic, chopped

Add the oil to a 3-quart saucepan, and heat over medium-high heat. Add the onion and fennel, and sauté for about 5 minutes until the onions are transparent. Add the garlic, and continue to sauté for about one minute until the garlic is fragrant. Transfer the sautéed vegetables and the sautéing oil to a food processor or blender, and set aside. The pan will be used again in step 3.

Step 2: Shrimp

1 c. dry white wine (Pinot Grigio preferred)
1 clove garlic, quartered
2 stalks of fresh basil, with tops and small leaves only (large
    leaves reserved for use in step 3)
3/4 lb. fresh extra-large shrimp (29–30 count per pound)
4 fresh colossal shrimp (9 count per pound)

Add the wine, garlic, and basil stalks to a steamer pot, and simmer covered over medium heat for about 5 minutes to evaporate the alcohol and infuse the herb flavors. While the wine stock is simmering, rinse and drain the shrimp.

Place the shrimp in the steamer basket, colossal shrimp on the bottom with small shrimp on top, and steam them covered over the wine stock. After the shrimp are cooked, about 3 minutes, completely shell and devein the small shrimp and set them aside. Shell and devein the colossal shrimp, leaving the tails, and set them aside. Strain the wine stock from the steamer pot, and reserve the liquid. Discard the solids.

Step 3: Sauce

1 c. heavy cream (option: half-and-half)
1/2 c. wine stock, reserved from steaming the shrimp in step 2
1 tsp. lemon zest
1/2 tsp. kosher salt (or to taste)
1/4 tsp. white pepper (or to taste)
1 pinch saffron
2 tbsp. *roux
4 tbsp. fresh basil leaves set aside in step 2, chopped

2 tbsp. fresh Italian flat-leaf parsley, chopped
1 tbsp. fresh marjoram leaves, chopped

Add cream, wine stock, lemon zest, salt, pepper, and saffron to the sautéed vegetables in the food processor. Blend briefly until smooth, and then return the mixture to the saucepan used in step 1.

Add the roux, basil, parsley, and marjoram to the saucepan. Simmer for about 3 minutes over medium heat to wilt the herbs and thicken the sauce. The consistency of the thickened sauce can be adjusted by either adding water a teaspoon at a time or continued reduction over low heat. Remove the pan from the heat and set it aside.

Step 4: Mushrooms and artichokes

2 tbsp. unsalted butter
1/2 c. cremini mushrooms, sliced (option: baby bella
       mushrooms)
1/2 c. artichoke hearts (bottled or canned)

Add the butter to an 11-inch sauté pan and heat over medium-high heat. Add the mushrooms and sauté for about 3–5 minutes. The liquid that sweats from the mushrooms should be slightly reduced, but the mushrooms should not be browned.

While the mushrooms are sautéing, drain and rinse the artichoke hearts. Prepare them by discarding the woody outer leaves and the interior chokes. Slice lengthwise to the approximate size of the small shrimp. Set aside.

Add the steamed small shrimp, sautéed mushrooms, and artichoke hearts to the saucepan set aside in step 3. Stir and bring the mixture to a simmer over medium-low heat. Heat thoroughly, but do not boil. Remove from heat, keep warm, and set aside.

Step 5: Finish

> 2 sections roasted sweet red bell pepper, large pieces (fresh
> roasted or jar)
> 2 servings angel hair pasta
> 2 qt. **salted water

I recommend fresh roasted peppers. If the roasted red peppers are from a jar, drain and rinse thoroughly. For either the fresh roasted or jar peppers, remove the roasted skin so that the surface is smooth and uniform in color. Cut two heart shapes from the sections. You can use a heart-shaped cookie cutter or cut the shape by hand. The hearts should be at least three inches long from top to bottom.

Prepare two servings of angel hair pasta in salted water according to directions. When the pasta is al dente, drain the pasta. In the empty pot used to cook the pasta, or a mixing bowl, dress the pasta with 1/2 of the sauce from step 4. Then divide the dressed pasta onto two dinner plates. Spoon the remaining sauce over the pasta. Place a red pepper heart on top of the sauce in the center of the plate. Arrange two colossal shrimp around each heart so that the tails form a point at the bottom of the heart and the heads touch in the notch at the top of the heart.

*Roux

Traditional roux is a paste made by cooking equal parts by weight of flour and clarified butter (about 1 part clarified butter to 2 1/2 parts flour by volume). Clarify unsalted butter by heating it gently. The butter will break, and the lighter milk solids will foam to the top. The heavier milk solids will sink. Allow the melted butter to rest off the heat. Skim the foam from the top. Carefully pour off the clarified butter to separate it from the solids on the bottom. In an appropriately sized saucepan, depending on the amount of roux being made, whisk together the flour and the clarified butter over medium heat. After about twenty minutes, the raw flour taste will have cooked out of the mixture, and the color will be blond. Roux can be cooked more for deeper levels of color, depending on the needs of the recipe.

**Salted Water

For cooking any type of pasta or vegetable, salted water translates to a 1 percent salt solution: about 1 1/2 teaspoons of salt in one quart of water.

PART 11

Travel with Emphasis on Food and Wine

CHAPTER 41

Business Trips with Extras

One aspect of my position at GEC Marconi Avionics that surprised me was the opportunity for business travel. I was promoted to higher positions in the company, first to vice president of engineering and programs and eventually to president, and the requirement for travel increased with the higher positions of responsibility in the company. There were a number of reasons to travel. The underlying reason for most was corporate oversight of the financial health of its subsidiaries. Other nonfinancial reasons included program partnership meetings with other companies, marketing presence at industry conventions, and social team-building events. The obligatory financial agendas for business travel were both boring and stressful, but I tried to piggyback a day or two to the business travel for my own sightseeing and entertainment. It was an efficient use of company-paid transportation to satisfy my wanderlust. An added benefit was that my position in the company authorized business class airfare.

The corporation conducted semiannual business reviews with its subsidiaries at corporate offices in Edinburgh, Scotland, and Basildon, England. These reviews focused on financial metrics; so data on revenue, profit, bookings, and backlog were presented. Program reviews were quarterly events focused on the cost, schedule, and technical performance of specific programs, and they were conducted in Edinburgh, Scotland, and Rochester, England. After these boardroom reviews were completed, I was on the road on my own time in Britain.

Edinburgh is steeped in medieval and Celtic history, and I really enjoyed my multiple trips there. The Royal Edinburgh Military Tattoo at Edinburgh Castle is a must-see event. Visiting the pubs and shops on Princes Street in Edinburgh will have you speaking in a brogue in no time. One evening, I drove a short distance to an inn on the Firth of Forth, which was reputed to be the inn Robert Louis Stevenson used as the setting in the opening scenes of his book *Treasure Island*. I ordered a traditional Scottish dinner consisting of Cock-a-Leekie Soup (chicken and leek soup), Stovies (Scottish skillet potatoes), Haggis (sheep's offal with trimmings boiled in the stomach), and Bannock Farls (Scottish flatbread). The dinner was interesting, and I really liked the Stovies, but I decided I would not order the Haggis again.

The most memorable part of my other personal post-business travel in England was sightseeing. London, of course, is filled with sites of cultural and historic significance, too numerous to list. Relatively short driving trips outside of London allowed me to visit the great gothic Salisbury Cathedral, the well-preserved Warwick Castle, Stratford-upon-Avon, and Stonehenge, to name a few. However, in my multiple trips to England and Scotland, I was disappointed in the paucity of fine dining. I am sure London has some world-class restaurants, but I have not had the pleasure of exploring them. On one trip, I stayed at the Brown's Hotel in Mayfair, and one evening I went to Corrigan's Mayfair, a highly rated restaurant. I recall I was pleased with the restaurant, but unfortunately, I do not recall the specifics of the dinner that night. At the risk of being accused of "damning with faint praise," let me offer a positive opinion about one type of English food. In my travels, I enjoyed midday pub food. A stop for lunch at a local pub, with a pint of the local brew, was always satisfying. Some tried-and-true pub food included Fish and Chips (battered fried fish and french fries with malt vinegar), Shepherd's Pie (minced lamb topped with mashed potatoes), Bangers and Mash (sausages and mashed potatoes), and one of my favorite pub dishes, Scotch Eggs (hard-boiled egg molded inside a deep-fried coating of bread crumbs and sausage). I also came to appreciate the full English breakfast, traditionally called the Full Monty. It is usually served buffet-style in a hotel, inn, or pub. I filled my plate with customary offerings such as bacon and sausage, the English version of baked beans, tomatoes grilled in bacon fat, eggs sunny-side-up with runny yolks, sautéed button mushrooms, hash brown potatoes, pan-fried bread, and accompanied with strong hot tea, HP sauce, and marmalade. The Full Monty was the way to start a full day of touring.

The most interesting bit of business travel was the annual air shows in Europe. The recurring events alternated annually between the Farnborough International Air Show in England and the Paris International Air Show in France. These annual expositions were the places where the entire global aerospace industry gathered to learn, network, and do business. These were huge events! All aerospace companies and all countries participated, so you had the opportunity to meet aerospace executive leaders and defense politicians. There were spectacular flight demonstrations, countless product displays, and hospitality chateaus offering food and drink. The excitement and scope of the Farnborough and Paris Air Shows were the highlights of annual business travel.

At one of the Paris Air Shows, I was invited by a marketing manager from one of the largest aerospace companies in the world to tour his company's display of leading-edge, high-technology products. Since his company was a competitor to mine in a number of product areas, I was interested in an escorted tour of his displays. In addition, there was always the possibility of a collaborative effort between our companies, so I would be looking for a business opportunity advantageous for both of us. The display was set up in a large hall on the mezzanine level of a five-star hotel where he and his associates were staying. I arrived at about 6:00 p.m. after a full day at the air show. He greeted me at the entrance, thanked me for coming, offered me a drink, and called for a waiter. I must admit, I wanted to take advantage of his hospitality with the best drink possible, and I assumed his marketing budget could cover just about anything. I turned to the waiter and asked for a glass of 1990 Chateau Margaux, Premier Grand Cru Classe. I knew this to be a very expensive exceptional wine, and I expected the waiter to flinch. He did not. He said, "Oui, monsieur," and hurried away. He soon returned with a goblet of wine on a tray. I was skeptical. Would they serve me a glass of simple house red wine because I would not know the difference as a naive American? I swirled, sniffed, and tasted. It was spectacular wine, and my sensory perception went into overload. This had to be the real thing, a 1990 Chateau Margaux. At this point, the marketeer started leading me through the displays, and I am sure he was giving me his best pitch, but I did not hear a thing. His lips were moving, but all my attention was focused on the wine. It was nearly a religious experience.

Another year at the Paris Air Show, I arrived a few days early so I could implement some of my routine personal travel. I drove to Normandy to see the World War II allied invasion beaches and the somber cemeteries of the fallen. I consider the Normandy invasion site a bucket list destination. While in the Normandy area, I also visited historic sites in Caen and Rouen. I had dinner on this trip that I ranked as one of the best I have ever had. Even in small restaurants, in obscure villages, French dinners are the pinnacle of fine dining. I have included the recipe for Lapin Normandie (braised Normandy rabbit) at the end of this chapter.

On a trip to France, I spent a weekend at the Chateau du Tertre in Normandy. On one evening, I had dinner in a nearby small village, Ambrières, and I enjoyed the meal entrée immensely. I don't recall the name of the village restaurant, but I do recall that it was one of the finest dinners I was ever served. When I returned home after the trip, I experimented in my kitchen, trying to replicate the entrée I ordered that evening. After a number of attempts with various ingredients, quantities, and techniques, I created a recipe that produced a result very similar in taste and presentation to what I had eaten. My recipe is below. Bon appétit!

Braised Normandy Rabbit
(Lapin Normandie)

Preparation: 1 hour
Cooking: 3 hours
Serves: 4–6

Step 1: Brown the rabbit

> 4 oz. slab bacon, only lightly smoked (option: thick-sliced packaged bacon, apple-wood smoke flavored preferred)
> 1 3 lb. rabbit, cut into serving pieces
> 1/2 c. flour
> 1 tsp. salt (or to taste)
> 1/2 tsp. ground black pepper (or to taste)
> 2 tbsp. *clarified butter (option: vegetable oil)

Dice the slab bacon into 1/4-inch cubes. (If more heavily smoked, thick sliced packaged bacon is optionally used instead of slab bacon;

blanch the bacon in boiling water for about one minute to minimize the heavy smoked flavor of the bacon, then proceed as directed.) Sauté the bacon in a 5-quart Dutch oven on the cooktop over medium heat until lightly browned and crisp. Monitor the heat so that the rendered bacon does not burn or smoke. Transfer the bacon to paper towels to drain, and set aside. Remove and discard excess bacon fat from the Dutch oven, leaving just a thin film for flavor.

Pat dry the rabbit pieces with paper towels. Dredge the rabbit in the flour, shaking off excess. Season the rabbit on all sides with salt and pepper. Heat the butter in the Dutch oven over medium-high heat, but not smoking. Add the rabbit to the Dutch oven and sauté for about 8–10 minutes until lightly browned, turning often. Depending on the size of the Dutch oven, the rabbit may have to be browned in two batches. Transfer the browned rabbit to a holding tray, cover, set aside, and keep warm (about 170 degrees Fahrenheit).

Step 2: Aromatic vegetables

> 2 tbsp. *clarified butter (option: vegetable oil)
> 1/2 lb. white pearl onions, peeled (about 25 per 1/2 pound)
> 4 oz. celery, cut to 1/4 inch crescents
> 4 oz. carrot, peeled and cut to 1/4 by 1-in. julienne bâtonnet
> 1/2 lb. chanterelle mushrooms, 1/4 inch slice (option: white
>   mushrooms)
> 3 garlic cloves, finely minced

Add the butter to the Dutch oven, and heat over medium-high heat, but not smoking. Add the onion, celery, carrot, and mushrooms. Sauté for about 5 minutes until the mushrooms sweat. Add the garlic and sauté for another minute until the garlic fragrance is released.

Step 3: Braise

> 1 c. aromatic dry white wine (Loire Chenin Blanc or Alsace
>   Gewürztraminer)
> 1 c. **tomato concassé

2 c. ***veal stock (option: chicken or vegetable stock)
3 tbsp. ****Fresh Fines Herbes, minced (or 3 tsp. dried)
6 lemon rind strips (1/4 by 2 in.)
1/2 tsp. kosher salt (or to taste)
1/4 tsp. white pepper (or to taste)
1 *****Sachet d'Epices

Preheat the oven to 350 degrees Fahrenheit.

Add the wine to the Dutch oven with the sautéed vegetables from step 2. Bring to a low boil on the cooktop over medium heat. Gently deglaze the Dutch oven by scraping up any brown bits on the bottom, but do not bruise the vegetables. Add the tomatoes. Reduce the liquid by half, about 10 minutes, stirring occasionally.

Add the stock, Fines Herbes, lemon rind, salt, pepper, and Sachet d'Epices to the Dutch oven. Add the crisp crumbled bacon from step 1. Nestle the rabbit pieces from step 1 in the Dutch oven on top of the vegetables, and bring to a low boil over medium heat. The liquid in the Dutch oven should cover the rabbit.

Remove the Dutch oven from the cooktop. With the cover slightly ajar, transfer to the oven, and braise at 350 degrees Fahrenheit for 15 minutes.

Reduce the oven heat to 200 degrees Fahrenheit, turn the rabbit, tightly cover the Dutch oven, and continue to braise for about 30 minutes. Then remove the Dutch oven from the oven. Using tongs, temporarily remove the rabbit from the Dutch oven. Using a slotted spoon or spider, transfer the vegetables to a holding tray, cover, set aside, and keep warm (about 170 degrees Fahrenheit). The vegetables should be tender, using the carrot as a test. Do not overcook the vegetables or they will become too soft, fall apart, and lose their integrity. Retain the lemon rind and Sachet d'Epices in the braising liquid.

Return the rabbit to the Dutch oven. The braising liquid in the Dutch oven should just cover the rabbit. If not, add additional veal stock or water, as necessary. Tightly cover the Dutch oven, and continue to braise at 200 degrees Fahrenheit for about another hour. Test the internal temperature of the rabbit with a meat thermometer, until it reaches 140 degrees Fahrenheit.

Step 4: Finish

> 6 oz. ******roux, blond
> 1 tsp. fresh squeezed lemon juice
> 1 tbsp. unsalted butter
> 1/4 c. heavy cream (option: half-and-half)
> 4 qt. *******salted water
> 1 lb. curly egg noodles (option: other medium-size flat pasta)
> 1/4 c. fresh chives, snipped for garnish

When the rabbit is tender, remove the Dutch oven from the oven. Using a slotted spoon or a spider, transfer the rabbit to a holding tray, cover, set aside, and keep warm (about 170 degrees Fahrenheit). Remove and discard the Sachet d'Epices and the lemon rind. Return the Dutch oven with the braising liquid to the cooktop. Add the roux, and simmer over medium heat until the sauce reduces and thickens to the desired consistency. Remove from the heat, and finish the sauce by whisking in the lemon juice, butter, and cream.

Bring the salted water to a boil in a 5-quart pot over medium-high heat. Cook the egg noodles according to directions. Drain.

Place a bed of noodles on warm dinner plates. Spoon half the sauce over the noodles, reserving the remainder of the sauce in the Dutch oven. Arrange the warm vegetables from step 3 on the bed of noodles. Then place the warm rabbit from step 3 on top of the vegetables and noodles. Drizzle the remaining sauce over the rabbit, then garnish with the snipped chives.

As suggestions for accompaniment to this entrée, start with a céleri-rave rémoulade (a classic French celeriac salad), haricots verts sautéed with butter, and shallots topped with walnuts. For dessert, serve marinated cherries with kirsch ice cream. This would make a French dinner to remember.

*Clarified Butter

Clarify unsalted butter by heating it gently. The butter will break, and the lighter milk solids will foam to the top. The heavier milk solids will sink. Allow the melted butter to rest off the heat.

Skim the foam from the top. Carefully pour off the clarified butter to separate it from the solids on the bottom. Discard the top foam and bottom solids.

**Tomato Concassé
Cut an X in the bottom of each tomato. Blanch the tomatoes in a pot of boiling water for 30 seconds. Using a spider or slotted spoon, transfer the tomatoes to an ice water bath to cool. When cool, drain. Remove the stems and peel off the skin from the X. Cut tomatoes in half lengthwise. Remove and discard the core and the seeds. Coarsely chop the tomato meat.

***Stock
Master Chef Auguste Escoffier says in his epic treatise *The Escoffier* on the fine art of French cuisine: "Stock is everything in cooking. Without it, nothing can be done. The cook mindful of success, therefore, will naturally direct his attention to the faultless preparation of his stock."

A great stock is judged by five criteria: flavor, clarity, color, body, and aroma. An excellent modern reference for preparing stock can be found in chapter 1 of *The Elements of Cooking* by Michael Ruhlman. If you prefer to use a commercially available stock product, the boxed Swanson brand or Kitchen Basics brand are good choices but not as good as homemade stock.

****Fines Herbes
An aromatic blend of herbs that usually includes equal parts of chervil, tarragon, chives, and flat-leaf parsley.

*****Sachet d'épices
Place four sprigs of parsley and two sprigs of thyme in a piece of cheesecloth. Add two bay leaves, twelve cracked Tellicherry black peppercorns, and a crushed clove of garlic. Fold opposite edges of the cheesecloth over the herbs, roll the cheesecloth from an open edge, and bind the roll with kitchen twine. As an alternative to cheesecloth, use a Number 4 Tea Filter Bag. (Adequate to flavor one gallon of liquid.)

******Roux, Traditional

Traditional roux is a paste made by cooking equal parts by weight of flour and clarified butter (about 1 part clarified butter to 2 1/2 parts flour by volume). In an appropriately sized saucepan, depending on the amount of roux being made, whisk together the flour and the clarified butter over medium heat. After about 20 minutes, the raw flour taste will have cooked out of the mixture, and the color will be blond. Roux can be cooked more for deeper levels of color, depending on the needs of the recipe.

*******Salted Water

For cooking any type of pasta or vegetable, salted water translates to a 1 percent salt solution: about 1 1/2 teaspoons of salt in one quart of water.

CHAPTER 42

Western Europe

While I was employed with GEC Marconi Avionics and we were living comfortably in our beautiful home in Nesbit Lakes, DL and I still followed our routine of annual international travel. As an aside, the travel was assisted by the fact I had accumulated tens of thousands of miles in my business travel, and company policy allowed me to bank these in my personal account. So DL and I used the mileage for free airfare when we traveled. We revisited the countries of Spain, France, and Italy, but we attempted to see parts of these countries we had not previously visited. Our goal was to experience something new each year. The scope of medieval and Renaissance art, architecture, museums, and treasures is nearly boundless. Regarding museums, three of the greatest museums on earth are bucket-list attractions: the Prado in Madrid, the Louvre in Paris, and the Uffizi in Florence. We also planned our itineraries to include wine-growing regions and wineries in the countries. Of course, Spain, France, and Italy are prolific wine producers. We covered key spots in Spain from Rias Baixas in the northwest to Granada in the southeast. Similarly, we touched France from Bordeaux in the southwest to Alsace in the northeast. Italy saw us visit Piedmont in the northwest to Sicily in the south. In addition to the wine, all the while we ate like royalty. Great meals in Spain, France, and Italy are the norm, and we joked that you would have difficulty finding a bad meal in any of these countries. From finger food to banquets, they are nirvana for foodies.

On one of our trips to Paris, we succumbed to the tourist temptation to have dinner at the Café Procope, reputed to be the oldest café in Paris. The word *café* does injustice to this fine restaurant. The interior was decorated in an eighteenth-century style of Pompeian red walls, crystal chandeliers, portraits of famous patrons, and waiters dressed in eighteenth-century livery. Famous patrons have included Voltaire, Benjamin Franklin, Robespierre, and Napoleon Bonaparte. DL and I were standing outside Procope, looking at the menu on the wall, when we noticed a couple standing behind us and talking in hushed tones. They had the look of young Americans on their honeymoon overwhelmed by the French menu. Although DL and I are not fluent in French, we had some experience ordering from French menus. We offered to help the couple with the explanation of some of the menu items we understood, such as moules dans le bouillon d'ail (mussels in garlic broth), champignons (mushrooms), and bifteck de cheval (horse steak). They were most appreciative, but they stayed outside discussing the menu as DL and I entered. I recall that we were seated near a large fireplace, and I ordered a four-course meal that included roast horse with red wine and onions. It was dark meat, lean, tasty, but a little chewy. It was the first time I had ever eaten a horse, and I have not had the opportunity or desire to order it again.

Another destination we added to our summer vacations was Ireland. We booked five-day hotel stays in Limerick, Dublin, and Belfast. While in each location, we traveled by rental car to visit places of interest in the surrounding areas. Celtic and Medieval sites abound. Some were anticipated and fun, like the Blarney Stone at Blarney Castle. Some were very surprising, such as the well-preserved New Grange burial mounds built during the Neolithic period, around 3,200 BC, making them older than Stonehenge or the Egyptian pyramids! The Book of Kells at Trinity College in Dublin dates from AD 800, and it is a masterwork of Western calligraphy and represents the pinnacle of manuscript illustration. It is also widely regarded as one of Ireland's finest national treasures, and I contend it is a bucket list item for travelers. Ireland is truly a beautiful country! However, from the perspective of fine dining, it is similar to England and Scotland. Evening dinners are mediocre, but pub food is good, and the hearty breakfast Fry-Up is nearly identical to the English Full Monty. For those who like a substantial breakfast, the Fry-Up is the way to start the day. I was pleasantly surprised by one dish on a number of menus. It was mussels. Irish lamb stew, yes, but mussels? I had never thought of Ireland as a source for mussels, but they were uniformly fresh and delicious, and relatively inexpensive, too. A mounded basket of mussels with broth was more than enough to satisfy an ardent seafood lover like me. The blue mussels in Ireland seemed larger than Mediterranean or stateside mussels, but not as large as New Zealand green mussels. I have eaten mussels in many worldwide locations, but in my opinion, the Irish mussels were the best I have ever had.

There was a lot more Western Europe for us to visit, so DL and I drafted a prioritized list of destinations. In addition, we added other worldwide destinations. We wanted to see as much as possible while we were young and healthy. We believe it is both a mistake and a tragedy to wait for retirement before undertaking international travel. The world is huge, and there are so many sights to see, cuisines to sample, wines to enjoy, and so little time to do it all. Travel opens up your perspective to the breadth of human complexity and achievement.

CHAPTER 43

South America

DL loves surprises. She especially loves surprises where there is a theme. For example, she would swoon over the gift of an emerald shamrock pendant on her birthday, March 17, St. Patrick's Day. Or she would be tickled if I gave her flowers to celebrate the day in September when we were engaged to be married. So as our twenty-fifth wedding anniversary approached, I wanted to plan a memorable surprise. The twenty-fifth anniversary is the silver anniversary, and a trip to the Rio de la Plata, the River of Silver, in Argentina seemed appropriate. An additional consideration was that we would be celebrating our January anniversary south of the equator in summer. I made reservations at a classic upscale hotel in Buenos Aires, the Hotel San Martin. The hotel was popular with foreign diplomats and other dignitaries. It is located in the Retiro neighborhood on Plaza San Martin at the northern end of the pedestrianized Florida Street, noted for its exclusive shopping. We would be in Buenos Aires for a week, and I hired a private car with a chauffeur to show us the highlights of the city. I also scheduled some sightseeing bus excursions for attractions well outside of Buenos Aires. DL was over the moon with this twenty-fifth wedding anniversary surprise.

Buenos Aires is an exciting city, sometimes referred to as BA, the Big Apple. There were many memorable events on the trip. Many of them were totally unexpected. On our first afternoon, we walked from the hotel along Florida Street. DL found some items to purchase and charged them on our credit card. As we were leaving the store after her first purchase, the saleswoman said "Ciao," an Italian greeting. I commented to DL how polite and sophisticated the saleswoman was to say "Ciao" after noticing our Italian surname on our credit card. However, we soon discovered that politeness had nothing to do with the surname on our credit card. In every store we entered, the salesperson greeted us with "Ciao." It was a standard greeting. We learned that Buenos Aires has a large population of Italians who emigrated to Argentina after World War II. It was part of the cosmopolitan character of the city. If you blinked for a moment and for an instant forgot where you were, you would open your eyes to find you could be in Milan, Madrid, or London. Our chauffeur offered a cliché-ish description of stereotypical residents of Buenos Aires: they dress in Italian fashion, speak Spanish, and have the self-confidence of the English. We found this description close to the mark.

On our first night in Buenos Aires, we asked the hotel concierge where we could find great restaurants and live entertainment. He directed us to the Recoleta neighborhood. The area is well-known for the most important Italian and French designers who have stores in Recoleta. It is also the gastronomic center of the city. A number of restaurants of international distinction are located along Ortiz Street, which is a pedestrian street. Clubs, cafes, and bars are scattered throughout the neighborhood. La Biella Café-Bar on the corner of Ortiz and Quintana Streets represents the area well. Our first night in Recoleta educated us to the evening heartbeat of the Big Apple. We arrived in Recoleta at about 7:00 p.m., and the area was calm and quiet. We walked the streets looking for a promising restaurant, but all were empty. At about 8:00 p.m. we were famished, so we entered a nice-looking restaurant, but only a very few customers. We had a four-course dinner with an excellent steak entrée, accompanied with grilled vegetables and a bottle of Malbec wine from Mendoza. Toward the end of our leisurely dinner, about 10:00 p.m., we noticed the restaurant filling with customers, but we were ready for some live entertainment, so we were back on the street again. As in our earlier search for a restaurant, we walked the streets looking for a promising club, but all were quiet with few customers. They started to fill as the dinner crowd finished their meals, and the clubs were bustling by midnight. We made our way back to the hotel a little after midnight, but the clubs were just hitting their stride in the wee hours of the morning. For the duration of our stay in Buenos Aires, we adjusted to the schedule of the locals, although we stayed on the early side of their schedule: dinner from 9:00 p.m. to 11:00 p.m. and clubbing from 11:00 p.m. to 1:00 a.m. This applied to weekdays and weekends.

For those who may not have had the same experience as DL and I had in Buenos Aires, let me summarize our observations of a typical day in the city. The city seems to awaken at midmorning, and the cafés are serving coffee, pastries, and beef empanadas to well-dressed business clientele at about 9:00 a.m. The retail stores are open from about 9:00 a.m. to 1:00 p.m. when they close for the midday meal and/or a siesta. This occurs from about 1:00 p.m. to 3:00 p.m. The midday meal is not lunch as we know it in the States. It is a multi-course meal with steak, chimichurri, and grilled vegetables. The retail stores reopen from about 3:00 p.m. to 7:00 p.m., and after closing, I believe the residents go home to prepare for the evening activities. How they can sustain this schedule is beyond me. DL and I participated for a week, and it took us a couple of days at home after the vacation to recover, but it was surely an exciting vacation.

If you are a beef lover, Argentina is the place to go. The quality and availability of beef are probably the best in the world. Per capita, beef consumption in Argentina is over two times greater than in the States (125 pounds per person in Argentina to 55 pounds per person in the USA). The general population is composed of connoisseurs of quality beef, and they are much more familiar with cuts of beef than average US consumers. The menus list a variety of cuts and in many cases show a schematic of where the cut is located on the animal. Most common are Bife de Lomo (tenderloin), Bife de Solomillo (porterhouse), Bife de Chorizo (NY strip), Entraña (skirt), Vacio (flank), and Asada de Tira (short ribs). DL and I ate beef in the morning, midday, and evening almost every day we were in Argentina. I recall only one evening when DL said in exasperation, "Let's have chicken for our protein tonight instead of beef," so we found a Spanish restaurant and ordered an entrée of Andalusian chicken with green olives and bitter oranges. Although our beef consumption may have been excessive by normal Stateside standards, it was a daily gourmet experience during our vacation. We even became accustomed to beef empanadas with our coffee in the morning. I have attached a recipe at the end of this chapter for a typical empanada we enjoyed to start the day.

A few years after our grand experience in Argentina, we decided to visit Argentina's neighbor to the west, Chile. The idea started with some neighbors who had immigrated to the States from Chile a decade earlier. DL fortuitously met the couple through her network of Spanish-speaking friends. They knew we had vacationed in Argentina, and they knew we were wine drinkers. With pride in their native country and the promotion of Chilean wines, they made a convincing case that we should visit Chile. Coincidentally, the man of the house, whom I will call Guillermo, was working on a career change that entailed the creation of a pharmaceutical company in Chile. Guillermo made frequent long-duration trips to Chile, and ultimately, he was spending more time in Chile than in the States. DL and I began planning a trip to Chile, and Guillermo graciously insisted that we spend a week in Santiago while he was there so he could show us the city and its surroundings. It is good to have worldly friends.

We flew to Santiago in January, summer south of the equator, and we flew business class for free with my banked mileage. Guillermo met us at the airport and drove us to our hotel. We stayed at the Marriott Santiago Hotel, a five-star hotel on Avenida Presidente Kennedy. At the time, the Marriott was the tallest building in Santiago, and we had a corner suite on an upper floor with breathtaking views north and east. The air was crisp and crystal clear, with visibility probably greater than twenty-five miles, so the snow-covered Andes Mountains seemed within arm's reach, and we could easily see ski lifts on some of the slopes. We coordinated with Guillermo for the itinerary over the next few days to tour wine producers, and he also gave us an extensive list of places in Santiago to see on our own.

On our first full day in Chile, Guillermo took us to the Maipo Valley, about an hour's drive from Santiago. We visited a couple of wineries, but the most memorable was Concha y Toro. The pre-eminent selection we tasted there was the Don Melchor Reserva Cabernet Sauvignon. It is reputed to be one of the finest Cabs in the world, and I will not disagree with that. A very interesting part of the Concha y Toro tour was the visit to the Casillero del Diablo, the Devil's Cellar. The tour guide told the story that some Concha y Toro workers decades ago were misappropriating wines, so the management moved the best wines to a cellar and spread the rumor that the cellar was haunted by the devil. The workers named the cellar Casillero del Diablo, and they feared to go in. The pilfering of wines diminished. During our tour, they momentarily turned off the cellar lights, and the place became pitch-black. The only sight that could be seen was a glowing red devil's face above the lintel of the cellar entrance, configured with a sinister smirk, a goatee, and horns. The tourists gasped!

One day, we traveled about one and a half hours to the Casablanca Valley. We visited the Matetic, Cono Sur, and Montes Alpha wineries. When we arrived at Matetic, the parking lot was totally empty, but we went to the entrance. A man came to the door and said the winery was closed to tours that day. Guillermo introduced himself and introduced us as his friends from the United States and asked for special consideration. The man said he was not too busy, and he would give us a private tour. Hooray for Guillermo! It was a very modern building and appeared brand-new. We appreciated the one-on-one hospitality and enjoyed the tasting and detailed analysis of Matetic's organically grown wines. I do not recall much of the visit to Cono Sur, but I have a unique memory of Montes Alpha unrelated to their wine, although I could be mistakenly assigning the memory to Montes Alpha. In any case, I was impressed by a large sitting room in the building that was decorated with an abundance of lapis lazuli. Lapis is mined in two places in the world, Afghanistan and Chile. It is a beautiful and relatively rare stone composed of blue lazurite. The sitting room had lapis chandeliers, lapis tabletops, lapis sconces on the walls, and a lapis fireplace mantle. It could have been a room at a museum. Up until this moment, DL and I did not know that Chile was a source for lapis lazuli, and I could have predicted that DL would buy some lapis jewelry while we were in Chile. It compliments her beautiful blue eyes.

On another day, we traveled north to Valparaiso. There were some small wineries on higher slopes overlooking the Pacific. I do not remember the winery names, but they advertised their locations as good for Pinot Noir. We took lunch on an open-air patio in Valparaiso, and it was a delicious spread of mixed seafood, and we drank the local Pinot Noir. The lunch was a precursor to seafood dinners we would enjoy in Santiago. With over three thousand miles of rugged Pacific coastline and its narrow east-west inland geography, Chile offers great cold-water seafood. Some delectable, unusual lunch and dinner seafood dishes were congrio, one of my favorites (firm, mild white eel, similar in taste and texture to monkfish), machas (pink, long, and flat razor clams), choritos (small black mussels), corvina (similar to bass and great in ceviche), and picorocos (barnacles with a taste between crab and lobster and tons of flavor). We ate seafood almost daily in Chile, analogous to our daily beef consumption in Argentina.

I looked forward to dining in Santiago. It was our first visit to Chile, and we did not know what to expect. We told Guillermo we favored fine dining venues, and we tried two restaurants that he recommended as the best in Santiago, in his opinion.

The first restaurant was called Azul Pacifica, and it was a striking midsized facility. It had an expansive menu, but the majority of the items were seafood. I saw Chilean sea bass in the list of entrées, and I thought, "What could be more appropriate?" I had ordered Chilean sea bass in Stateside restaurants, and I anticipated making the comparison with the local product. There was no comparison. The dish I was served was lemongrass and panko-crusted baked thick fillet of Chilean sea bass. The meat was bright white in color with a rich melt-in-your-mouth flavor. It was so much better than stateside Chilean sea bass I wondered if the fish I ate in the States was really Chilean sea bass. I suspect the major difference was that my entrée at Azul Pacifica was fresh, never frozen, and the product exported to the States is lesser quality frozen fillets. In any case, my entrée was so impressive that I do not recall the other courses in the meal. Since this dinner in Santiago, I have been reluctant to order Chilean sea bass elsewhere.

The second restaurant was called Gardel's. It was a large thriving facility filled with active customers. I quickly learned that the restaurant was named after Carlos Gardel, an Argentinian songwriter, composer, and tango singer. A neon-lighted portrait of smiling Carlos Gardel wearing his signature fedora adorned the restaurant entrance. Gardel's proudly advertised the best Argentinian beef in Santiago. I had hoped for a venue with typical Chilean food, but since we were already at Gardel's, and we were familiar with great Argentinian beef, we decided to dine there. The kitchen lived up to the advertisement, and the porterhouse steak I ordered was as good as steak can be. I was served a large bone-in steak, medium rare, tender, juicy, and packed with flavor. The beautiful, uniform char on the outside was indicative of a high-temperature grill. Besides the high quality, well-cooked steak, the memorable aspect of the service was the presentation at the table. The steak filled the plate, and the waiter asked if I wanted him to slice it for me. I did, and with a surgeon's precision, he sliced the strip and the fillet tableside into overlapping ribbons about one inch thick. It was obvious that the steak had been properly rested because the juice remained in the meat. Any remnant of disappointment I may have had dining in Santiago on Argentinian beef disappeared with the presentation and the first bite. But the evening was not entirely at a loss for Chilean influence. We ordered a vintage bottle of Don Melchor Cabernet Sauvignon to pair with the steak. I do not recall the vintage year, but I do recall that the wine was the most expensive part of the meal. It was plated ecstasy!

DL and I plan to visit Argentina and Chile again in the future. Unfortunately, there are a few other destinations we have not visited that are ahead in the queue. There is so much global cuisine and wine yet to be sampled. The world is large, and time is short.

On our first trip to Argentina, my spouse and I learned how much the Argentinians love their beef. Beef was consumed for breakfast, lunch, and dinner. For comparison, per-capita beef consumption in Argentina is about 125 pounds per year whereas in the United States, the per-capita beef consumption is about 55 pounds per year. Why? I offer two reasons: first, cattle ranching is one of Argentina's main businesses, and second, the quality of Argentinian beef is world-class! One of the pleasant surprises we experienced was the common practice of having beef empanadas for breakfast. These juicy meat hand pies are also a hit at lunches, brunches, and buffets. The recipe below is my attempt to replicate the beef empanadas we enjoyed for breakfast with our morning coffee in Argentina. Enjoy!

Argentinian Beef Empanadas

Preparation: 1 hour
Cooking: 30 minutes
Serves: 8 (2 per person)

Step 1: Brown the ground beef

> 1 lb. 85 percent lean grass-fed ground beef or high-quality equivalent

Cook the beef in a 10-inch cast-iron skillet over medium-high heat. Stir and break up the lumps into a uniform granular consistency. Cook until the beef is no longer pink, about 6 minutes, but do not heavily brown the beef. Use a slotted spoon to transfer the beef to a platter lined with paper towels. Pour off and discard the oil remaining in the skillet.

Step 2: Onions and extras

> 1/4 c. black raisins
> 2 tbsp. hot water
> 3 tbsp. unsalted butter
> 2 medium yellow onions, chopped
> 2 large eggs, hard-boiled and chopped
> 16 medium Manzanilla green olives, pitted and minced
>   (option: Castelvetrano olives)
> 1/2 tsp. ground cumin
> 1 pinch ground allspice
> 1 pinch ground nutmeg
> 1/2 tsp. salt
> 1/4 tsp. ground black pepper

Plump the raisins in the hot water for about 10 minutes. Drain and set aside.

Melt the butter in the 10-inch cast-iron skillet used in step 1 over medium heat. Add the onion and sauté until tender, about 6 minutes. Return the beef from step 1 to the skillet. Add the eggs, olives, spices, and seasonings. Stir to thoroughly mix, reduce the heat to low, and allow the flavors to blend for about 5 minutes.

Transfer the mixture to a shallow bowl and cool at room temperature for 10–20 minutes.

Step 3: Fill the empanadas

> 2 packages frozen puff pastry (2 sheets per package for a total
>   of 4 sheets)

Defrost the puff pastry sheets according to directions.

Line two shallow half-size baking sheets, 13 × 18 inches, with parchment paper.

Position two racks in the center of the oven. Heat the oven to 425 degrees Fahrenheit.

Unfold a pastry sheet onto a lightly floured surface. Dust the top with flour. Roll the sheet into a 12-inch square. Cut four 6-inch rounds from the sheet. Brush a 1/2-inch border around each round with water. Spoon about 3 tablespoons of filling from the shallow bowl in step 2 onto 1/2 of the round. Fold the other half of the round over the filling and press the edge together, then crimp the edge with a fork. Transfer the half-moons to one of the prepared baking sheets, positioning them at least 1 1/2 inches apart.

Repeat the process with the three remaining puff pastry sheets to make 12 more empanadas in the same manner. This will yield eight empanadas on each of the two baking sheets.

Step 4: Finish

1 large egg, lightly beaten

Brush the tops of the empanadas with the beaten egg. Bake for about 8 minutes, then switch the position of the baking sheets in the oven and bake for about another 7 minutes until the empanadas are golden brown. The empanadas can be served hot or at room temperature.

PART 12

Relocating
to Austin

CHAPTER 44

Flux in the Business World

As president of GEC Marconi Avionics in Atlanta, I had some insight into the corporate headquarters' business strategy and plans. It was not total insight, but it was enough for me to deduce the future plans of the corporation. My deductions were corroborated with the unusual executive travel I observed. Ultimately, I was finally informed about the acquisitions and corporate reorganization that were in progress. Now I could start to anticipate the effect these changes would have on my company and on me personally.

A number of significant events occurred sequentially over a two-year period. The corporation made a number of acquisitions of private companies in the United States. This growth necessitated a new high-level reorganization of the corporation where companies were grouped into sectors, which meant that my company would be part of a US sector. Inevitable consolidations for efficiency followed the reorganization. My business was relocated from Atlanta to Austin, Texas. Then came a major merger between GEC Marconi and British Aerospace to form a huge new corporation called BAE Systems. This merger resulted in another round of organizational changes and consolidations. Personally, it was a dizzying and unsettling flurry of activity.

Coincidentally and unrelated to this business activity, DL and I had been looking ahead to retirement. Our personal financial situation was healthy, so the most important factor to us was where to retire. We went as far as creating a spreadsheet with weighted decision considerations, which we populated with factors that were both very important and less important to us. Our weighting was based on detailed research and personal experience. We wanted the low cost of living, warm weather, cultural activities and, of course, fine dining. We were not that concerned with public transportation and school districts. Based on our analysis, we selected five possible retirement locations: Alpharetta, Georgia, where we were currently residing; Savannah, Georgia; Charleston, South Carolina; the Research Triangle area of North Carolina; and Austin, Texas. This was the point in time when our personal retirement planning and the chaos in my business world coincided. Fate had delivered us an ideal scenario. I would be relocating my company to Austin, which was one of the retirement locations we had already independently selected.

CHAPTER 45

A New Home in Austin

Prior to this, I had no discussion of retirement with corporate management. More than ever now, I decided to not raise the subject. Instead, I worked diligently with the sector staff to relocate the company from Atlanta to Austin in the most efficient manner possible. Part of the planning was the negotiation and incentives for me to move with the company to Austin because it was not a "given" that I would want to relocate or that the corporation would want to retain me in my position. As it turned out, we reached an agreement for me to relocate to Austin with the company, and this agreement included a relocation package including a furnished apartment, real estate services, and shipment/storage of our personal property. It may sound a little Machiavellian on how we manipulated the situation, but it was nearly a perfect solution for both our career and retirement plans. It would have been difficult to foresee a better outcome.

I moved into my apartment in Austin, while DL remained in our home in Alpharetta. I traveled between Atlanta and Austin about every two weeks, in the complex and time-consuming process of relocating the company to Austin. The transportation and installation of administrative, engineering, and manufacturing assets were a challenge; but equally challenging was the staffing and training of new employees in Austin. Of the approximately 350 employees in Atlanta, we made offers of employment with relocation incentives to about 50 of those employees whom we believed had the secret sauce for the success of the business. About 25 of those accepted the offers.

Fortunately, there was a large pool of potential skilled employees in Austin, so restaffing the company proceeded quickly.

While I was busy with the relocation, I was also searching for a new home. The real estate agent provided by the company was the best I had experienced in any of my previous searches. She was very professional, and she filled my scarce free time with visits to homes, lots, and community developers. Once again, I took the lead on the new home, and DL took the lead on selling our Alpharetta home. With the diligent help of my real estate agent, we found a half-acre lot with a view in the River Place Country Club community. With DL's concurrence, I contracted a custom builder to start on the home in River Place, and DL put the Alpharetta home on the market. We decided to downsize to a single-floor home, about 3,300 square feet. It would be an open floor plan ideal for entertainment, a gourmet kitchen, three bedrooms, and a three-car garage. I monitored the construction progress in River Place every weekend and sometimes on weekdays. DL sold the home in Alpharetta in a month, put our household goods in storage, and joined me in the apartment in Austin while we awaited the completion of our new home.

A humorous conversation with a member of the sector staff occurred during the transition period. The sector president had invited me to a get-acquainted dinner with his staff. We went to Sullivan's, a popular, well-rated steakhouse in Austin. As the evening started, the wine steward began pouring red wine for the table. I noticed that the wine was a 1994 Stag's Leap Cabernet Sauvignon. I knew the wine. It was highly rated and cost about $100 per bottle. I asked the gent sitting next to me who ordered the wine because it was a superb selection, especially paired with Sullivan's steaks. The gent answered that the sector president had ordered it and added that he was a wine enthusiast. He then asked if I was also a wine enthusiast. I told him I had received basic sommelier training from the Court of Master Sommeliers and that I had a 1,200-bottle-capacity wine cellar in my Alpharetta home. When I said, "1,200-bottle capacity," he nearly spat out the sip of beer he was taking. It was then that I realized he was not drinking wine but Shiner Bock bottled beer. I further explained that my wife and I had been purposefully consuming our wine cellar without replenishment over the last year with the expectation of relocating to Austin, and the cellar now contained fewer than five hundred bottles. He still found "five hundred bottles" incredulous. To further clarify, I told him I maintained a spreadsheet of the wine cellar contents, so I knew that my wife and I consumed about five hundred bottles a year through personal daily consumption and frequent entertaining. He wrinkled his nose in apparent disgust at the thought of daily wine consumption. Then he gave me an odd, raised eyebrow look, somewhere between disbelief and fear of my eccentricity. He was one of the few people I have ever met who had a genuine distaste for wine. So sad! I recalled a quote from the nineteenth-century medical innovator Louis Pasteur, who said, "A meal without wine is like a day without sunshine."

As the situation began to stabilize in Austin, DL and I started to explore the area. We knew Austin had a great reputation for fine dining and live entertainment, and we were anxious to partake. During the better part of the year when I was living in the apartment, I was so busy I had reverted to an eat-to-live lifestyle. When we closed on the new home in River Place and our household goods were delivered, DL and I eased back into our normal life of dining, wine, and travel. It was a new adventure, and Austin did not disappoint.

CHAPTER 46

Howdy, Austin!

In both my military and industry careers, DL and I relocated every three years on average. We became well-versed in all the aspects of adapting from one location to the next. We learned that one of the quickest techniques to establish ourselves in a new area was to join every social organization possible. Some organizations were a good fit with like-minded friends and others that we found less compatible were eventually displaced. We followed our system in Austin. We became members of food and wine groups, including the International Wine & Food Society, Les Ami du Vin, Wine and Food Foundation, Tasting Collective, and Zinfandel Advocates and Producers. We became season subscribers to music entities, including Austin Symphony, Austin Lyric Opera, Chamber Music Society, and Austin Classical Guitar. We joined social groups, including Austin Newcomers and the Italian Cultural Association. With financial contributions, we earned membership privileges in KMFA Classical Music, Blanton Museum of Art, and Bullock State History Museum. We promptly became part of the Austin social scene with an extended group of new friends.

Adapting to Austin was one of the easiest relocations we ever experienced. The people were so friendly! A smile and a "Howdy" from just about everyone you met exemplified the Texas-friendly attitude that seemed pervasive. Let me cite a few examples.

On one of the first evenings in our new home in River Place, we were exhausted from unpacking boxes of our household goods. We went to the clubhouse for dinner. While we were seated, a number of club management and clubhouse service staff personnel visited our table to welcome us as new members. It was a great first impression. Then one of the management people brought a couple to our table for introductions. We went through the obligatory get-acquainted questions, "Where did you move from?" and "What street do you live on?" Then they told us they were having a few folks over to their home the next evening and asked us to join them. We accepted, and when they left our table, DL and I commented with a bit of amazement on how we knew these people for only a minute or two and they invited us to their home. When we arrived at their home the next evening, we were surprised to discover it was an engagement party for their daughter and about fifty guests! They had catered an enormous buffet with beer, wine, spirits, and a Margarita machine. Talk about Texas-friendly! We knew we were going to be happy in Austin.

Another example was our affiliation with the Bullock State History Museum. It was under construction at the same time as our home in River Place. We made a respectable contribution to the museum. When the museum opened, we were surprised to receive an invitation to opening ceremonies. It was a grand event with Tex-Mex appetizers and drinks. At one point in the ceremony, donors were recognized and thanked. In our specific case, the museum management issued us official-looking cards as naturalized Texas citizens. In an instant we became Texans. From then on, we used the cliché, "We may not have been born here, but we came as soon as we could." We really liked being Texans.

It is common practice for neighbors to introduce themselves to new homeowners, but in River Place, the practice seemed more far-reaching than our previous experiences. Yes, we received our share of casseroles, in this case mostly King Ranch casseroles, but we also received invitations to join neighborhood poker groups, bridge groups, golfing groups, and dinner groups. We joined a dinner group of about twelve couples that was still going strong after a decade. The members were gourmet cooks, and they were wine enthusiasts. Once again, there is no explicit competition in dinner service, but the implicit competition is fun and results in great meals with fine wine. One subset of this dinner group was a tight-knit group of three couples that choose to meet more regularly than the group at large. DL and I are members of this smaller group, and we called ourselves the Six Pack.

Another typically Texan group I joined was a group of six wild game hunters. The group had exclusive hunting privileges leased on 1,100 acres of ranchland about two hours north of Austin. The land was about 50 percent pasture and 50 percent wooded. Wild game was abundant. I had hunted in previous locations in North Carolina, Virginia, Georgia, and California, but that was an activity that infrequently yielded whitetail deer, cottontail rabbits, gray squirrels, mallard ducks, Canadian geese, and feral hogs. Both DL and my young daughter had become accustomed to occasionally consuming the wild game I brought home from the hunt, and they professed to enjoy it. In Texas, I was much more engaged in the sport. Frequent successful hunts on our leased ranchland yielded whitetail deer, wild turkey, mourning dove, and chukar. I needed to buy a seven-cubic-foot chest freezer to store the game. One whitetail deer would provide about thirty to forty pounds of hams, backstrap, sausage, and chili-cut meat. One of the issues with wild game is the inconsistent quality of the meat. Younger game was tender and mild, and older game was tougher and gamey, but it was difficult to know what you had. That is why so many game recipes are stews, fricassees, braises, chili, and sausage dishes. In any case, an occasional wild game entrée served at home was a unique treat. I particularly liked wild game birds. At the end of this chapter, I have attached a menu DL and I served to our Six Pack dinner group with a wild turkey entrée harvested in one of my hunts.

Hunter Gathering

Appetizer
Smoked Salmon Spread with Rice Crackers
Comte Audoin de Dampierre Brut Champagne

Soup
Wild Turkey Consommé with Custard Royalé
Les Charmes Macon-Lugny Chardonnay

Salad
South-of-the-Border Coleslaw

Entrée 1
Wild Turkey Breast Sous Vide with Onion, Apple, and Calvados
Salsa Verde
2010 Amisfield Central Otago Valley Pinot Noir

Entrée 2
Wild Turkey Breast Smoked
Mole Don Vicente
2001 Anciano Gran Reserve Valdepeñas Tempranillo

Side 1
Sweet Potatoes with Orange and Chipotle Glaze

Side 2
Grilled Zucchini Fingers with Brown Butter Sauce

Side 3
Oatmeal Bread with Compound Herb Butter

Dessert
Blackberry Ice Cream with Chocolate Drizzle
Cordial
Limoncello di Enzo

CHAPTER 47

Food, Wine, and Entertainment

The effort to relocate my company from Atlanta to Austin and establishing our new home in River Place decreased the amount of time we would have otherwise spent on our preferred array of activities: gourmet dining, fine wine, live entertainment, and leisure travel. However, as our life stabilized, we returned to these sensual and pleasurable aspects of the good life, and Austin was a fertile place to do so.

The fine-dining scene in Austin was active and extensive. Notable chefs treated us with their expertise, including Tyson Cole of Uchi (James Beard award), Aaron Franklin of Franklin Barbeque (James Beard award), Bryce Gilmore of Barley Swine (James Beard nominee), Kevin Fink of Emmer and Rye (James Beard nominee), and Michael Fojtasek of Olamaei (James Beard nominee). I previously mentioned an organization DL and I joined after arriving in Austin, the local chapter of the International Wine & Food Foundation. This group organized monthly private wine dinners in other highly rated Austin restaurants, and it is our favorite organization for gourmet dining and fine wine. The format for these dinners is an off-menu assortment of dishes to allow the chef creativity, and we strive for ideal wine pairings with upscale wines for each course. As an example of an IW&FS dinner, we planned a dinner at the Austin Club on the one hundredth anniversary of the sinking of the Titanic to replicate the eleven-course dinner served in first class on the night it sank, and most of us wore formal regalia of the period. It was the epitome of plated ecstasy on a night to remember.

We also discovered the embryonic wine industry in Hill Country west of Austin. Although Hill Country in Texas cannot compete with established wine appellations in California, Oregon, and Washington, we a found a few wineries with bottlings worth a purchase, including Becker Vineyards Viognier and Flat Creek Estate Super Texan. We enjoyed weekends in Fredericksburg, in the center of Texas Hill Country wineries, staying at a bed-and-breakfast and touring multiple wineries on the weekend. The wines may not be world class, but the setting in Hill Country reminds one of Tuscany in Italy. I did not intend to store any Texas wines in my wine cellar, although I would be tempted to occasionally buy a bottle for consumption the same day. The wine cellar in our new home could store up to about 350 bottles, and they were still a slowly revolving inventory of Old World and New World wines we tasted and deemed worthy of purchase.

As for entertainment, Austin is informally known as the Live Music Capital of the United States because it reputedly has more live music per capita than any other US city. Whether you book a concert in a major venue, visit the raucous scene on Sixth Street, go to a bar for happy hour, or dine at a fine dining restaurant or even a run-of-the-mill café, you will be entertained with live music. It is pervasive. For those who favor classical music, the Austin Symphony under Maestro Peter Bay is as good as anywhere in the States, and we were season subscribers seated in the Parterre section of Dell Hall.

Membership in the Atlanta Symphony provided us an unexpected benefit for one year. In addition to purchasing season tickets to the monthly classical series, we also contributed periodic additional donations to the symphony. For one fundraiser, we purchased a $100 raffle ticket for the chance to win what was advertised as an "instant wine cellar." Our intent was just to donate money to the fundraiser with no real expectation that we had a chance to win the prize. We were in attendance at the weekend event when the winner was announced, and we were not surprised our name was not called. The next Monday, we received a call from the symphony office.

The caller introduced himself and congratulated us for winning the instant wine cellar. We thought the phone call was some kind of scam. We told the caller that we were in attendance at the weekend event when the winner was announced, and we knew it was not our name. He informed us that the announced winner was not a resident of Texas and thus was disqualified according to the raffle criteria. He further stated that the symphony had drawn another ticket over the weekend, and we were the winners. I was still a little skeptical, so I asked when I could pick up my prize. He said, "Today," and I said without hesitation that I would arrive at the symphony office shortly. DL and I drove to the symphony office, and the instant wine cellar was waiting for us. The prize consisted of eight mixed cases of wines, ninety-four bottles, and six other loose bottles. The value for this bonanza was listed as $5,000! Fortunately, there was space in our wine cellar. One of the loose bottles was noteworthy. It was a 1.5-liter bottle of 1997 Domaine Bouchard Père & Fils Le Corton Grand Cru. The bottle had been donated to the raffle by the lieutenant governor of Texas with a value listed as $800! We put the bottle to good use at a French dinner we prepared for close friends. It was truly grand and a perfect pairing for the main entrée, Cailles Roties Grand-Mere (roast quail with root vegetable cakes). Our guests autographed the bottle, and we retained the empty bottle as a memento of an evening of plated ecstasy.

CHAPTER 48

Retirement Decision

DL and I were comfortable in our new home in Austin, my company had recovered from the trauma of relocation, and it was time to seriously plan for my retirement. DL had already been retired from her high school teaching career for about a decade, and now it was my turn.

We had planned well for our future, and we were in a position for me to retire early. We were in a retirement location of our choice. We were financially healthy and debt-free. We had a plan to bridge our health care coverage until we qualified for Medicare. So the basic question distilled down to, "What activities will we choose to fill our golden years? Would I pursue a part-time business consulting position? No. Although I enjoyed my time in both my military and aerospace careers, I was ready for something entirely different. Should I volunteer to work in the private nonprofit sector? No. The four-letter word w-o-r-k ruled against this. I wanted to do things that I considered fun, not w-o-r-k, and I wanted to do them at a time and place that suited me. I give DL credit for getting to the heart of the matter. She asked, "What is your passion?" Then she immediately answered her own question, "Dine, wine, and travel." There, in three words, she set the theme for my retirement.

I announced my decision to retire to the corporation, family, and friends. Some were surprised because I had not reached the standard age of sixty-five. Others were pragmatic and agreed if I could retire, why not. All asked what I was going to do in retirement. I gave them the short answer, a variation of DL's synopsis, that has become my mantra, "Eat, drink, and travel!" The next stage of my life as a culinarian was about to begin.

PART 13

A New Beginning

CHAPTER 49

Transition into Retirement

Our previous experiences with adjusting to new jobs, moving to new locations, building new homes, and developing new circles of friends had taught us the skills to succeed in complex career transitions. Compared to those previous, the transition into retirement was easy. Our geographic location, our home, our country club lifestyle, and our finances were already in place. The skeletal framework for retirement activities—"Eat, drink, and travel!"—had been created, and we eagerly anticipated putting meat on those bones. I also wanted to punctuate the magnitude and importance of this retirement transition with some personal optics. I gave most of my business suits to either consignment shops or charity donations, keeping only a couple for special occasions. I noticed that the wait staff at our club wore white shirts and ties, so I gave my inventory of white dress shirts and silk ties to the club, keeping only a few for special occasions. I would no longer be conducting business on the golf course, and I did not intend to include golf as a hobby, so I donated my golfing equipment to charity. I changed the style of my hairdo from a left part and relatively short sides to longer hair combed straight back without a part. I replaced my business card with a social card that said, "Donna Lee and Vince DiLoreto, Passionate Consumers of Gourmet Food and Fine Wine." Additional minor changes enhanced the transformation. Almost overnight, my persona went from a captain of industry to a purveyor of the good life. Laissez les bon temps roullez!

CHAPTER 50

Formal Culinary Training

DL and I had continued our practice of enrolling in cooking classes after we moved to Austin. Two supermarkets, in particular, became our favorites: Whole Foods and Central Market. Both of these maintained a schedule of frequent events, and we liked their professional instructors and facilities. We did not attend all their classes, but we did enroll in those classes whose topics appealed to us. However, after my retirement, I had the time and the desire for more formal culinary instruction. I wanted more than a series of one-hour nonparticipative demonstrations of recipe preparation. I wanted a full curriculum of hands-on culinary training. I discovered there were a few culinary training organizations in the Austin area, and I investigated them. One that was flexible enough to satisfy my requirements and was conveniently located was the Texas Culinary Academy. When completed, training at the TCA would lead to an accredited certificate in culinary arts. I had no intention to be a full-time student, and my desire was to take individual blocks of training at my own pace. The normal educational process for culinary students at the TCA was equal time in the classroom and the kitchen. Once I explained my intentions, and I had been interviewed about my general knowledge of the culinary arts, the TCA allowed a modified course of instruction for me consisting of primarily the kitchen curricula. The TCA could accommodate my desire, although I would be an exception to their normal process of an organized class of students proceeding sequentially through the curriculum. I had the option to enroll and pay tuition for various blocks of training as they were being conducted without concern for the standard sequence. I was also an exception from the perspective that I had no goal for employment in the culinary industry. I just wanted the formal education for my own edification, and I had the time to do it.

After I had arrived at an agreement with the TCA, I went to a restaurant supply retailer in Austin, Ace Mart, and I purchased some essential material I would need. Based on the recommendation from *Cook's Illustrated* magazine, I bought a set of knives that had been evaluated as a "best value": a Victorinox brand eight-inch chef's knife, six-inch fillet knife, three-inch paring knife, eight-inch bread knife, protective plastic blade covers for the knives, and a knife-carrying bag. I also bought black chef trousers, a white chef coat, and black Fila brand shoes that were waterproof, shockproof, and slip-proof, suitable for standing long periods in a kitchen. I would need more equipment in the future, but this was a start.

My unusual situation was immediately apparent in my first block of training. I was the oldest by far in a class of about twelve male and female students probably in their midtwenties. My presence aroused curiosity in both instructors and students. Who was this old guy, and why is he here? After introductions, it did not take long for everyone to understand my intentions, accept my eccentricity, and respect my desire to learn just for the sake of learning. They seemed genuinely interested in the extent of my travel experiences and the associated exposure to different cuisines. Inwardly, I was in high spirits to take on the challenge of formal culinary training. I knew it would be an ideal marriage with the formal sommelier training I had previously completed. As one who was obsessed with food and wine, I was almost giddy thinking about my future as a Passionate Consumer of Gourmet Food and Fine Wine. My formal culinary training progressed over a two-year period to a point where I was satisfied that I had learned enough to be competent in both commercial or private kitchens. I chose not to enroll in the patisserie and pastry block of training or the garde-manger block of training, but I had studied all that I considered essential. I knew the basics of French lexicon (*vocabulaire culinaire*), techniques, and kitchen organization.

Upon completion of the curriculum at the TCA, it was customary for the graduate to do about an eight-week stage (like an internship that the French call stagiaires) at an area restaurant, and the TCA helped with placement, but this was another aspect of my training that I declined. Although a novice, I was now on my own as a classically trained chef. I had been collecting and creating favorite recipes for a couple of decades, and this training motivated me to transform my collection into a standard format. The format I used was a composite of the formats recommended by the TCA, the Culinary Institute of America, and culinarian Michael Ruhlman. The recipes attached at the end of some chapters are in this format. I compiled my reformatted digital collection in early 2008 and have been adding to it ever since. With pride in my accomplishment, I adopted a nom de guerre. Henceforth, I would call myself Chef Enzo, and DL had the name embroidered on my white chef's jacket.

CHAPTER 51

New Food and Wine Activities

After the completion of my formal culinary training, I was pleasantly surprised by a number of unexpected outcomes. Friends and relatives responded in ways I had not imagined. I had decided to pursue formal culinary training and also my previous sommelier training strictly for personal reasons, so I did not intend to elicit any social recognition of my training. However, others seemed to be as interested in my efforts as I was. I was humbled by the extent of unforeseen compliments, but I will admit, they quietly stroked my ego.

While in culinary training, I had acquired a chef's knife bag with a decent set of knives. As a novice with no professional intent, I did not invest in the highest quality knives, which can cost $100–$200 for an eight-inch chef's knife. My generous brother, Denis, gave me a set of custom, handmade knives: an eight-inch chef's knife, a six-inch boning knife, a three-inch paring knife, and a ten-inch bread knife. They were the highest quality works of art made by custom knifemaker T. Vasler. The blades are numbered, like fine art prints, and engraved with my name and the name of the knifemaker. The handles are beautiful laminated multicolor hardwood. What a gift! I am proud to open my knife bag in a public setting and lay out my one-of-a-kind set of knives.

I mentioned earlier that DL and I were members of a dinner group of about twelve couples in River Place who were gourmet cooks and wine enthusiasts. One member of the group had been promoted to a management position at Dell Company. She knew about my formal culinary and sommelier training, and she asked if I would be willing to prepare a dinner at her home for twelve employees who now reported to her. I was flattered and a little intimidated, but I agreed. We established that she would reimburse me for the cost of food and wine, my chef service was free, and I would prepare the dinner in her kitchen. I sat with her to develop a menu with wine pairings. I would serve a four-course dinner: first, salmon butter spread with crostini and crudité, paired with Mumm's Brut Prestige; second, céleri-rave rémoulade salad, paired with Kendall-Jackson Chardonnay; third, chicken breast with a cheese and herb spread in a pastry crust, with a side of roasted asparagus and hollandaise sauce, paired with 2007 Michele Chiarlo Barbera d'Asti La Court; and fourth, pears poached in spiced wine, paired with Vin Santo. DL acted as my sous chef, and she helped serve the dinner. The dinner went smoothly, and the attendees seemed impressed with the effort. I have a clear memory of this event because it was the first catered dinner I was contracted to prepare, but it would not be the last. I would be called upon in the future by friends and acquaintances to cater other dinners. I have attached my recipe for the chicken breast in pastry crust at the end of this chapter.

Two years in a row, I teamed with another chef to prepare buffet dinners for the annual January members' meetings of the International Wine & Food Society. They were large gatherings for about forty-eight people. We hired kitchen help and wait staff to assist, and we rented tables, chairs, linens, plates, cutlery, and stemware. The quantity of food was a challenge to prepare, but the buffet format simplified the service. One year we had a French theme for the buffet dinner. The next year we opted for a Texas barbecue theme. This was my first experience with large numbers, and it was a good learning experience.

One summer I was part of a team of volunteers assembled to prepare a plated dinner for the Austin Chamber Music Society, an Austin nonprofit organization. The team was led by an executive chef who had experience with this type of event. It was a semiformal fundraising dinner attended by over two hundred patrons, where each 8-top table cost $2,000. The venue was outdoors at the beautiful Umlauf Sculpture Garden in Austin. Once again, equipment had to be rented and service staff hired. I do not recall the entire menu, but I remember that the entrée was beef tenderloin, which presented its own complexity for doneness-level to satisfy the attendees. This was the largest event I ever served, and I decided not to volunteer for anything like this again. It was not fun. Even though it was for a worthwhile cause, I classified it with the four-letter word, W-O-R-K.

In addition to food preparation, I volunteered to moderate wine tastings. I conducted wine tasting events for a number of organizations, including the International Wine & Food Society, the Italian Cultural Association, River Place Country Club, and Texas Wine Guild. I really enjoy conducting wine tasting events. I have created a library of PowerPoint presentations and hard-copy handout material applicable to a number of wine tasting themes. One of the most interesting events was one I moderated for the Austin Wine Guild. The members were amateur winemakers. I found them to be very focused on the wines they made, but they were generally lacking in global knowledge about varietals, appellations, and techniques outside their specific area of interest. I chose a theme of rosé wine to present to the Guild because they did not make rosé wine and were unfamiliar with the worldwide variety of rosé. The theme generated a very lively discussion of rosé wine, including single-grape bottlings, blends, saignée, free-run techniques, aging, and food pairings. After tasting and scoring six rosé wines, both old world and new world styles, I was pleased but not surprised that they voted a Provençe blend their favorite. Provençe rosé blends are my favorite too. In my opinion, the crisp, pale-pink Provençe blend of Grenache, Syrah, Mourvèdre, Cinsault, Clairette, and Tibouren makes the quintessential rosé wine.

The extent of these new food and wine activities prompted me to create a new business card. I refer to it as a business card, but I had no intention of starting a business. I planned to only do pro bono activities of my choice, without the specter of the four-letter word, W-O-R-K. The card said, "Events by Enzo, Wine Tastings and Wine Dinners." This card was not a replacement for our previous social card that said, "Donna Lee and Vince DiLoreto, Passionate

Consumers of Gourmet Food and Fine Wine." We use the Passionate Consumer card when we first meet new people, and I use the Events by Enzo card in specific situations where someone expresses an interest in my free food and wine services. Both cards are excellent conversation starters that enhance our lifestyle.

PART 14

Travel and Fine Dining in Retirement

CHAPTER 52

Visiting International Friends

I previously mentioned that senior military officers from twenty-six allied countries were enrolled in the Monterey Naval Postgraduate School while I was there earning postgraduate degrees. DL and I developed some close friendships with many of these foreign students and their families. A few of the friendships have endured the test of time, and we have maintained contact, sharing the growth of our families and the changes in our lives with cards, letters, photos, and emails. When some have vacationed in the States, we hosted them with accommodations and sightseeing. Others have hosted us when we traveled to their countries. Let me relate three memorable episodes of visiting our international friends.

One of our trips was a tour focused on Central Europe, including northern France, Belgium, and the Netherlands. We contacted our friends, Henny and Rob Seegar, who lived in the Netherlands, and told them we would be touring their country, including a couple of days in Amsterdam, and asked if it would be convenient to meet with them. Rob said they did not live in Amsterdam, but they would love to meet with us there. He laughed and added that the Netherlands is so small you can drive anywhere in the country in less than an hour. They spent a day showing us the sights in Amsterdam, and we went to dinner in what is arguably Amsterdam's finest restaurant, De Silveren Spiegel (The Silver Mirror). The venue is a classic European building that dates to the seventeenth century, the Dutch Golden Age. I ordered a four-course dinner paired with four wines selected by the sommelier. My entrée was braised veal garnished with marrow and potato foam accompanied with a mélange of local vegetables. My comments usually focus on the entrée, but the vegetables with this dish were remarkable. Their color and presentation were like a still-life masterpiece by the Dutch master Vermeer, with al-dente texture and on-point seasoning. I would describe the chef's creative effort as delicate and unadorned, but all the courses were freshly delicious. Henny and Rob said this was their first visit to De Silveren Spiegel, and surprisingly, they thanked us for triggering the experience.

When we arrived at the Monterey Naval Postgraduate School, we were asked if we would sponsor the family of a foreign student. Sponsorship entailed providing information and assistance to the foreign family as they adapted to unfamiliar situations in the States, such as buying a previously owned car, elementary school enrollment, sources for general retail shopping, etc. DL was enthused with the idea of sponsorship, but I was not. I told her I would be too busy with my studies, but she persisted until I relented, setting what I thought was an insurmountable criterion. I told her I would only consider sponsoring an Israeli fighter pilot. To my complete surprise, she found an incoming student family of an Israeli fighter pilot! So we sponsored Shmulik and Yaffa Ben-Rom and their twin daughters, who were the same age as our daughter. We have been fast friends with the Ben-Roms ever since. They retired near Caesarea, about fifteen miles south of Haifa. A tour of Israel included a visit with the Ben-Roms. Reuniting with them was enjoyable, but it was made even more enjoyable by touring the archeological site at Caesarea, which was an important Roman port in Roman times and the location of King Herod's palace as governor of Palestine. After touring the archeological site, we went to dinner at Limani Bistro located on the ancient Caesarea harbor waterfront. I was delighted by a dinner menu recommended by Shmulik, including an appetizer of hummus with pita bread, Israeli salad with pomegranate and avocado, whole grilled Denees (the Israeli name for gilt-head bream), accompanied by mejadra with bulgur wheat, and malabi milk pudding for dessert. The wine was a white blend from Yarden Mount Hermon Galilee.

It was a delicious dinner, and Shmulik was pleased that I thoroughly enjoyed it all.

Our next-door neighbors at the Monterey naval Postgraduate School were a Greek couple, Miranda and George Germanos. Miranda taught DL how to make her spanakopita, and DL took Miranda to San Francisco to see the sights, and we maintained contact with the Germanos after Monterey. On a trip to Greece, we reunited with the Germanos in Athens. Miranda was our tour guide for an entire day, setting a frantic pace to see the highlights of the city, including the Parthenon and other classic ruins on the Acropolis. We met George for dinner at the iconic Athenian restaurant Orizontes. The restaurant was located on the top of rocky Lycabettus Hill, the highest point in the city. The view of Athens and the lighted Acropolis at night was astonishing. The menu was also an overwhelming list of gastronomical offerings. As we sat for dinner and with typical pride in all things Greek, Miranda summarized our sightseeing adventures of the day, described the sweeping panoramic view of Athens, and made menu recommendations for a dinner fit for Greek gods. The appetizer was rigani white bean and garlic slather on pita bread served alongside a bowl of black Kalamata olives. An avgolemono soup followed. Of course, there was the obligatory Greek salad with romaine, cucumber, tomatoes, roasted red bell pepper, and feta cheese. For my entrée, I selected the spiced Peloponnesian braised lamb shanks, accompanied with a side of eggplant ratatouille. Dessert was creamy yogurt topped with quince spoon sweet. We drank white wine, Muscat Blanc a Petit Grains from Samos, and a red, Agiorgitiko from Nemea. What a feast to remember! I have used the expression "bucket list" before, and I would definitely apply it to fine dining with a view at the Orizontes restaurant in Athens.

CHAPTER 53

International Cruising

Cold logic told me that I would be the manager of my daily schedule in retirement. I knew that I would no longer be shackled to a weekday work schedule, an alarm clock, or a honey-do task list for weekends. However, I did not fully appreciate the freedom and flexibility I would have. I went to bed when I was tired, and I awoke when I was rested, regardless of the time. When I awoke, I did not care what the day of the week was because they flowed together in a seamless stream. I stopped wearing my iconic business executive Rolex wristwatch, but I started wearing a fitness and health tracking device. Do not assume I turned into an aimless brain-dead couch potato. On the contrary, I was more meticulous with entries in my smartphone calendar to keep track of the things that were important and pleasurable to me. "Eat, drink, and travel" was still the mantra, but DL and I filled in the blank spaces with other activities, including mentoring high school students, social volunteer activities, adult education through the University of Texas Quest program, and a daily exercise regimen at our gym. The change with the most significant impact on our lives was the ability to plan long-duration vacations. We were no longer limited to a total of two weeks of vacation a year, three-day holiday weekends, and one-week summer vacations. This opened up access to two-week, three-week, or one-month cruise ship international vacations.

DL and I were initially a little apprehensive about the concept of cruising. We had never done it before. Would we feel trapped aboard a ship? Would there be sufficient entertainment activities to keep us from being bored? Would the passenger demographics allow us to socialize with others like us? All our apprehensions were dismissed on our first cruise. We booked a fifteen-day Mediterranean cruise with the Oceania cruise line. Oceania catered to a mature clientele who were interested in luxury service and adult excursions. There were about six hundred passengers on the ship with a crew of about four hundred, resulting in a level of service that made you feel like minor royalty. For example, there was a roving classical string quartet aboard and wine tasting ashore instead of Disney characters or ski boat rentals. The ship was essentially a hotel that traveled at night while you slept, so you only had to unpack once. Each day you awoke at a new destination with multiple excursions to choose from. More than a hotel, the ship offered a myriad of onboard activities from stage shows, a casino, a spa, a gym, afternoon tea, a library, art auctions, and more. By far, the most impressive aspect for me aboard the ship was the food.

Chef Jacques Pépin was the consultant to Oceania for menus. Breakfast, lunch, and dinner in the grand dining room were definitely appropriate for minor royalty. Dinners in the specialty restaurants would satisfy major royalty. Even the offerings in the less formal venues at the terrace buffet and on the pool deck were world class. The fifteen days spent on our first cruise lavished us with the best fifteen sequential days of plated ecstasy we had in our lives up to this point. Oceania advertised the "finest cuisine at sea," equivalent to a Michelin star rating ashore, and DL and I would endorse that claim. So do other sources, such as Condé Nast Traveler magazine. We tried a couple of other cruise lines with similar destination and demographic formats, but the dining experience in Oceania was the siren that seduced us to return. Since that first cruise, DL and I have cruised on Oceania to destinations including Australia, New Zealand, Scandinavia, the Baltic, the Aegean, the Adriatic, the Mediterranean, and the Caribbean. We have been toying with the idea of a 180-day around-the-world cruise, although that would take some major adjustments to the administrative and logistic aspects of our home life.

I became captivated by the concept of luxury cruising. I have already touched on an all-inclusive aspect of carefree life aboard a ship, the unrivaled level of customer service, and the superlative cuisine. However, I must add that the excursions ashore at the daily ports of call are ideally selected for the luxury cruise clientele demographic. In reality, you can spend about half of your vacation ashore, so the experience has to be equally gratifying to your time on board. From the perspective of "dine, wine, and travel," I will offer a few examples of the total cruising experience.

CHAPTER 54

Cruising the Aegean

DL and I had never traveled to the Greek islands in the Aegean Sea or to the western coast of Turkey, so we booked a ten-day cruise on Oceania. The itinerary was a circuitous island-hopping route from Athens to Athens. On a whim, we called my brother, Denis, and his wife to ask if they would be interested. Denis had never been on a cruise, so he was a little hesitant. I told him I would send him all the cruise information, and I would also send him the detailed arrangements DL and I had made. After his review, he decided to join us on the cruise. He replicated our arrangements, except for air travel, and we were all excited about sharing a travel adventure. A few days later, Denis called me to ask some questions about the amenities aboard the ship. One of his questions was "Vince, I see that our room enjoys the service of a butler. What does the butler do?" I suggested that he call Oceania to get a more definitive answer than I could give him. He called me later to say he had spoken to Oceania. Denis said he had spoken to a polite gentleman with an English accent who told him, "The butler aboard the ship will do the same things your butler at home does." Den was not entirely satisfied with the answer, but he was happy with the expectation of first-class customer service.

DL and I had an uneventful flight to Athens, then we were shuttled to the port of Piraeus, where the ship was docked, and we boarded about midday. Once aboard, I asked the concierge if my brother had arrived, and I was told he had. We went to our stateroom, unpacked, and called my brother. He was in a penthouse on the same deck, and he invited us to his suite. As this was his first cruise, I asked him about his experience checking in and boarding the ship. He said that everything had gone smoothly, but he had made one mistake. He had left the charger for his camera in his suitcase that had been moved to a storage area after he unpacked. I said that was not a problem. Just call the butler. He dialed for the butler, and not thirty seconds later the door chime to his suite rang. When he opened the door, the butler standing there gave him a polite nod. Denis was surprised at the quick response and explained to the butler what he wanted. Before the butler went to retrieve the camera charger, he noticed the that complimentary fruit basket and bottle of champagne on the coffee table were untouched. He asked if he could serve the champagne. He entered the room with a flourish, unwrapped the foil, placed a white towel over the bottle, and pulled the cork. He poured four flutes, served two to the ladies, and then excused himself to run his errand. Denis attentively observed the episode, and after the butler left, he said, "I may get accustomed to the butler."

From the observation deck, we watched the departure process with interest from the port of Piraeus. After we cleared the harbor, we went to the grand dining room for dinner. We were seated at a table with a view of the frothy churn of the wake as we headed to Mykonos at a leisurely pace. Denis was perusing the à la carte menu and was impressed with the extensive gourmet selection of dishes. So many items tempted him that he was unable to decide. Having experienced the same bewilderment on my first cruise with Oceania, I offered advice.

I said, "Denis, you have already paid for all this, so order all that you want. You don't have to eat it all."

He said to clarify, "You mean I could order two or more appetizers, entrees, garnishes, or desserts?"

I said, "Yes, there is no limitation, and no one is keeping score." Along with an appetizer, soup, and salad, he decided to order two entrees. One was roasted pancetta-wrapped rack of lamb over roasted potatoes perfumed with garlic and rosemary, and the other was Wellington of veal tenderloin with Cabernet Sauvignon reduction and harvest vegetables. Denis was impressed and asked if this was what he could expect for the next ten days. I said, "Yes, for breakfast, lunch, and dinner."

When we woke the next morning, we were docked at Chora, the principal city on Mykonos, and the first of nine other ports of call on this cruise. Mykonos's nickname is the Island of the Winds because of the very strong winds that regularly blow. The island is composed mostly of granite, and the hilly terrain has been eroded by the strong winds. Windmills are a defining feature of the Mykonian landscape, and there are many dotted around the island. Tourism is a major industry, and we spent an entire day ashore visiting tourist sites and relaxing in cafes featuring Mykonian cured ham and fresh seafood snacks. Mykonos is also known for its vibrant nightlife. Paradise Beach is one of the famous areas to party in, and here you can find one of the best nightclubs in the world, Cavo Paradiso. We visited the beach, but we did not have time to sample the nightlife, so we would have to be satisfied with the late-night stage show in the lounge aboard the ship. We returned to the ship in the late afternoon and prepared ourselves for another sumptuous fine-dining experience with a variety of gourmet entrées of seafood, fowl, pork, and beef. Although the ship was stocked with a first-rate selection of wines, we could bring wine to the dining room that we had purchased ashore, and the staff was happy to serve it. I liked to offer the waiters a taste of the local wine we bought, and they usually accepted the offer. The sharing seemed to help them remember our name.

An unforgettable destination was the island of Santorini. The island is volcanic in origin and has been formed, destroyed, and reformed a number of times over tens of thousands of years. Some scientists theorize that the cataclysmic explosion about twenty thousand years ago was one of the largest volcanic eruptions in the history of the world, and smoke and ash from the eruption filled the atmosphere and caused four years of winter in the northern hemisphere. The current configuration of the island is like a half-moon remnant of a giant caldera. The ship anchors in the seven-by-five-mile giant central lagoon, up to four hundred meters deep, formed by the collapse of the volcanic cone. Passengers are taken to shore by tenders, and an incline lift transports them from the narrow, rugged shoreline to the top of the three-hundred-meter cliff of the caldera wall. At the top of the cliff, the city of Fira decorates the edge like a white-and-blue tiara. Even if you have never been to Santorini, you would recognize the white-walled buildings with their Grecian blue domes, roofs, shutters, and doors from tour guides, advertisements, and photo galleries you have seen. Santorini and Fira are probably the most photographed scenery in the Aegean Sea. A stroll through the bright, beautiful, narrow, quiet streets of Fira is comforting. Lunch at an open café on a terrace overlooking the lagoon and the ship at anchor is breathtaking. The best restaurant in Fira may be Lombranos, but exceptional food is available everywhere. You would expect a variety of fresh seafood dishes, and you would not be disappointed. Santorini shrimp, a sizzling dish of sautéed tomatoes, plump shrimp, and rich feta cheese, is a local standard. DL and I shared this dish for lunch at a terrace café. I have attached my recipe for Santorini shrimp at the end of this chapter. Octopus and local Dentex fish (a variety of sea bream) grilled whole are also favorites. Other specialty lunches and dinner dishes include tomato keftedes (local tomato fritters), moussaka made with local eggplant, and laganaki (fired cheese in filo dough spread with honey). Santorini also has a thriving wine business. An exceptional white wine made from the Assyrtiko grape, indigenous to Santorini, has a minerality and acidity that make it a perfect pairing for seafood. A full-bodied red wine made from the Mandelari grape is produced in less quantity, but it is a good pairing for heartier dishes. One of the most interesting aspects of wine production in Santorini is the unique method the grapes are grown. The vines are not grown on trellises, but they are trained to grow wound in a basket shape low on the ground with the grape bunches in the center. The reason for this growing method is to protect the grapes from the high winds that periodically blow in Santorini. When you travel to Santorini, make it a point to visit wineries to taste the best wines in Greece.

On the western coast of Turkey, we docked at the port of Kusadasi. A thirty-minute bus ride from the port brings you to the archaeological site of the ancient city of Ephesus. The city was founded in the tenth century BC, but the visible ruins primarily reflect Greek and Roman heritage. The city came under the control of the Roman Republic in 129 BC, and it was a major Roman city until it was destroyed by the Goths in AD 263. Ephesus is unique. It is unlike the ancient Acropolis standing in the center of urban Athens or the ancient Forum in the heart of bustling Rome. Ephesus stands alone in quiet solitude without modern urban distractions. As you exit the bus at Ephesus, in one step you are transported from the twenty-first century to the second century. The well-preserved remains of impressive structures include the Library of Celsius, the Temple of Hadrian, and the Terrace Houses where the wealthy lived during the Roman period. Nearby are the ruins of the Temple of Artemis, one of the seven wonders of the ancient world. I was particularly moved to tread on the stone walkways of the Theatre of Ephesus, an amphitheater that seated over twenty thousand people, where St. Paul walked and preached. We returned to the port of Kusadasi in midafternoon and decided to have a late lunch ashore at one of the many small cafés within walking distance from the ship. We started lunch with corba, a comforting soup made with lentils and tomato. The soup was followed by typical lamb shish kebabs skewered on wooden sticks and grilled over hot charcoal. We finished with a dessert of kunefe, a sweet dish made with cheese, bread crumbs, and pistachio nuts. The lunch was a fitting punctuation to the excursion in western Turkey.

While visiting the Aegean island of Santorini, I ordered a lunch of sizzling fresh shrimp on a bed of local tomatoes and feta cheese. The dish was advertised as a Santorini specialty. I expected the local tomatoes to be very tasty due to the rich volcanic soil of the island. I was initially wary of the feta cheese because of its tangy flavor profile and because cheese is rarely used with seafood in most cuisines. The dish was delicious and balanced. I enjoyed it so much I decided to try to replicate it when I returned home. After some experimentation, the following recipe is my version of Santorini shrimp. If you are tempted to try the recipe, I offer some tips. Use Greek olive oil. Use heirloom tomatoes. Use Greek oregano. Enjoy!

Santorini Shrimp

Preparation: 20 minutes
Cooking: 40 minutes
Serves: 2

Step 1: Prepare the shrimp

1 lb. jumbo shrimp, 21–25 count
1 tbsp. Greek extra virgin olive oil
1/2 tsp. sea salt
1/4 tsp. fresh ground black pepper

Peel and devein the shrimp. Place the shrimp, oil, salt, and pepper in a bowl. Toss to evenly coat, and set aside.

Step 2: Prepare the tomato mixture

2 tbsp. Greek extra virgin olive oil (option: Italian extra virgin
    olive oil)
1/2 c. white onion, chopped
2 cloves garlic, minced
1 lb. heirloom tomatoes: blanched, peeled, cored, and coarsely
    chopped (option: canned San Marzano tomatoes)
1/2 c. dry Assyrtiko Santorini white wine (option: dry Italian
    white wine such as Vermentino or Soave)
1 tsp. dried Greek oregano (option: dried Italian oregano)
1/2 tsp. sea salt
1/4 tsp. fresh ground black pepper
1 pinch red pepper flakes
2 tbsp. fresh flat-leaf parsley, chopped

Heat the oil in a 10-inch sauté pan over medium heat. Add the
onion and cook until translucent, about 5 minutes. Add the garlic
and cook until fragrant, about 1 minute. Add the tomatoes, wine,
oregano, salt, pepper, and pepper flakes. Sauté over medium heat for
about 5 minutes, stirring frequently. Reduce heat to low and simmer
for about 15 minutes until the sauce thickens. Stir in the parsley and
simmer another minute until the parsley is wilted. Adjust the seasonings to taste. Remove from the heat.

Step 3: Finish

1/4 c. Kalamata olives, pitted
4 oz. Greek feta cheese, large crumbles
1 tbsp. fresh flat-leaf parsley, chopped
1 tbsp. fresh squeezed lemon juice

Position an oven rack in the center of the oven, and heat the
oven to 425 degrees Fahrenheit.
Spread the tomato mixture from step 2 into an oven-proof
9-inch round baking dish or deep Pyrex pie pan. Arrange the shrimp

from step 1 over the tomato mixture in one layer. Interspace the olives among the shrimp. Spread the feta cheese crumbles over the top. Bake the dish for about 10 minutes until the shrimp are medium pink in color and the feta cheese is slightly browned. Do not over-cook the shrimp.

Remove the dish from the oven, and garnish with parsley and lemon juice. Serve hot while the dish is still sizzling. Serve with crusty bread.

CHAPTER 55

Cruising the French Riviera

Another memorable cruise was the inaugural cruise on Oceania's newest ship, MS *Sirena*. The port of departure was Barcelona, Spain, and we had arranged a two-day precruise visit to the city. We stayed at the Majestic Hotel, reputed to be one of the finest in Barcelona, and we had hired a private car with a tour guide and driver to show us the sights in Barcelona. It is a beautiful city with architecture by Gaudi, the famous Sagrada Familia cathedral, and the spectacular Park Güell. On the day of embarkation, there was a huge inaugural festival pier-side, and Chef Jacques Pépin's daughter, Claudine, had the ceremonial honor of christening the ship by breaking the traditional bottle of champagne on the bow. Jacques and Claudine would be passengers on this cruise. Well in advance of the cruise, DL had purchased a Little Mermaid doll at the Disney Store because the ship's name, *Sirena*, is the Spanish and Italian word for mermaid. One evening, we were fortunate to share a dinner table with Jacques and Claudine. DL had Jacques and Claudine autograph the Little Mermaid doll, and Claudine gave us a copy of her cookbook for children, which she autographed with a personal note to our grandsons that said, "Ross, Mitch, and Troy, don't forget to help in the kitchen." Some senior members of the ship's crew, including the captain, witnessed the autograph session, and they asked to participate by also signing the Little Mermaid doll. That doll is one of our prized travel souvenirs. I also prize the memory of dining with Chef Jacques Pépin and discussing his contributions to the scrumptious menus aboard the ships of the Oceania cruise line.

We departed Barcelona and awoke the next morning docked in Palma de Mallorca. A tour of the city unveils a mix of Medieval, Moorish, and modern Spanish characters. The famous cathedral La Seu impressively dominates the shoreline. Its ornate Catalonian Gothic construction was started in 1229. Below the cathedral, along the shoreline, is the tropical-looking Parc de la Mar (Park of the Sea). Behind the cathedral is the old city of Parma with a maze of quiet, narrow pedestrian streets. Walking in the old city of Parma is reminiscent of walking in the old Trastevere district of Rome. A short distance west of Palma is a well-preserved fourteenth-century castle, Bellver Castle, one of the few circular Gothic-style castles in Europe, and it is currently the city's History Museum. After a tour of Palma, we relaxed with a leisurely lunch at a café in the Plaza d'Espanya. We started with Sopas Mallorquinas, a soup that includes onion, garlic, tomatoes, cabbage, beans, pork, paprika, and sliced local bread. Next, we tried a Mallorcan classic, tombet, which is a combination of fried eggplant, potatoes, red peppers, tomatoes, olive oil, and garlic, and it can be compared to ratatouille from Provence. To finish lunch with a flourish, we ordered a glass of Hierbas, Mallorca's unique 40 percent proof aniseed-flavored herbal liqueur made from distilled molasses and infused with an assortment of herbs. Residents routinely drink Hierbas after a meal, but I caution you that it is an acquired taste. I did not buy a souvenir bottle.

The day after Palma de Mallorca, we docked at Marseille, France. We spent no time touring Marseille, just a transit of the city on an excursion to Aix-en-Provence. As we approached the city, fields of light-purple-hued lavender plants stretched to the horizon. Whenever Provence is a topic of conversation, Aix-en-Provence is the vision that appears in my mind's eye. To me, it epitomizes Provence. The city was founded by the Romans in 123 BC, but it has been occupied and plundered by a number of factions up through the Renaissance period. Today, it is a center for education, culture, arts, and entertainment. The city has a Mediterranean climate that encourages a leisurely stroll along the Cours Mirabeau, a beautiful thoroughfare lined with mature trees, bordered by impressive homes, and decorated by fountains. In fact, the city boasts hundreds of fountains. Beautiful Medieval, Romanesque, and modern architecture can be found throughout the city. Cafés and brasseries line the Cours Mirabeau, and the most famous is probably the Deux Garçons, which was a favorite of Paul Cezanne and Ernest Hemingway. Food and wine are significant parts of the appeal of Aix-en-Provence, and that is to be expected in a locale that is the birthplace of three world-renowned dishes: salade niçoise, bouillabaisse, and ratatouille. DL and I enjoyed lunch on an outdoor terrace on the Cours Mirabeau, and we ordered and shared these three typical dishes. The salade niçoise was an entrée-sized bowl layered with greens, vine-ripened tomatoes, boiled new potatoes, haricots verts, sliced hard-boiled eggs, green olives, pieces of seared tuna, and dressed with a lemon vinaigrette. Freshly caught shrimp, langoustines, mussels, and clams comprised the main ingredients in luscious fennel and saffron bouillabaisse vegetable broth served over a toasted baguette slathered with garlic aioli. The ratatouille was simple, but the dish was elevated by the artistically arranged fresh summer vegetables: eggplant, zucchini, tomatoes, and onions in a shallow bath of fruity, garlic-flavored olive oil. Equally noteworthy to the food was the wine, a bottle of classic Provence rosé made from the six-grape blend of Grenache, Syrah, Mourvèdre, Cinsault, Clairette, and Tibouren. I looked forward to a daily provision of Provence rosé as we toured the French Riviera.

After Aix-en-Provence, our ship made daily successive transits to Toulon, St. Tropez, Cannes, and Nice on the French Riviera. These destinations were the ultimate standards for "dine, wine, and travel." Tourism is a key business on the French Riviera, and travelers can share the high quality of life expected by the inhabitants of these famous locations. Although all four have their individual character, they share some common attributes: Mediterranean climate, the provincial cuisine of southern France, accessibility to fine French wine, and the proliferation of glamourous residences and estates of wealthy and celebrity residents.

Toulon has been an active Mediterranean port since the seventh century BC. It grew in size and importance under the Roman empire. Today, Toulon is an important commercial center, and it is also the military port for the French Mediterranean fleet, but DL and I were more interested in the historic old town of Toulon between the port, the Boulevard de Strasbourg, and the Cours Lafayette. We spent the day in the old town with its narrow pedestrian streets, Medieval squares, and many restored fountains. Shops and cafés abound, with the interesting tourist sites of the Toulon Cathedral, Opera House, and the celebrated Provençal Market. Once again, we lunched at an outdoor terrace in the shade of a small square treated to the fresh seafood and produce of Provençe. That evening, upon return to the ship, we dined at one of the specialty restaurants, Jacques' Parisian Bistro. We wanted to stay in character with the theme of French dining. We started with escargots, followed by a braised oxtail salad. I opted for the provincial roasted lamb with Tarbais bean puree, and DL chose the lobster thermidor. We finished with a tarte aux pommes, an apple tart that seemed a perfect ending after the roasted lamb and creamy lobster. Although I do not remember the producer, the wine was an excellent Provence rosé, a requisite choice as we feasted on the French Riviera.

We awoke the next morning in St. Tropez. No place epitomizes the French Riviera more than St. Tropez. It is an internationally known seaside resort famous for artists, music, beaches, and jet-set tourists. Wealthy jet-setters frequent two world-class hotels, Hotel Byblos and Les Caves du Roy. Similar to Toulon, St. Tropez has been a Mediterranean port since the sixth century BC, and it grew in importance under the Roman empire when wealthy Romans built opulent villas in this idyllic area. The trend continued into the modern era. Many notables reside in St. Tropez, and probably the most well-known is Brigitte Bardot. She starred in the movie *And God Created Woman* filmed in St. Tropez, and she popularized the clothing-optional beaches in St. Tropez. An assortment of art exhibits, music venues, traditional parades, and sailing regattas entertain the locals and tourists in St. Tropez. DL and I enjoyed the scenic vistas from a tour tram, and we strolled in the quietly sophisticated town, but our focus turned to a number of local wineries for wine tasting and light hors d'oeuvres. An interesting cellar was Bertaud

Belieu. One of their Provence rosé offerings was bottled in a shapely, wasp-waist bottle. The moderator made a lighthearted comment that the shape of the bottle honored Brigitte Bardot, and they even nicknamed the wine B-B, both for Brigitte Bardot and Bertaud Belieu. I've already mentioned how much I like Provence rosé wines, and this one was no exception. When we returned to the ship, we took a brief late-afternoon nap (probably induced by the serious wine tasting ashore), and we made late-evening reservations at one of the specialty restaurants, the Polo Grill. DL started with fried calamari followed by a lobster bisque. I started with an escargot casserole followed by baked onion soup with a crust of Gruyère. For her entrée, DL chose the Surf and Turf, and I opted for the Dover Sole with lemon-brown butter emulsion. We finished with a light dessert of fresh fruit with Chantilly cream. Once again, we stayed in character with an excellent Provence rosé, reminiscent of the B-B we enjoyed earlier that day.

After a restful night recovering from a fabulous dinner, fine wine, and the plush memory of St. Tropez, we awoke in Cannes. Like St. Tropez, Cannes is noted for its association with the rich and famous, only on a larger scale. Luxury hotels and restaurants cater to this clientele. Cannes is probably most known for the annual Cannes Film Festival. We were there in late May, soon after the festival was finished. The red carpet was still in place at the entrance to the Palais des Festivals et des Congrès, so DL and I were photographed there to be festive. We spent the day strolling on the Promenade de la Croisette, a palm-tree-lined waterfront avenue known for its luxury hotels, restaurants, and picturesque beach. Nearby, the old town called Le Suquet offers the characteristic charm of the well-restored and well-maintained historic French Riviera. DL and I had lunch in a quiet café in Le Suquet on a terrace under a shade umbrella with a view of the hustle and bustle on La Croisette. We were treated as if we were rich and famous, which made us feel like we belonged on the French Riviera. The feeling continued after we boarded the ship, and we made reservations for another of the ship's specialty restaurants, Toscana. DL was in the mood for her favorite vegetable, asparagus, so she started with an appetizer of steamed asparagus with coppa and then followed with a salad of grilled asparagus with romanesco sauce. I started with red beets and goat cheese in balsamic vinegar, followed by a classic Caesar salad. DL choose a shrimp dish, gamberoni allo scoglio, for her entrée. I went with the filetto di branzino with artichokes a la barigoule. We both selected a chocolate mousse for dessert. We had been drinking so much Provence rosé wine, we decided to try a different Provence white wine with our seafood entrees. We chose a wine made from the grape called Rolle in southern France but called Vermentino elsewhere. Its acid and body are qualities that make a good pairing with seafood. This dinner was the third night in a row where we had dined in the specialty restaurants aboard ship. This series of fine dining was probably the best three-night sequence of gourmet dining in my life. Of course, the memory was enhanced by the fact that it occurred on the French Riviera.

The next morning opened to the promise of another day in the seat of luxury as we docked in Nice. This would be our final destination on the cruise. Nice is like Toulon, St. Tropez, and Cannes on steroids. It is one of France's most visited cities with over four million tourists a year. Nice has the second-largest hotel capacity in France, and it has the third busiest airport in France after the two Parisian airports. Even with its size and economy, it is still stereotypically the French Riviera. The beautiful environment of Nice was discovered by the English upper classes in the eighteenth century when aristocratic families started their winter vacations there. In fact, a main seaside promenade is named Promenade des Anglais, Walkway of the English. Others who frequented Nice include family members of Tsar Alexander II of Russia and notable French painters such as Henri Matisse and Marc Chagall, whose works are commemorated in many of Nice's museums. With only one day to tour metropolitan Nice, DL and I visited a few notable landmarks, including the palatial Hotel Negresco on the Promenade des Anglais, the Opera de Nice in Vieux Nice (Old Nice), Place Giribaldi named after Guiseppe Giribaldi, who promoted the union of Nice with Italy, and the Place Rossetti, which is a major pedestrian square in the heart of Vieux Nice. We paused for lunch at a café in Place Rossetti and ordered some typical cuisine of Nice. We shared a salade niçoise and a pan bagnat, a healthy sandwich mounded with a variety of fresh provincial ingredients. Naturally, we accompanied the lunch with more Provence rosé wine. Ah, the sophistication of wine with lunch in Nice! We boarded the ship in the late afternoon and prepared ourselves for dinner in the grand dining room. I do not recall the specifics of the dinner, but I remember we decided to have Mediterranean seafood for the appetizer, soup, and entrée courses. I believe we selected a seafood-friendly Italian white wine, Gavi, which is made from the Cortese grape of Piedmont. I do recall the decadent French dessert Puits d'Amour, pastry hearts filled with rich vanilla custard ice cream, aptly named for lovers celebrating their last night on the French Riviera. I would consider an extended trip to Nice in the future to see more of the cultural attractions and to try more of the local provincial cuisine influenced by the Italian cuisine of nearby Liguria and Piedmont.

CHAPTER 56

Cruising the Adriatic

After the glamour, notoriety, and ambiance of the French Riviera, one may believe no other cruise destination could match its enchantment. In reality, many others are equally entertaining with their own unique character. I contend the Dalmatian coast on the Adriatic Sea is such a destination. For the most part, it is little-known and under-appreciated by American travelers. DL and I decided to take a cruise focusing on the western Adriatic Sea coast. It was a decision we do not regret. The cruise itinerary started in Athens and ended in Venice with a number of ports of call on the eastern shore of the Adriatic from Corfu to Trieste, and a couple of ports of call on the Italian coastline on the western shore of the Adriatic. I will focus on a few of the memorable coastal destinations on the Dalmatian coast along the way.

The islands and coastal waterways of the Dalmatian coast are beautifully Mediterranean in character. The inland areas of Croatia and Bosnia Herzegovina are rugged hills and valleys much like the terrain of Abruzzi province in Italy. Most of the cities and towns along the coast show their medieval origins with city walls, arched gates, squares, fountains, and remnants of Greek, Roman, Medieval, and Byzantine architecture. As a major bonus, do not underestimate the food and wine. Traditional Dalmatian cuisine is based heavily on seafood, green vegetables, olive oil, and Mediterranean seasonings like garlic, rosemary, and flat-leaf parsley. If you like the food of coastal Greece, Italy, and France, you will be at home on the Dalmatian coast. The wines are surprisingly good too, although it seems the wine industry in this part of the world is not interested in global distribution, and most of the wine is consumed locally. About two-thirds of the wine production is white wine from the cooler interior appellations. One-third is red wine from the warmer coastal regions. DL and I preferred the red wines.

We arrived in Athens and shuttled directly to the port of Piraeus to board our ship. Since we had been to Athens on previous trips, we did not opt for any precruise hotel accommodations or city excursions. While we recovered from the jet lag with a long snooze that first night, the ship traveled around the southern coast of Greece and docked at our first destination, the town of Corfu on the large island of Corfu. Corfu is the northwestern frontier of Greece, bordering the country of Albania to the north. Corfu is studded with whitewashed houses, Byzantine churches, and the remains of Venetian fortresses and Greek temples. The beautiful landscapes and seascapes have made Corfu a desirable setting for many movies. One of the movies from the James Bond series, *For Your Eyes Only*, was notable for its underwater scene of an ancient sunken Greek temple.

The old town of Corfu City is a UNESCO World Heritage Site. The old town's architectural character is strongly influenced by the Venetian style because it was under Venetian rule for four centuries. Its small and ancient streets and the old buildings' trademark arches are particularly reminiscent of Venice, without the canals. DL and I spent the midday strolling through the old town, captivated by its serenity and medieval ambiance. The local cuisine in Corfu is also influenced by its Venetian heritage, and DL and I stopped for an alfresco lunch in a small square. We sampled one of the most popular dishes in Corfu, pastitsada. Although we were informed pastitsada can be made with fish or beef, the version we were served used chicken. It was a savory, spicy dish with onions, garlic olive oil, cinnamon, cloves, and some other exotic spice flavors, served over thin pasta. The flavor of Venetian Corfiot cuisine was obvious and enjoyable. We did not dwell on the wine list because we saw one of our favorite Greek white wines listed, an Assyrtiko from the Aegean island of Santorini, and it paired well with the pastitsada. We returned to the ship and prepared ourselves for another sumptuous late evening meal in the grand dining room. Have I mentioned there are no mediocre dining experiences aboard Oceania cruise lines? Oh, yes, I have, but we were still amazed by the "finest cuisine at sea."

We awoke the next morning docked in the port of Dubrovnik, Croatia. After a substantial breakfast in the Terrace Café aboard ship, DL and I went ashore with the first group of passengers. We had planned a full day of touring the city, known as the Pearl of the Adriatic, which has become one of the most popular vacation destinations in Europe. With its pleasant weather, beautiful architecture, and incredible food and drink, it is surprising Dubrovnik is not more popular than it is. As with Corfu, the Venetian influence resulting from four centuries of control in the Adriatic is apparent in the architecture and cuisine of Dubrovnik.

The walled city of Dubrovnik is a World Heritage Site. We started with a walk along the famous medieval fortress walls of the Old Town. The pathway on the walls provides ideal vantage points to look down on the red-tiled rooftops of the city and the azure waters of the Adriatic. We then proceeded into Old Town, which is the most beautiful part of Dubrovnik. There are no cars in Old Town, and the architecture, shops, museums, and cafés lining the narrow street paved with stone gives the impression you have gone back in time. After a few hours of taking in the captivating ambiance of Old Town, DL and I stopped for an early lunch at an outdoor café on a street that was featured in the TV series *Game of Thrones*. We were surprised that the menu listed an assortment of dishes from the interior of Croatia and from former Yugoslav countries, in addition to the local dishes of the Dalmatian coast. We opted for some specialties of Dubrovnik. We started with salata od hobotnice (octopus salad), followed by brudet (a fish stew in the style of Italian brodetto). We each had a glass of the local dry red wine made from the Plavac Mali grape, and we were surprised to conclude that this wine could be compared to better-known fine red wines from any more famous global appellations.

After lunch, we joined a tour group from the ship for a wine tasting at a local winery. I do not recall the name of the winery, but it seemed to be a first-class operation of moderate size. We focused on Plavac Mali wine, which we were told was the origin of the genetically identical grapes of Italian Primitivo and American Zinfandel. We bought a bottle of their reserve Plavac Mali to take back to the ship for dinner. Returning to Dubrovnik, DL and I refreshed ourselves at the Buza Bar, reputed to be the best in Dubrovnik. We sat at an open-air terrace located on a cliff overlooking the Adriatic. We shared a charcuterie board with another glass of sumptuous Plavac Mali wine while watching cliff divers make their breathtaking dives off the cliff. In the late afternoon, we returned to the ship for a light workout in the gym, then another superb dinner in the grand dining room with our bottle of reserve Plavac Mali wine, followed by a song-and-dance stage show in the lounge. It was a grand day for dining, wine, and touring.

That night, the ship sailed southwest across the Adriatic to the city of Bari on the heel of the Italian boot. We spent an interesting day in Bari (but that is the subject for another time) before we sailed the following day north across the Adriatic back to the Dalmatian coast to visit the city of Split, Croatia. DL and I went to the observation deck of the ship at sunrise to watch our approach and docking at Split. The ship navigated through tranquil waterways and around numerous wooded islands as it approached the vista of the red-tiled rooftops of the city. Split is the largest city on the Dalmatian coast, but it still displays its Roman, Medieval, and Byzantine history.

The historic center of Split is also a UNESCO World Heritage Site. Although there are a number of attractions for sightseeing, the remains of the palace of Roman Emperor Diocletian (ruled AD 282 to 305) are the most impressive. The original palace was an opulent and heavily fortified structure fronting on the sea. It was square in shape, measuring about six hundred feet on each side. Two roads bisected the interior, dividing the palace into four equal quadrants, with gates in the middle of each side except the side on the sea. Diocletian and his servants occupied one quadrant, his Roman military guards another, his family another, and his administrative staff another. Diocletian had many accomplishments during his reign, and he is noted for two historical facts. First, he was the most notorious emperor for persecuting Christians. Second, he was the only Roman emperor to retire from power instead of dying from assassination, warfare, or rebellion. He retired to his palace in Split in AD 305 and died there in AD 311, where he was laid to rest in the palace mausoleum. It is ironic that this domed, circular mausoleum for the infamous persecutor of Christians became part of the Cathedral of Saint Domnius consecrated in the seventh century and is the second oldest Christian cathedral in the world.

DL and I spent the better part of the day touring Diocletian's palace, the Cathedral of Saint Domnius. and the neighborhood around Narodni Trg, the town's main square. As we walked back to the ship along the Obala Hrvatskog narodnog preporoda, the thoroughfare along the harbor, we stopped for lunch at Zoi, an upscale café for lunch. The view from the terrace of the restaurant was the sparkling waters of the port and seaside facade of Diocletian's palace. We shared a marvelous lunch of smoked seabass salad, accompanied by black risotto with squid and shrimp cooked in a seafood broth. At the recommendation of the waiter, we ordered glasses of a local white wine called Degarra Marastina, a dry medium-bodied wine with good acidity, which paired well with the seafood dishes. I was so intrigued by the risotto I made my own version of the dish at home, and my recipe is attached at the end of this chapter.

We returned to the ship in midafternoon and went to afternoon formal tea before we retired to our stateroom to prepare for dinner. We had made reservations at one of the specialty restaurants aboard ship *Red Ginger*. The restaurant served bold Asian cuisine, and DL and I were ready for a change from the cuisine of the Dalmatian coast. We started with a platter of skewers, sushi, and tempura for two. We also shared one of our favorite Thai soups, tom kha ga, and then a salad of spicy duck, melon, nuts, Thai basil, and sweet fish sauce. For the entrée, DL ordered the red curry chicken with Thai eggplant, baby corn, kaffir lime leaves, and Thai basil. I ordered the seven-spice-crusted rack of lamb with wasabi lamb jus, shitake mushrooms, and snow peas. The sides were steamed jasmine rice and green asparagus with miso glaze. We were satiated, but we could not resist the dessert offerings. I ordered the steamed ginger cake with apple-cardamon ice cream, and DL ordered the exotic fruit sherbet trilogy. We enjoyed two wines with the meal. The first was a Gekkeikan sake that carried us through the salad. The second was an Alsatian Gewurztraminer by Trimbach which we savored through the entrée and up to our departure from *Red Ginger*. This was probably the best upscale Asian dinner we ever ate. We went to bed full, happy, and looking forward to another day of plated ecstasy.

A few days later, we sailed northwest along the Adriatic coast to the city of Pula, situated at the southern tip of the Istrian peninsula in Croatia. Like so many of the cities on the western coast of the Adriatic, Pula's character has been formed over centuries by the influences of multiple overlayed cultures from the ancient Mediterranean to modern Central European. Known for its mild climate and docile sea, Pula has had a tradition of winemaking, fishing, and shipbuilding for millennia. Located beneath seven hills with views of the Adriatic, Pula's unspoiled natural surroundings are stunning.

The city's old quarter is a warren of narrow streets surfaced with ancient Roman paving stones and lined with Medieval and Renaissance structures. For tourists interested in architecture, the city is blessed with many diverse sites, including the Roman Temple of Augustus, the Byzantine chapel of Santa Maria del Canneto, the Romanesque-Byzantine-Gothic fusion design of the Cathedral of the Assumption of the Blessed Virgin Mary, and the star-shaped Venetian castle built on top of the central hill of the old city. However, the most famous and best-preserved site is the first-century Roman amphitheater. It is one of the six largest Roman arenas in the world, built in the same style as the Flavian Coliseum in Rome. It is still in use today for concerts, operas, and film festivals, although, fortunately for civilized tourists, gladiator combat has been prohibited since the fifth century.

After an extensive and detailed tour of the Roman amphitheater, DL and I asked the docent to recommend an excellent nearby restaurant for lunch. She said with enthusiasm, Street Food Two, a restaurant about a quarter of a mile away, and she added that it was the number 1 rated restaurant in Pula. With a name like Street Food Two, we were skeptical, but we decided to try it. We were not disappointed. With all the cultural fusion in Pula, the cuisine is an adventure, and the menu at the restaurant lived up to the expectation. We decided to share a substantial one-dish lunch of a Croatian specialty called hobotnica pod pekom (octopus under the bell). The description of how this traditional dish is prepared overwhelmed my curiosity. I enjoyed it immensely, probably more than DL. When we returned from the cruise, I decided to reproduce the dish to my best recollection. My recipe, with some modifications of ingredients and techniques, is attached at the end of this chapter. In the late afternoon, we returned to the ship for a well-deserved nap, then another superb dinner in the grand dining room, followed by after-dinner cocktails and live piano music in the Martini Bar. Thus ended a fabulous experience of food, wine, and touring along the eastern coast of the Adriatic Sea.

This Croatian dish is a favorite along the Dalmatian coast, where seafood is abundant. The creamy rice, squid ink, and seafood make a dish with a minimalist appearance, but the complex Adriatic flavors offer a taste that belies the monochromatic form. Unlike northern Italian risotto, this Croatian recipe is loaded with seafood so that it can be the protein course in a dinner menu or a one-dish lunch. Buon appetito!

Black Risotto
(Crni Rižot)

Preparation: 30 minutes
Cooking: 1 hour
Serves: 4–6

Step 1: Prepare the seafood

> 1 lb. frozen calamari rings (option: 1 1/2 pounds fresh squid)
> 1 lb. fresh jumbo shrimp in the shell, 21–25 count
> 1 qt. *seafood stock
> 1/2 c. dry white wine
> 1/2 c. yellow onion, coarsely chopped
> 1/4 c. carrot, peeled and coarsely chopped
> 1/4 c. celery stalk, coarsely chopped
> 1/2 tsp. salt, or to taste
> 1/4 tsp. fresh ground black pepper, or to taste

Defrost the calamari rings in a colander under cold water. Set aside.

If optional fresh squid is used, clean the squid. Start by holding the body with one hand and the head and tentacles with the other. Pull the squid apart, and the gut should come out. You may have to reach into the body to grasp and remove the long body cartilage. Discard the gut and the cartilage. Grasp the spotty skin at the top of the body and peel back toward the flukes at the end. Discard the skin. Cut the tube body into 1/2-inch rings. Cut the tentacles from the head, and discard the eyes and the beak. Thoroughly rinse the rings and the tentacles, and set them aside. Although some folks may balk at using the tentacles, I recommend using them in the recipe because they add a textural crunch to the dish.

Peel the shrimp, including the tails, and retain all the shells. Remove and discard the intestinal vein. Rinse the shrimp and set it aside.

Place the stock, wine, onion, carrot, celery, salt, and pepper in a 3-quart pot. Add the shrimp shells to the pot. Bring to a boil over medium-high heat, then reduce the heat to medium low and simmer covered for 30 minutes. Drain the cooked mixture through a chinois into a 2-quart pot, and discard the solids. Retain the strained stock, cover, and keep hot over low heat. You should have at least 3 1/2 cups of finished stock which is required in step 3 of this recipe. If less than 3 1/2 cups, add additional stock or water to make up the difference. Clean the 3-quart pot so it can be used in step 3 of this recipe.

Step 2: Aromatics

> 1/4 c. EVOO
> 1 large yellow onion, diced
> 2 cloves garlic, minced
> 1 tbsp. tomato paste
> 1/4 c. dry white wine
> 1 tbsp. fresh squeezed lemon juice

Heat the oil in a 12-inch sauté pan over medium-high heat. Add the onions, and sauté for about 5 minutes until the onions are transparent. Do not brown. Add the garlic and tomato paste, and sauté for about a minute until the garlic is fragrant. Deglaze the pan with the wine and lemon juice until the liquid is reduced by half. Remove from the heat, and set aside.

Step 3: Rice

> 2 tbsp. EVOO
> 1 1/2 c. Arborio rice (option: Carnaroli rice)
> 1 tsp. squid ink (available online or in upscale food markets)

Heat the oil in the 3-quart pot from step 1 over medium heat. Add the rice, and stir to coat thoroughly. Lightly toast the rice for about three minutes, stirring frequently. Add one cup of hot stock from step 1. Stir frequently for about 10 minutes until the stock is almost completely absorbed. Add a second cup of hot stock and the reserved aromatics from step 2. Stir frequently for about 10 minutes until the stock is almost completely absorbed. Add a third cup of hot stock and the squid ink. Stir frequently for about 10 minutes until the stock is almost completely absorbed. At this point, the rice should be tender but still al dente, and the mixture should be creamy, black, and slightly wet.

Step 4: Finish

> 2 tbsp. unsalted butter
> Salt, to taste
> Fresh ground black pepper, to taste
> 1/4 cup flat-leaf parsley, chopped

Add the reserved squid and shrimp from Step 1 to the risotto. Add about 1/2 cup of the hot stock from step 1, and gently stir to mix. Cook over medium heat for 3–5 minutes until the squid rings and shrimp are cooked through and tender. Add additional stock or water as required to achieve the desired consistency. Do not overcook or the seafood will become tough. Off the heat, stir in the butter, and adjust seasonings to taste. Spoon the risotto onto four shallow serving plates, and garnish the top with the parsley. Serve immediately.

*Stock

Master Chef Auguste Escoffier says in his epic treatise *The Escoffier* on the fine art of French cuisine: "Stock is everything in cooking. Without it, nothing can be done. The cook mindful of success, therefore, will naturally direct his attention to the faultless preparation of his stock."

A great stock is judged by five criteria: flavor, clarity, color, body, and aroma. An excellent modern reference for preparing stock can be found in chapter 1 of *The Elements of Cooking* by Michael Ruhlman. If you prefer to use a commercially available stock product, the boxed Swanson brand or Kitchen Basics brand are good choices but not as good as homemade stock.

Hobotnica ispod peke is a popular Dalmatian dish, especially in the cities of Split and Dubrovnik. It is traditionally prepared in a peka, a domed covered vessel, and cooked on hot coals and covered with hot coals in a wood-burning fireplace. This recipe is my attempt to replicate the traditional technique using a Dutch oven in a conventional convection oven. The intent is to cook a one-dish meal that seals in juices and creates a depth of flavor that makes seafood and vegetables taste like the Croatian homeland. If you have never cooked with octopus before, this may be the recipe that expands your culinary range. Buon appetito!

Octopus under the Bell
(Hobotnica Pod Pekom)

Preparation: 30 minutes
Cooking: 1 hour 15 minutes
Serves: 4

Step 1: Clean and cook the octopus

    2 lbs. medium-sized fresh octopus
    2 qt. *salted water

Carefully cut the tentacles from the head of the octopus. Cut out the beak from the center of the tentacles. Cut out and discard the eyes from the head. Slit one side of the head and body, and scrape out any gut from inside. Rinse the cleaned octopus under running water to remove any remaining gut and grit.

Heat the water in a 3 1/2-quart Dutch oven over medium-high heat. When the water starts to simmer, reduce the heat to low. Place the cleaned octopus in the pot, and simmer for about 15 minutes. Simmering helps to tenderize the octopus and also removes excess gelatinous moisture from the octopus.

Remove the cooked octopus from the Dutch oven and allow it to drain in a colander. Then cut the tentacles and body into serving-size segments. Set aside.

Step 2: Vegetables

> 2 cloves garlic, minced
> 1/2 cup EVOO
> 1 lb. russet potatoes, peeled and quartered
> 2 large carrots, peeled and quartered lengthwise
> 1 medium pointed cabbage, cored and quartered (also called cone cabbage or white cabbage)
> 1 medium leek, white and light green parts only, quartered lengthwise
> 5 medium shallots, peeled and quartered
> 1 tsp. kosher salt
> 1/2 tsp. fresh ground black pepper
> 1/2 c. **vegetable stock
> 1/2 tsp. liquid smoke (hickory flavor preferred)

Position a rack on the lower level of the oven, and heat the oven to 350 degrees Fahrenheit in the Convection Roast mode.

Clean the Dutch oven from step 1. Combine the oil and the garlic. Drizzle half of the oil-garlic mixture into the bottom of the Dutch oven. Line the bottom of the Dutch oven with the potatoes. Then distribute the carrots, cabbage, leek, and shallots on top. Season with salt and pepper. Drizzle the remaining oil-garlic mixture over the vegetables. Now place the octopus from step 1 on top. Pour the vegetable stock and liquid smoke over the contents. Tightly cover the Dutch oven, and place it in the oven. Cook for 30 minutes.

Step 3: Finish

2 tbsp. fresh squeezed lemon juice, divided
1/4 c. fresh flat-leaf parsley, chopped
1 tbsp. fresh dill, chopped
1/4 c. dry white wine

After cooking for 30 minutes, remove the Dutch oven from the oven. Add one tablespoon of the lemon juice and the remaining step 3 ingredients. Turn the contents with a large wooden spoon. (It's traditional!) If the liquid in the mixture has evaporated more than you desire, add a little more oil and wine to remoisten. Cover, and return the Dutch oven to the oven. Cook for an additional 30 minutes.

When finished, remove the Dutch oven from the oven. Apportion the contents onto four shallow serving plates. Drizzle the remaining lemon juice on top. Serve immediately.

*Salted Water
For cooking any type of pasta or vegetable or poaching in water, salted water translates to a 1 percent salt solution: about 1 1/2 teaspoons of salt in one quart of water.

**Stock
Master Chef Auguste Escoffier says in his epic treatise *The Escoffier*, on the fine art of French cuisine: "Stock is everything in cooking. Without it, nothing can be done. The cook mindful of success, therefore, will naturally direct his attention to the faultless preparation of his stock."

A great stock is judged by five criteria: flavor, clarity, color, body, and aroma. An excellent modern reference for preparing stock can be found in chapter 1 of *The Elements of Cooking* by Michael Ruhlman. If you prefer to use a commercially available stock product, the boxed Swanson brand or Kitchen Basics brand are good choices but not as good as homemade stock.

Road Trips

The travel aspect of our mantra, "Dine, wine, and travel," still included spontaneous short weekend trips to US destinations and had expanded to include international cruising. Now, with the time available to us, we added a third format for travel which we called *road trips*, lasting about two weeks or more driving through a multistate section of the country to visit a series of old friends or scenic areas such as national parks. We only formulated an approximate itinerary for our road trips to allow us spontaneity and flexibility. We made most of our overnight reservations while on the road on the day of travel, except when we planned ahead to stay with friends at their invitation. Routine overnight accommodations were usually at a Holiday Inn Express, Hilton Garden Inn, or Marriott Courtyard because they were consistently clean, good quality, and offered a fresh buffet breakfast to start the day. Selection of diners or restaurants for meals was for the most part an impromptu activity, except when friends took us to one of their favorite venues or if we knew about a particularly fine restaurant on the route. I particularly liked to visit the fifty-plus national parks in the United States for their overwhelming grandeur, and as seniors, we are eligible for free entry to all these magnificent places. DL and I have visited many of the national parks, although we may never have the time to visit all of them. I suggest that touring the major National Parks should be a bucket list item for all Americans.

Regarding our road trips, I must admit two items. First, neither DL and I like driving long distances, so we limit our daily driving to a few hundred miles. Second, most of the dining on road trips is routine, not gourmet. Our main intention on road trips is to visit national parks (Grand Canyon, Yosemite, Big Bend, etc.), national military parks (Shiloh, Gettysburg, Fredericksburg, etc.), festivals (Mardi Gras, New Orleans, Louisiana; Pageant of the Masters, Laguna Beach, California; Monterey Jazz Festival, Monterey, California; etc.), and scenic routes (Skyline Drive, Virginia; Columbia River Gorge, Oregon; Grand Teton/Snake River, Wyoming; etc.). However, we occasionally are treated to a fine dining experience on our road trips.

CHAPTER 58

Washington, Oregon, and Northern California

One year we hit the road for nearly a month to visit the coastal northwest of the United States. We planned to fly into Seattle, rent a car, drive south, and fly home from San Francisco. We had friends, Steve and Diane Harper, who lived about ten miles east of Seattle in Sammamish, and they were first on our list. They took us to the Space Needle to enjoy a spectacular view of Seattle and Puget Sound while savoring a cup of Seattle's best coffee. Then we went to Pike Place seafood market to watch the unbelievable athletics of the vendors who made a show of tossing and catching large fish. For dinner, we went to a restaurant called El Gaucho in Bellevue. Our friends told us it was a chain restaurant but added that it was a cut above the standard restaurant chain. I recall two dishes from that dinner. The first was a salad with a base of grilled romaine lettuce. I had never been served grilled romaine before, and it was probably one of the best salads I have ever eaten. The entrée was a flaming sword of beef tenderloin, presented and served tableside, with cremini mushrooms and béarnaise sauce. The awesome tableside presentation was easy to remember.

When we left our friends in Sammamish, we went to Mt. Rainer National Park followed by Mt. St. Helens National Volcano Monument. Continuing at a leisurely pace, we stopped to visit Dave and Ellen Ludwig, friends in Lake Oswego, about five miles south of

Portland, Oregon, where we spent about five days. Over two days, we toured the Columbia River Valley for both the impressive scenery and a few wineries. Then we spent a day in the Willamette Valley touring more wineries. I was most impressed with the Willamette Pinot Noir wines, especially the bottlings of Domaine Serene. For dinner one night, we went to the Portland City Grill. Their seafood menu was so extensive I found it difficult to choose, and their wine list was also impressive. My entrée that night was cioppino with Dungeness crab, halibut, and other fresh seafood, paired with a bottle of the aforementioned Domaine Serene Pinot Noir.

As much as we enjoyed the long visit with our Lake Oswego friends, we hit the road again and headed west then south along the scenic Pacific Coast Highway toward California. We took our time to travel the 250 miles of the Oregon coast, stopping frequently to enjoy scenic views and lunch in quaint seaside towns. Crossing into California, we spent one overnight at a seaside resort in Crescent City; and on the next day, we visited the Redwood National Park.

Our next destination was Mendocino wine country, about two hundred miles south on the scenic Pacific Coast Highway. Although not as well-known as Napa Valley and Sonoma, Mendocino has twelve American Viticultural Areas (AVA) with significantly different climates and soils that produce a wide variety of wine. We spent the night in Ukiah and toured a number of wineries the following day. Navarro and Parducci wineries had first-class tasting room operations.

Our final destination was San Francisco. We had reservations for a couple of nights at our go-to hotel, the Marines' Memorial on Sutter Street. One night we thought we would try to dine without making reservations at Postrio, a very popular Wolfgang Puck restaurant. The restaurant was in the Prescott Hotel on Post Street, a few blocks from our hotel. We walked there, entered through the lobby of the Prescott Hotel, and approached the host at the restaurant entrance. He asked if we had a reservation, and I answered in a confident but polite tone, "No, we do not have a reservation, but we are ready to be seated now if you have a table for two available." To our surprise, he looked at the ledger on the kiosk and said, "Yes, sir.

This way please." In the past, we had previously dined at two other Wolfgang Puck restaurants, Spago and Chinois on Main, and Postrio was the same Michelin star quality. That night, my entrée was baby lamb shanks with an apricot-walnut-cilantro sauce and grilled baby fennel bulbs. Upon our return to Austin, we mentioned to friends that we had dined at Postrio, and they asked how long in advance did we have to make reservations. We told them our story, and they were amazed. I guess we were lucky, and by the way, we were very well dressed that night.

CHAPTER 59

Arkansas, Tennessee, Mississippi, and Louisiana

Another of our road trips was planned to be a three-week loop through northeast Texas, southern Arkansas, western Mississippi, southern Louisiana, returning via eastern Texas. We did not plan to meet any friends or family, did not expect much fine dining, and we would focus on national parks, Civil War sites, and scenic highways.

The first leg of the trip was a short drive north to the village of Salado, where we planned to have lunch at the Stagecoach Inn. The Stagecoach Inn, built in 1861, is the oldest continuously operating hotel in Texas. Distinguished patrons who found lodging and meals at the inn include Sam Houston, Robert E. Lee, George Custer, Charles Goodnight, and Jesse James. The lunch menu is typical Texas-style substantial offerings of salads, sandwiches, and specialties like chicken fried steak. The tasty and hearty lunch was good preparation for the next leg of travel.

We continued to McKinney, Texas, a little northeast of Dallas. We spent the night at a landmark in McKinney, the Grand Hotel and Ballroom on the square downtown. The restaurant in the hotel is Rick's Chophouse, which at the time was known for Chef Paul Peterson, proclaimed by *Southern Living* magazine as the best grilling and barbecue chef in Texas. Of course, we had to have Chef Peterson's rib eye steak seasoned with his signature spicy rub. It was a succulent, tender entrée, but I need to pause here for an editorial comment. As much as I like medium-rare steak perfectly grilled, I usually do not order steak in a fine dining venue. In my opinion, there is not much difference in restaurant steaks when any good chef properly grills a cut of FDA Prime beef. I tend to order more difficult entrée preparations that challenge the chef. However, out of respect for Chef Peterson's culinary expertise, I was happy to order his version of a rib eye steak.

The following morning, we were back on the road heading east to Texarkana. We stopped for a leisurely, simple lunch of burgers and fries and proceeded to the national park in Hot Springs, Arizona. Without reservations, we approached the desk at the Arlington Resort Hotel and Spa on historic Bathhouse Row and were fortunate to find that accommodations were available. The Arlington was an impressive historic hotel, the largest in Arkansas. Built in 1875, it has been in continuous operation hosting tourists visiting the hot springs for their therapeutic value. The Arlington boasted an elegant fine dining restaurant, the Venetian Dining Room, where we dined our first night in Hot Springs. The restaurant offered a classic multicourse Italian dinner menu, and I could not resist the temptation to order one of my favorite Italian secondo piatto entrees, veal osso buco. In upscale Italian restaurants, my benchmark to measure the star-quality of the kitchen is their ability to make osso buco. The Venetian Dining Room measured up. I have included my recipe for osso buco at the end of this chapter. We spent the next day touring Bathhouse Row and hiking trails in the park and museums and art galleries downtown. That night we relaxed in the Arlington's thermal bathhouse, where you soak in the famous mineral waters of the natural hot springs. Until our visit, I was unaware that the Hot Springs National Park even existed, so the stay in Hot Springs was enlightening.

We headed east to Memphis, Tennessee. When one thinks of Memphis, the thoughts usually run to Overton Square entertainment, the Blues on Beale Street, and Elvis Presley's Graceland mansion. Food takes second place, although many folks praise Memphis barbecue, fried chicken, catfish, greens, and hush puppies. We had previously traveled to Memphis, so we decided to stay in a brand-name motel about twenty miles north of Memphis in Millington. Millington is home to the Naval Support Activity (NAVSUPP) which employs over 7,500 military, civilian, and contractor personnel. I had been assigned there once on temporary duty while on active duty. As a retired officer, I still had access to the Officers' Club on base, so DL and I went there for their famous Friday night seafood buffet. It was a sumptuous buffet of almost every seafood imaginable, including lobster tails, peel-it-yourself shrimp, oysters, mussels, fried seafood medley, and all the accompaniments you would expect with a Southern seafood dinner. It may not be classified as fine dining, but it was certainly satisfying.

Our next destination was the Shiloh National Military Park about one hundred miles east of Memphis. I have always been interested in the Civil War. My interest started when my parents took me to tour the Gettysburg Military National Park when I was a child. Since then, I have collected a small library of the Civil War, and my favorite historical narrative is the three-volume set titled *The Civil War* by Shelby Foote. I had been to a number of Civil War sites, some more than once, including Gettysburg, Antietam, and Fredericksburg, but I had never been to Shiloh. Shiloh was unique. On the day we visited Shiloh, it seemed that we were the only tourists in the park, very much unlike the other popular Civil War parks I had previously visited. The place was as serene as an unoccupied church. The stillness almost seemed unnatural. I recall seeing the plaque and the tree where Confederate General Albert Sidney Johnson rested as he bled to death from a leg wound sustained near the Hornet's Nest. I saw the Bloody Pond where wounded soldiers from both sides crawled to slake their thirst before they succumbed to their wounds. In the tranquility at the Bloody Pond, a spiritual person may have felt the presence of souls in eternal rest at peace. It was a sobering and evocative experience. DL and I needed something to offset the sobriety of our day in Shiloh, so we decided to find a popular and typically Southern place to eat dinner. Fortunately, there was a place close by that fit the bill, Hagy's Catfish Hotel. The building stands alone, isolated in the middle of nowhere, on the undeveloped banks of the Tennessee River. The place has stood there since 1825, and it is reputed to be one of the oldest family-owned restaurants in the country. It was a well-kept rustic place, completely rebuilt in 1976. When we visited the restaurant, it was still owned and operated by a fourth-generation Hagy. Naturally, we had to try their specialty, Southern-style fried whole catfish, accompanied by stuffed potato skins, fried green tomatoes, and hush puppies. It was a fitting conclusion to a memorable day.

The next morning, we headed southwest about one hundred miles to Oxford, Mississippi. We wanted to have a brief windshield tour of the University of Mississippi and then lunch before we continued southwest to Vicksburg. The small town of Oxford and the university grounds were picturesque. Trees and green space were plentiful, and antebellum character prevailed. We had heard about the Ajax Diner which had been serving Oxford and the Ole Miss community for over twenty tears, so that was our choice for lunch. We continued with our Southern food dining theme, and the Ajax Diner did not disappoint us with its comfort food. Our substantial lunch included the Ajax salad, chicken and dumplings, and butterbeans. We were told that best-selling author John Grisham, probably the most famous citizen of Oxford, frequented the Ajax Diner, but we did not see him on our brief visit.

We checked into the Holiday Inn Express in downtown Vicksburg for a couple of nights. The motel was within a minute of the Vicksburg National Military Park and a number of restaurants. The next day we toured the park and the museum. The siege of Vicksburg during the Civil War was one of the most prolonged and most desperate for the Confederate Army and the citizens of Vicksburg. After nearly two months, Vicksburg surrendered on July 4, 1863, coincidentally the same day as the Confederate defeat at Gettysburg. The Vicksburg National Military Park is not as pastoral as Shiloh or Gettysburg because urban development has erased much of the original battlefield. As a result, it seemed busier and less somber than our previous experience at Shiloh. The touring during the day stimulated our appetites, and we took dinner at the Beechwood Restaurant, a Vicksburg landmark since 1956. Staying with our Southern food dining theme, we ordered breaded and fried dill pickles, fisherman's mixed grill plate, accompanied by sweet potato fries. It was an excess of fried food, but it was delicious in the southern tradition. The next morning, after the Holiday Inn breakfast buffet, we headed south to Baton Rouge.

We chose Baton Rouge over New Orleans on this road trip because we had never been to Baton Rouge, and we had visited New Orleans numerous times. On the way to Baton Rouge, we drove the scenic Natchez Trace Parkway and stopped for lunch in the classic antebellum town of Natchez. We made a reservation for two nights at the Renaissance Baton Rouge Hotel, which is located near Louisiana State University and a number of downtown entertainment attractions. On the first day, we took a windshield tour of LSU, much like we did at their Southeastern Conference rival, Ole Miss, and we also visited the Louisiana Capitol and the Mall of Louisiana. As an aside, let me confess to favoring the SEC in college football. I have visited many of the attractive SEC campuses, and I have attended many SEC football games. I just feel an affinity to the SEC. A secondary aspect is that I enjoy Southern cooking, so it should not be a surprise that DL and I sought a notable restaurant for dinner in Baton Rouge. We asked the concierge at the Renaissance for a restaurant recommendation other than the Renaissance's restaurant, and he directed us to The Chimes Restaurant. The Chimes was a moderately priced, family-friendly venue that had been serving Baton Rouge and LSU for over twenty-five years. We had a relaxed dining experience with well-prepared and well-presented made-from-scratch Southern dishes. I started with raw oysters, then crawfish étouffée, accompanied by a sauté of collard greens and pork belly with peach cobbler for dessert. The Chimes had an extensive selection of beer and spirits, but the wine list was limited. However, we found an unpretentious Napa Chardonnay that paired well with the creamy étouffée. We rested well that night. As we discussed the travel plans for the next day, we decided we had had enough on this road trip. So instead of a stop in the Houston area on the way back to Austin, we decided to drive the 450 miles straight through to Austin. I guess you could say we had a case of "get-home-itus." It was a great road trip with memorable touring and some fine dining, but we were happy to finally sleep in our own bed after nearly a month.

PREFACE

In my opinion, osso buco is the benchmark dish to determine the caliber of a great Italian ristorante. Osso buco takes time, attention, and quality ingredients. If the restaurant can prepare an osso buco worthy of praise, then there is high confidence that other dishes on the menu will be equally praiseworthy. Following is my recipe that attempts to replicate a style of osso buco that I have enjoyed. Buon appetito!

OSSO BUCO

Preparation: 1 1/2 hours
Cooking: 3 1/2 hours
Serves: 4

Step1: Brown the veal shanks

    1/4 c. EVOO, divided
    4 oz. pancetta, 1/4 in. dice
    4 large veal shank crosscuts, 2+ in. thick, about 4+ lbs. (option: lamb shanks, beef shanks, or venison shanks)
    1 tsp. kosher salt (or to taste)
    1/4 tsp. freshly ground pepper (or to taste)
    1/2 c. flour, for dredging
    2 tbsp. unsalted butter

Heat two tablespoons of the oil in a 12-inch sauté pan over medium-high heat until it is shimmering but not smoking (350 degrees Fahrenheit). Add the pancetta and sauté for about 5 minutes until golden brown. Monitor the heat so that the pancetta does not smoke or burn. With a slotted spoon, transfer the pancetta to paper towels to drain, and set aside. Remove and discard excess fat and oil from the skillet, leaving just a thin film for flavor.

Pat dry the veal shanks. Tie each shank around the circumference with kitchen twine to keep the meat attached to the bone. Season the shanks on all sides with salt and pepper. Dredge the shanks in the flour, shaking off excess. Heat the remaining two tablespoons of olive oil and the butter over medium-high heat in the sauté pan. Sear the shanks for about 8 minutes, browning well on all sides, turning frequently. When browned, transfer the shanks from the sauté pan to a 6.5-quart Dutch oven or oven-proof pot. Arrange the shanks in one layer.

Step 2: Aromatic vegetables

2 tbsp. EVOO
1 c. yellow onion, chopped
1/2 c. carrot, grated
1/2 c. fennel bulb, white part only, chopped
1 small shallot, minced
2 cloves garlic, minced or pressed
4 large *plum tomato concassé (option: 15 oz. canned diced
     tomatoes)
2 c. dry red wine (Barolo, Barbaresco, Chianti, or Primitivo
     preferred)

Add the oil, onion, carrot, and fennel to the sauté pan from step 1. Sauté over medium-high heat until the onions begin to turn transparent, about 5 minutes, stirring frequently. Add the garlic, shallot, and tomato, and sauté for about an additional 2 minutes. Transfer the vegetable mixture to the Dutch oven in step 2, and spread it on top of the layer of shanks. Also, spread the browned pancetta from Step 1 on the shanks.

Add the wine to the sauté pan, and bring to a low boil over medium heat to deglaze the skillet. Scrape up the brown, caramelized bits clinging to the bottom and sides of the skillet. Reduce the liquid by one-half to about 1 cup, about 15 minutes. Strain and pour the reduced wine over the shanks in the Dutch oven. Discard the solids.

Step 3: Braise

> 2 c. **veal stock (option: beef stock or chicken stock)
> 1 fillet anchovy, mashed to paste (optional)
> 1 sachet: 2 sprig fresh oregano
> 2 sprig fresh sage
> 2 sprig fresh rosemary
> 4 strips lemon rind, about 1/4 by 2 inches
> 2 bay leaves
> 12 whole black peppercorns, cracked
> 1 whole clove
> 1 Parmesan rind, about 1 by 3 inches

Preheat the oven to 350 degrees Fahrenheit. Position an oven rack in the lower third of the oven.

Pour the veal stock into the Dutch oven. The stock and wine should barely cover the shanks. Add the anchovy paste. Construct the sachet by enclosing the oregano, sage, rosemary, lemon rind, bay leaf, peppercorns, and clove in a cheesecloth packet and bind with kitchen twine. As an alternative to the cheesecloth, a size-2 tea bag can be used to make the sachet. Nest the sachet among the shanks.

Bring the mixture in the Dutch oven to a low boil over medium-high heat on the cooktop. Remove the Dutch oven from the cooktop, cover with the cover slightly ajar, and place on the oven rack in the preheated oven.

Braise for 15 minutes at 350 degrees Fahrenheit, then reduce the temperature to 200 degrees Fahrenheit, and adjust the cover on the Dutch oven to a tight fit. Check the meat every half hour. Turn the meat after one hour, and add a small amount of stock, wine, or water as necessary to offset any evaporation. Stop the cooking when the meat is easily penetrated by a fork, or when the meat is separating from the bone, about 150 degrees Fahrenheit internal temperature. The approximate time at 200 degrees Fahrenheit is 1 1/2 to 2 hours.

Step 4: Sauce

>
> 1/4 c. dry red wine (Barolo, Barbaresco, Chianti, or Primitivo
>   preferred)
> 1/4 c. tomato paste
> 1 tbsp. fresh basil, minced (or 1 tsp. dried basil)
> 1 tbsp. fresh marjoram, minced (or 1 tsp. dried marjoram)
> 1 tbsp. fresh thyme, minced (or 1 tsp. dried thyme)
> 1/4 c. fresh flat-leaf parsley, minced (or 2 tbsp. dried parsley)
> Kosher salt (to taste)
> Freshly ground pepper (to taste)
> 2 tbsp. unsalted butter (option: robust olive oil)

After braising is complete, remove the Dutch oven from the oven. Remove the shanks from the Dutch oven and set them aside, but keep them warm in a covered container or in a foil tent so they do not dry out. Remove the sachet and discard.

Using a strainer or a conical chinois, strain the mixture from the Dutch oven into a 3-quart saucepan, and discard the strained solids. Skim and discard any excess fat from the surface of the braising liquid. Bring the liquid to a low boil over medium heat. Add the wine, tomato paste, basil, marjoram, thyme, and parsley. Reduce the sauce by 1/2 for about 20 minutes. Add salt and pepper to taste. Remove the sauce from the heat, and whisk in the butter.

Step 5: Finish

>
> 1/2 c. gremolata: 1/2 c. fresh parsley, minced, loosely packed
> 1 tbsp. lemon zest
> 1 tbsp. garlic, finely minced
> 4 servings of fettuccine (option: polenta or risotto)
> 6 qt. ***salted water

While the sauce is reducing, prepare the gremolata by mixing the parsley, lemon zest, and garlic in a small bowl. Set aside.

While the sauce is reducing, prepare 4 servings of fettuccine according to directions until al dente. Drain. Place a portion on each of the 4 plates as a bed. Place a shank on each bed. Pour equal portions of the sauce over the bedded shanks. Any extra sauce can be placed in a gravy boat for use at the table. Sprinkle the gremolata over each serving.

*Tomato Concassé

Cut an X in the bottom of each tomato. Blanch the tomatoes in a pot of boiling water for 30 seconds. Using a slotted spoon, transfer the tomatoes to an ice water bath to cool. When cool, drain. Remove the stems and peel off the skin starting from the X. Cut tomatoes in half lengthwise. Remove and discard the core and the seeds. Coarsely chop the tomato.

**Stock

Master Chef Auguste Escoffier says in his epic treatise *The Escoffier* on the fine art of French cuisine: "Stock is everything in cooking. Without it, nothing can be done. The cook mindful of success, therefore, will naturally direct his attention to the faultless preparation of his stock."

A great stock is judged by five criteria: flavor, clarity, color, body, and aroma. An excellent modern reference for preparing stock can be found in chapter 1 of *The Elements of Cooking* by Michael Ruhlman. If you prefer to use a commercially available stock product, the boxed Swanson brand or Kitchen Basics brand are good choices, but not as good as homemade stock.

***Salted Water

For cooking any type of pasta or vegetable, salted water translates to a 1 percent salt solution: 1 1/2 teaspoons of salt in one quart of water (10 grams of salt in one liter of water).

CHAPTER 60

New Mexico, Arizona, and West Texas

A year or more had passed, and we were ready for another monthlong road trip. Although we would only travel in three states, they were large western states. The size of our country and the diversity of its geography can be fully appreciated with travel through the American West. What an amazing undertaking for the early pioneers in covered wagons! On this road trip, we would experience less fine dining and more time on the road than previous road trips. However, we would be compensated by the grandeur of the national parks we intended to tour. The long-range forecast for our trip was warm weather and clear skies. We packed the car and headed west; however, we had some trepidation about the amount of time we would spend on the road.

Our first stop would be lunch in Fredericksburg, the heart of Texas Hill Country. We anticipated that we would be passing through Fredericksburg again in about a month on our way home, so we just opted for a lunch of German cuisine before proceeding westward. There are a lot of choices for German restaurants in Fredericksburg, and almost anyone can provide a delicious, traditional lunch of sausages, rye bread, kohlrabi, and apple strudel. In my opinion, Eastern European cuisine is underrated, but for those of us that like it, central Texas has its share.

From Fredericksburg, we started the long drive, about 270 miles, to the Midland/Odessa area in the Permian Basin, which is a huge oil-producing area. After clearing the verdant western edge of Hill Country, the scenery became a boring and seemingly endless expanse of flat, semiarid, brown terrain. Like an immense herd of prehistoric beasts in the basin, countless pump jacks rhythmically dipped their heads to feed on the ground. We had no specific plans for the Midland/Odessa area except as a rest stop. I am certain there are luxury accommodations and fine dining venues that serve the oil barons, but DL and I were road weary. All we needed was rest at one of our brand-name motel preferences and a nongourmet eat-to-live dinner.

The next morning, we were on our way to Carlsbad Caverns National Park. We planned to tour the park and spend the night in Carlsbad, New Mexico. I was dazzled by the caverns! After an elevator ride into the bowels of the earth, you entered an unworldly scene of huge grottos filled with stalagmites, stalactites, and columns. The interior lighting was spectacular, accentuating the natural wonder. Carlsbad Caverns has been described as the Grand Canyon with a roof on it. I suggest the caverns are a bucket list destination. After a remarkable day in the park, we were happy with accommodations at one of our brand-name motel preferences in the town of Carlsbad and a simple sit-down dinner.

From Carlsbad to Roswell, New Mexico, was a seventy-five-mile trip from the spectacular to the bizarre. We planned a quick visit to the International UFO Museum and Research Center in Roswell, then lunch, then on to Santa Fe. It seemed that everything in Roswell was UFO-centric. Even the tourists had a spacey look. We ate an ordinary lunch gawking at the tourists then headed to Santa Fe and the beautiful Sangre de Cristo mountains.

Up until this leg of the road trip, DL and I had not sought luxury accommodations or fine dining. Santa Fe changed that. We had made reservations for two nights at the luxury hotel, La Fonda on the Plaza. Authentic New Mexico architecture, a prime location on the plaza, indulgent amenities, and a choice of unique dining options place La Fonda a cut above other hotels. On our first night, we dined at the hotel's La Plazuela restaurant. I started with a bowl of roasted green chili corn chowder, followed by a roasted beet and

Brazilian seared cheese salad. My entrée was bison short rib tacos, probably the best tacos I have ever eaten. Do not wrinkle your nose at the thought of gourmet tacos in a fine dining restaurant until you have tried them. My dessert was sopapillas stuffed with sweet Queso Chihuahua and drizzled with honey. I always find it difficult to pair a wine with New Mexico cuisine, but the wine steward at La Plazuela was accustomed to this dilemma, and he recommended a bold, deep-purple Petite Sirah from Napa. Good choice. The next day we leisurely visited art galleries, old churches, and Native American historic sites. We had lunch outdoors at Santacafé, where we enjoyed traditional New Mexico enchiladas with green and red chili salsa, New Mexico-style Christmas decorations. I live in Texas, so what I am about to say may be considered heretical, but I prefer the style of northern New Mexico cuisine over the Tex-Mex style. There seems to be more authenticity and refinement in northern New Mexico cuisine. On our second evening, we took an early light dinner at the Luminaria restaurant in the Inn at Loretto, because we had reservations for a performance of La Bohéme by Giacomo Puccini at the Santa Fe Opera. The Santa Fe Opera House is one of a kind. It is an outdoor facility, partially open to the sky, and the sets are transported to the stage by an elevator from two stories below the stage. If you love opera or even if you like it a little, you must visit the Santa Fe Opera House. DL and I enjoyed our luxurious respite in charming Santa Fe, but now it was time to move on.

We headed south through Albuquerque, with the strains of "Quando m'en vo," the famous aria from the second act of La Bohéme still resonating in our memory, then turned west toward Arizona. We crested the Continental Divide in the vicinity of Thoreau, New Mexico. Our intermediate goal was early lunch in Gallup New Mexico, a freeway-fast two hundred miles. After lunch, it was only another hour to the Petrified Forest National Park. We toured the park from the north entrance to the south entrance and then spent the night at one of our brand-name motel preferences in the town of Holbrook with an ordinary motel restaurant sit-down dinner.

The next day's travel promised some spectacular scenery. First, we drove about sixty miles west to the Meteor Crater near Winslow.

The crater is an impressive scar on the surface of Mother Earth. A nickel-iron meteorite hit the Earth about fifty thousand years ago with the estimated impact force of a ten-megaton thermonuclear weapon, a good example of the power of nature. After a short visit to the crater, we drove another hour west to Flagstaff for an early lunch. From our open-air lunch patio, we could see Humphrey's Peak, the highest point in Arizona at over twelve thousand feet. The area around Flagstaff is some of the most beautiful in the States, but we did not linger in the area because we planned to enjoy more time there later on the road trip. So we headed northwest on designated scenic highways toward the south rim of the Grand Canyon National Park. The seventy-file-mile drive was National Geographic quality.

Before we departed on this road trip, we made reservations over sixty days in advance for two nights at the El Tovar lodge, located directly on the canyon's south rim. At the time it was built in 1905, many critics considered El Tovar the most elegant hotel west of the Mississippi. Countless notable luminaries have stayed there, including Theodore Roosevelt, prolific western author Zane Grey, and Albert Einstein. Even today, El Tovar is considered the crown jewel of historic national park lodges. The dining room at the hotel offers fine dining appropriate for its spectacular, one-of-a-kind location. I opted for a French dinner theme. I started with French onion soup gratinée, then DL and I split the El Tovar salad composed of baby greens, fresh julienned or sliced vegetables, nuts, fruit, and a balsamic vinaigrette. For my entrée, I selected a roasted half duck with a cherry Merlot demi sauce. The duck seemed a perfect choice for the setting: an untamed protein next to wild terrain. Dessert was an apple and almond tart with honey butter presented beautifully in an individual shallow ramekin. What a way to end the day in anticipation of the next day's impressive sightseeing! We packed in a full day of absorbing the awe of the Grand Canyon. Standing on the edge of a cliff looking down three thousand feet into the muddy Colorado River, seeing the multishades of ochre, red, and yellow in the stratified layers of the gorge walls, and witnessing the western sunset as it filled the canyon with colors and shadows that would challenge the artistic photographic talents of Ansel Adams. There cannot be another place on earth as awe-inspiring as the Grand Canyon. The dinner on our second night was as superb as the first night, although I do not recall the details because my senses were still saturated from the remembrance of the day. Although I have already mentioned bucket lists a number of times, I contend that a visit to the Grand Canyon should take the number one position in your bucket list.

After our luxurious stay at El Tovar, we headed south back to Flagstaff. Our ultimate goal for the day was Tucson, with an intermediate stop in the Phoenix area for lunch. But first, we wanted to spend some leisurely time touring the scenic highway south of Flagstaff through Sedona and Oak Creek Canyon. If you have never been to Sedona or Oak Creek Canyon, let me tease you with a prediction. When you visit, you will look around and say, "Hey, I've been here before!" Expect a strong dèjá vu experience. The reason is that this gorgeous area has been used in countless commercials that you have no doubt seen. DL and I stopped at an outdoor café for coffee and a croissant to enjoy the quiet, stunning vistas. Then we continued with the more mundane freeway driving to Phoenix. We stopped on the south side of Phoenix for a late lunch, and it was an ordinary sit-down lunch. As an editorial comment, I must mention that in all our everyday lunch stops, we never ordered a fast-food hamburger. We made that decision a matter of principle. With our hunger quelled, we headed one hundred miles southeast to Tucson and our next national park.

We found accommodations for two nights at one of our brand-name motel preferences in the Tanque Verde area on the eastern edge of Tucson within a short distance from the Saguaro National Park. It had been a long day, and we were ready for a late meal and a long night's rest. We discovered a Fleming's Restaurant relatively close by. Although Fleming's is a chain, it is a fine-dining chain that DL and I like. We have dined at Fleming's restaurants all over the country and have never been disappointed with a Fleming's meal. As a benefit from our frequent attendance, we have a membership in their Magnum Club, which guarantees seating without reservations at any of the restaurants. As Magnum Club members, the staff treats you like family, with courtesy visits to your table by the manager and occasionally the wine steward or chef. We had not had red meat for a while, but this was the night. DL and I started by sharing a lobster bisque and a wedge salad. For the entrée, DL ordered the petite filet mignon, her go-to selection at Fleming's, with herbed horseradish sauce. I ordered the Angus beef rib eye, thick and juicy, with béarnaise sauce. We also shared a side of sautéed mushrooms to complement the steaks. We were so satiated that we could have passed on dessert, but we decided to share a bowl of fresh fruit with Chantilly cream. Fleming's has an extensive wine list, so we had no problem finding a nonvintage sparkling split to start and then a big, bold Coach Insignia Fisher Vineyards Napa Cabernet Sauvignon to pair with the steaks. Without hesitation, I could enthusiastically repeat this meal monthly with no risk of becoming jaded. The next morning, we slept in, had the motel's buffet breakfast, and headed for the Saguaro National Park. The park was briefly interesting, but we had seen all we needed by noon. We made an impromptu decision to visit the Pima Air and Space Museum adjacent to Davis-Montham Air Force Base. We had a simple soup and salad lunch at the museum and then toured the exhibits, both inside and outside. Predictably, based on my background and education, I am fascinated by aerospace technology. On the way back to the motel, we stopped for dinner at El Charro Café downtown, reputed to be the nation's oldest Mexican restaurant in continuous operation by the same family. The restaurant's founder, Tia Monica, is credited with inventing the chimichanga. So we ordered Tia Monica's classic chimichangas accompanied by Arroz Sonora and frijoles charros. The chimichanga was eye-popping: huge with a perfect deep-fried exterior. DL had a slushy margarita, and I had Mexican cerveza. We rarely have a dessert with Mexican food, but this night we decided to try a tres leches cake. That dessert capped the day.

After another motel buffet breakfast, we got an early start on a long day of driving. Our next destination was El Paso Texas, about three hundred miles east, with an intermediate stop in Lordsburg, New Mexico, for lunch. We had no plans for touring parks, scenic highways, or fine dining, so we just gritted our teeth and drove the interstate. Arriving in Lordsburg, we unwound with an ordinary sit-down lunch in a nondescript restaurant. For being a small town, Lordsburg has some notoriety. It was the epicenter of the Lincoln County War when Billy the Kid worked for a Lordsburg businessman, John Henry Tunstall. It has been the setting for numerous western movies and has been referred to in numerous others, including the iconic 1939 movie *Stagecoach*, with John Wayne in his breakthrough role. Heading east from Lordsburg, we crested the Continental Divide once again. We found accommodations at one of our brand-name motel preferences on the south side of El Paso. After a circuitous trip, we had finally returned to our Texas home turf, so we opted for a standard Tex-Mex dinner of chile relleno, rice, and refried beans. If I see chile relleno on a Tex-Mex menu, I usually order it. It is difficult to make, so I do not make it at home, but when it is done well, it is a very satisfying dish. We slept in, had the buffet breakfast, and then drove about 190 miles to our next destination, Fort Davis.

Fort Davis is at one apex of the triangle formed with the towns of Marfa and Alpine. These are the wide-open spaces many folks envision when they think of Texas ranchland. Marfa was the location for the ranch house set in the 1956 movie *Giant*, starring Rock Hudson, Elizabeth Taylor, and James Dean. Alpine is a popular overnight destination for tourists vising Big Bend National Park. The highways connecting Marfa, Alpine, and Fort Davis are listed as scenic highways, as is the highway from Alpine to Big Bend National Park. DL and I wanted to visit the Fort Davis National Historical Park, a post-Civil War US Cavalry outpost, so we had made reservations for two nights at the Limpia Hotel in Fort Davis, a two-story structure built in 1912 with pink stone and generous porches. After checking in and having an early lunch at the Limpia Hotel, we spent the afternoon touring the Fort Davis National Historical Park, and then sightseeing on the scenic Marfa, Alpine, Fort Davis loop. That evening, we ate at the Blue Mountain Bar and Grill in the Limpia Hotel, the only fine dining restaurant and the only bar in Fort Davis. To start, DL and I shared a braised brisket street taco appetizer. We also shared an entrée-sized house salad. I selected the grilled whole mountain trout with lemon chimichurri for my entrée. Chimichurri with fish seemed unusual, but the lemon in the chimichurri made it a great match. The wine list was minimal, so we had an unpretentious California Sauvignon Blanc. For dessert, we shared a simple dessert of Texas peach cobbler with vanilla ice cream. The next morning, we planned an early departure to Big Bend National Park, so we went to a small diner across the street from the Limpia Hotel for a quick breakfast. As it turned out, this was a memorable breakfast. Even at the early hour of the morning, the diner was nearly full of locals, and they were a colorful crowd dressed in western hats and boots. In addition to the standard offerings of fried eggs, hash brown potatoes, sausage, and cowboy coffee, I had an unforgettable serving of biscuits and gravy. It was an unexpected treat! We spent the better part of the day at Big Bend National Park, returning to the Limpia Hotel after sunset. We were tired, so we decided to order a simple dinner of chips, salsa, and burritos in rocking chairs on the porch outside our room. As it turned out, this was also a memorable event. The elevation of Fort Davis is about five thousand feet, the air is crystal clear, and there is little-to-no light pollution. Looking at the sky from our rocking chairs, the stars were unflickering pinpricks in the black dome. And there were so many more stars than I was accustomed to seeing, even the familiar constellations seemed to be decorated with stunning excess. It was a sight I will never forget. The next morning, we returned to the diner across the street for breakfast with the locals. Naturally, I ordered the biscuits and gravy. Then we were back on the road again for a long haul to the Texas Hill Country.

Our trek took us north to the interstate, then east through Fort Stockton, and on to Sonora for lunch. We had soup and sandwiches in a sit-down roadside diner, stretched our legs, and continued east on the interstate. Our destination was Fredericksburg. Although Fredericksburg is only about one hundred miles from our home in Austin, we wanted to spend some time there. We arrived at dusk and booked two nights at a rustic bed-and-breakfast on Main Street, a few blocks from the National Museum of the Pacific War. Dinner that night was a forgettable eat-to-live event. We were exhausted and thought more about sleeping than eating. We slept in, had our B and B, and walked to the museum. If you have never visited the museum, you would be surprised to see a Pacific War museum in the middle of landlocked central Texas. The reason, of course, is because Fredericksburg is the home of the great admiral of World War II Admiral Nimitz. It is an extensive facility that can easily fill the better part of a day. After the museum, we strolled the heart of Fredericksburg looking at the antique shops and art galleries until it was time for dinner. We returned to a restaurant where we had dined on previous trips to Fredericksburg. Otto's Restaurant was fine dining in the German tradition. I started with seared foie gras and peach butternut chutney, followed by Otto's salad of pickled vegetables and candied nuts. My entrée was duck schnitzel with cranberry marmalade and pickled peppers. The duck dish was so sophisticated: beautiful, delicious, and unique. Dessert was apple strudel and vanilla ice cream. Otto's restaurant may not be worthy of a Michelin star, but the food is consistently good, and I would go back there again. We slept in again the next morning, had our B&B breakfast, and then headed home.

On the way home, we stopped at Becker Vineyards for wine tasting and lunch. I do not buy much Texas wine, but I like the Viognier made by Becker. DL and I drink it as an everyday white wine when we want a break from our standard selections of French, New Zealand, and California white wines. The short trip home was uneventful, and we both let out a great sigh of relief when we pulled into our garage and turned off the engine. Like Dorothy said in *The Wizard of Oz*, "There's no place like home!"

PART 15

Expanded Horizons

CHAPTER 61

First Class in the Golden Years

Our wonderful life in the golden years continued. We were living true to our mantra, "dine, wine, and travel," but the sophistication of that triad had evolved. We had come to appreciate the highest quality food products, wines of the best vintages, and first-class travel. Intrinsic excellence became overwhelmingly more important than cost.

Let me offer our perspective on food, using proteins as an example. FDA prime beef tenderloin, Berkshire pork chops, and wild-caught halibut cost about $25 per pound. DL and I would buy about one pound of these products for our dinners, which computes to about $12 of protein for each of us. At a restaurant, an entrée with those quality products would cost more than $30 per person, two and one-half the retail cost of the protein. Yes, you can buy less-marbled FDA Choice strip steaks, insipid shrink-wrapped pork chops, and previously frozen cod fillets for half the cost, and they can make good dinners, but they lack the character to make gourmet dinners. I might think differently if I had to feed a family of ravenous teenagers with inexperienced palates, but for the two of us, DL and I chose to buy the best products available.

Most of our friends drink wine regularly, but some are so parsimonious that they judge wine by the cost, not the taste. I do not understand their logic. When they brag about buying two-buck Chuck at Trader Joe's, it is difficult not to be judgmental. Others buy decent wine, but they set a hard ceiling on what they are willing to spend, and they agonize at the thought of spending more than $20 per bottle. I believe this is backward thinking. I know there are some excellent $20 bottles of wine, and we have some in our cellar, but my point is that we consider the characteristics of the wine first before we ever ask the question, "How much does it cost?" An estate-bottled wine sourced from a single vineyard, produced by a reputable wine-maker in an excellent vintage year, and tasted by us to verify that it meets our standard of fine wine are some of the criteria we consider before price. In some cases, this process raises the stakes of the game. For example, we may try a Brunello or a Chateauneuf du Pape that we love only to find it costs $100 per bottle. That may be suitable for a special occasion but too much for our everyday consumption. However, even on those special occasions, a French proverb reminds us that "Only the first bottle is expensive." DL and I are firm believers that life is too short to drink cheap wine.

In the realm of travel, DL and I have come to appreciate the value of first-class service. Compare a twelve-hour flight from the USA West Coast to New Zealand in coach class or first class. DL and I have done both, and let me say loud and clear, "There is no comparison!" On another trip to Barcelona, we upgraded to a deluxe city-view room at the Majestic Hotel, while friends of ours opted for a standard interior room. We paid about one and one-half more than they did, but when they visited our room, they were stunned at the differences. In addition, our deluxe accommodations included a number of amenities not available to them. Our friends said they regretted their decision. Another example was a recent twelve-day cruise we took on Oceania cruise lines to the Adriatic and the Aegean. On previous cruises, we booked a nice stateroom with a veranda on the concierge level, but on this cruise, we booked a penthouse. The penthouse cost about one and one-quarter more than the concierge stateroom, but the features and amenities, including a butler, were worth the price difference.

A hard-sell travel agent once said to us, "It only costs a little more to go first class." It may be more, but it is worth the cost difference. If you need to rationalize the added expense for your annual vacation, just think about amortizing the difference over the entire year. If the additional expense is $3,500 to go first class, then this calculates to about $10 per day. Do not worry about rationalizing. Just do it. You will not regret your decision. At our current stage and state of life, DL and I are committed to a first-class lifestyle.

CHAPTER 62

Entertaining with a Theme

DL and I frequently entertain our friends with wine dinners, and they reciprocate. There is no need for them to reciprocate. DL and I love to entertain, and we would do so even without reciprocity. We do not keep score. Probably the biggest issue we have with entertaining is the challenge to avoid a routine. Little things can add variety, such as using different sets of china, special stemware like Riedell or Waterford crystal, and eye-catching color-coordinated table linens. No doubt the most important and most memorable aspect of a dinner with friends is the menu. Our solution to menu selection is a theme. DL is a master at selecting a theme. I would summarize her philosophy as "Any excuse for a party."

Look at any annotated calendar. There are numerous historic events, important milestones, and what I call Hallmark occasions in addition to standard religious or secular holidays. DL and I select a theme that links a calendar event to a projected dinner date. After choosing a theme, we plan together the appropriate food and wine. We print the menu, roll it like a scroll, wrap it with a colored ribbon, and arrange it at all place settings. Let me cite just three examples of entertaining with a theme as well as the associated menu. I hope I am tempting you to say, "I would like to go to dinner at their house!"

CHAPTER 63

A Theme for January

Some options in January include New Year's Day, the first; college football bowl games; Orthodox Christian Christmas, the sixth; MLK Day, the eighteenth; and Scottish poet Robbie Burns' birthday, the twenty-fifth. DL is favored with Scottish ethnicity and appearance, so we like to celebrate the poet's birthday. At the end of this chapter, I have attached a dinner menu we routinely use for the celebration. Although not listed in the menu, we had a selection of wine available for those who wanted wine, but we primarily promoted wee drams from our inventory of single-malt Scotch whisky. As part of the theme during the dessert course, we ask our guests to read a Burns' poem of their choice from *The Works of Robert Burns* published by the Wordsworth Poetry Library. By the time the dessert course was served, guests had a few wee drams of Scotch whisky, so their Scottish brogue and enthusiasm were in fine form. For our guests who have not traveled to Scotland, the food, whisky, and poetry made a memorable evening. The appetizer of Faux Haggis was cautiously approached by attendees, but the savory roast grouse with Prince Charles sauce appealed to both the eyes and the palate. Sláinte!

Dinner Menu
In joyous celebration of
Robbie Burns' Birthday

Appetizer
Wee Drams
Smoked Firth of Forth Salmon with Dill Sauce
Faux Haggis with Scotch Sauce

First Course
More Wee Drams
Cock-a-Leekie Soup (Chicken, leek, and barley)
Bannock Farls (Oatcake Wedges)

Main Course
Additional Wee Drams
Roast Grouse with Prince Charles Sauce
Skirlie (Oat Stuffing)
Stovies (Skillet Potatoes)
Braised Buttered Carrots
Oat Bread Cockaigne

Dessert
Final Wee Drams
Cranachan (Berries, Oats, Cream, and Drambuie)
Bergamot Tea
Coffee

CHAPTER 64

A Theme for June

Some options in June include the end of the high school academic year, the eleventh; Flag Day, the fourteenth; Father's Day, the twentieth; and the summer solstice, the twenty-first. DL and I like to celebrate the summer solstice for a number of reasons. We were introduced to one of the reasons on a trip to St. Petersburg, Russia in June during the summer solstice. There was a weeklong celebration called White Nights. On June twenty-first, the longest day of the year, at the latitude of sixty degrees north, sunset in St. Petersburg is about 10:30 p.m. and sunrise is about 3:30 a.m. It never really gets dark at night, and even at 1:00 a.m., the sky is dusky. Peter the Great, Russian Tsar, moved the Russian capital from Moscow to St. Petersburg in 1712 and built the early stages of Peterhof Palace as his summer residence in 1714. There were strategic reasons for the move to St. Petersburg, but I am sure Peter the Great also liked the idea of long summer days and short summer nights. The current residents of St. Petersburg surely do. As a counterpoint to long summer days, we asked some residents what they do in December during long winter nights, and they said, "We drink vodka and sleep!" At the end of this chapter, I have attached a dinner menu for the celebration of White Nights at Peterhof Palace. Try the chlodnik soup for a gourmet version of borscht from Mother Russia. Za vashe zdorovie!

Replication of a Dinner at Peterhof Palace of Czar Peter the Great

Appetizer
Wild Mushroom Blinchiki

Salad
Kohlrabi Caesar Salad

Soup
Chlodnik Soup

Entrée
Beef Stroganoff
Haricots Verts

Dessert
Plum and Almond Tart
Black Tea and Coffee

Dinner Wine Selections
2018 Chateau Tour de Bonnet Entre Deux Mers
2018 Chateau la Vivonne Côte de Provençe
2014 Vinum Russian River Pinot Noir

CHAPTER 65

A Theme for July

July includes some expected themes, such as Independence Day, the Fourth of July. For a Spanish theme, there is the running of the bulls in Pamplona at the festival of San Fermín on the seventh. There is also the anniversary of the first manned moon landing, July 21, 1969. Since DL and I like French cuisine, we like to celebrate Bastille Day on the fourteenth. Bastille Day in France is analogous to the Fourth of July in the USA. The friends we invited to our Bastille Day dinner were Francophiles, and they thoroughly enjoyed the five-course meal. They enjoyed the exceptional French wines with equal gusto. The dessert of marinated cherries with our homemade kirsch ice cream received high praise and requests for second servings. Overall, this was one of our better theme dinners, especially from the perspective of wine pairings. À votre santé!

Dinner with Friends
A French Theme for Bastille Day

Appetizers
Pâté de Maison sur Crostini
Saumon sur Concombre
Veuve Clicquot Brut Champagne

Soup
Milliessoise
2012 Sous le Puits Puligny-Montrachet 1er Cru

Salad
Céleri-Rave Rémoulade
2012 Sous le Puits Puligny-Montrachet 1er Cru

Entrée
Filet de Boeuf dans Pâtisserie
Oignons Caramélisés
Asperge avec Sauce Hollandaise
1997 Bouchard Père and Fils Le Corton Grand Cru
2007 Domaine des Croix Beaune les Bressandes

Dessert
Cerises Marineés à Glace de Kirsch
2013 Chateau Guiraud Sauternes 1er Grand Cru Classé

CHAPTER 66

La Dolce Vita

To say that DL and I are content in our golden years would be an understatement. Our palates are still fine-tuned to crave the luxury of gourmet dining, either in Michelin star restaurants or creations in our own home. Our expanded appreciation of fine wine has driven us to drink the best, to explore the bounty of worldwide varietals, and to recognize the nuances of pairing fine wine with gourmet food. We are thankful for our good health and physical vigor that allow us to travel the world without restrictions. We cherish our circle of friends—locally, nationally, and globally—who give us great comfort and who tolerate our eccentric focus on "dine, wine, and travel." We are gloriously living la dolce vita.

PART 16

Continuation and Anticipation

CHAPTER 67

Reprise: Fine Dining

Somewhere, a chef is planning a spectacular dinner. The chef has a sequence of courses, where each course stands on its own with an artful presentation to match Michelangelo's *Pieta* and complements its predecessor while seamlessly flowing to its successor with the perfect balance of an Olympic gymnast. The sight, aroma, taste, and texture of each course tantalize the senses with unrivaled pleasure. Patrons who are fortunate to partake of this masterpiece will carry the memory for life. I intend to seek and find this dinner. Or maybe I will be the chef to prepare it.

I have learned over time how little I know of the culinary arts. The more I learn and the more I practice, the more I am humbled by the limits of my expertise. The scope of the culinary arts is analogous to the scope of the cosmos. It is infinite and expanding. Even those few culinarians who are afforded the title and respect as grand chefs are only masters of a finite piece of the culinary cosmos. Novice chefs, like me, are only a mote in the culinary cosmos. Regardless, grand chefs and novice chefs pursue with equal enthusiasm the perfectly prepared, perfectly presented dinner. I have also come to realize the truth that there is no such concept as a perfect dinner in the absence of friends and family. The French statesman, diplomat, and clergyman Charles-Maurice de Talleyrand philosophized, "Show me another pleasure like dinner [with family] which comes every day and lasts an hour." People are the most important ingredient when planning a fine dining menu. I believe the conjunction of extraordinary food, served to faithful friends, in a beautiful setting is the stuff that lifelong memories are made of. In my unremitting obsession with plated ecstasy, I intend to bank as many of these memories as possible.

CHAPTER 68

Reprise: Exceptional Wine

Somewhere, a cask of wine ages that will be bottled as the best wine I will ever taste. Its characteristics of acid level, alcohol percentage, floral scent, fruitiness, residual sugar, and tannin structure will be in perfect balance. This will be the quintessential wine in the long history of exceptional wine. I intend to sample the world of wines until I find this elusive zenith.

Wine experts generally agree that 99.9 percent of the wines in the world are made from the Vitus-vinifera genus-species, of which there are thousands of grape varieties. However, of these thousands, fewer than eight hundred varieties have historically been made into wine. Furthermore, of these eight hundred varieties, seven are traditionally categorized by wine masters as noble grapes (Cabernet Sauvignon, Chardonnay, Merlot, Sauvignon Blanc, Pinot Noir, Riesling, and Syrah) because they are associated with the highest quality wines, and they adapt to growing conditions worldwide. Americans generally consume and cellar very few varieties beyond the noble grapes or blends of the noble grapes, with a few exceptions, such as Malbec from Argentina or Zinfandel from California. Why not try some of the other eight hundred varieties made into wine worldwide? The reason is probably because of purchasing habits, comfort factors, and risk aversion. Many varieties can produce wine of equal quality to the Noble Grapes. Until I earned my sommelier certificate, I was happy in a narrow comfort zone. After my sommelier training, augmented by worldwide travel, DL and I broadened our repertoire of wines.

Expanding our experience with wine also created more options for pairing wine with food. Try an Italian Aglianico with roasted, smoked, or grilled meat. Try a Spanish Albariño with a flaky baked fish. Try an Argentinian Torrontes with Indian curry or a spicy Thai dish. When traveling internationally, try the local wines that do not get exported to the USA. We have enjoyed some exceptional wines in Croatia, Hungary, and Israel. The indigenous population has been drinking their local wines with their ethnic cuisine for hundreds of years, and they know the tried-and-true pairings. Never heard of the grape or the producer? So what? Relish the adventure! You may be pleasantly surprised.

CHAPTER 69

Reprise: Stimulating Travel

Imagine a spectacular, lavishly decorated throne room in a Renaissance palace that is poorly lit by one feeble candle. Your perception of the room would be a colorless, unimpressive small space. Such a scene is analogous to the ethnocentric mind of a person deprived of the richness of world travel. Now imagine lighting a bevy of crystal chandeliers in that throne room, spreading bright, refractive light into every nook and cranny. All of a sudden, your vision is overwhelmed by the colorful artwork on the walls, the details of the statuary, the high vaulted ceiling with its delicate ribs sprouting from the Corinthian capitals on columns, the inlaid pattern of the marble floor, the prismatic leaded glass windows, and the meticulously carved artisan furniture. Now the scene is analogous to illuminating your mind to the wonders of travel, but travel is so much more than a spectacular throne room.

When DL and I travel, we try to live in the moment. We focus on the present. Dwelling on past memories fades in importance. Speculating on the future is preempted by the mindfulness of the present. We try to see the beauty in everything, although from our experience, not everyone sees it. Some folks see the Roman forum as a pile of rubble, unable to see the grandeur of the Roman architecture. When some folks visit the Burren in western Ireland, they only see a huge expanse of barren rock and not the geological wonder of its creation. Other folks visit Tanzania by safari and see third-world poverty and not the complex circle of life in the untamed savannah. DL and I believe world travel provides the opportunity to find beauty in all its forms: architecture, art, ethnic festivals, exotic scenery, strange customs, unusual cuisine, wild flora and fauna, and many other unanticipated encounters. I close this thought by paraphrasing John Kenneth Galbraith, "There is certainly no absolute standard of beauty. That precisely is what makes its pursuit [through travel] so interesting."

DL and I still continue with our three-pronged approach to travel: weekend adventures in the states, monthlong road trip in the states, and annual international vacations of two weeks or more. There are so many remarkable destinations we have yet to visit. The Galapagos Islands, Machu Picchu, and South Africa are high on our list for international travel. Yellowstone National Park, Mount Rushmore National Memorial, and Hawaii Volcanoes National Park are on our stateside list. We would also like a road trip on the Atlantic coast from Cape Hatteras to Key West. We have the time, we have the health, we have the finances, and we have an appreciation of the importance of travel in a life well lived.

CHAPTER 70

Living the Mantra

In moments of quiet mediation, I often contemplate how many things in life truly give me enjoyment. Invariably I find gourmet food, fine wine, and exhilarating travel at the top of the list. Am I being too obsessed with hedonistic, sexual, and sensual, pleasures? I think not. Each of us finds satisfaction in one or more hobbies, interests, or talents to give sense and meaning to our lives. In this memoir, I have attempted to convey the breadth of my passion for dine, wine, and travel. If I have fallen short, it is because my choice of words and my literary skill are inadequate to adequately describe the flame within me. Suffice it to say, the flame burns hot and bright.

In closing, consider this scene that encapsulates my memoir. It is the first Saturday of summer. The weather is perfect, and all of nature seems fresh and alive. I feel compelled to prepare a dinner for DL and me that would pay homage to Mother Earth's seasonal splendor. I decide on a seven-course French menu that I hope will transport our minds and palates to Lyon, the gastronomical capital of France: warm hors d'oeuvres, savory soup, seafood dish, citrus sorbet intermezzo, meat entrée with vegetables, green salad, and sweet dessert. My spirit is high, and I feel like a maestro in the kitchen directing an orchestra of knives, whisks, pots, and pans. I am in the zone. The courses come together in a timely sequence with spot-on flavors, contrasting textures, balanced spices, and clean presentations. The dinner reaches the pinnacle of plated ecstasy with the service of the meat entrée. I deliver the main course to DL. She sits for a moment with her hands in her lap examining the presentation like a critic analyzing a work of art. Then she takes a couple of polite forkfuls sampling the depth of flavor, and she sips some garnet wine from a crystal goblet between forkfuls. She wrinkles her brow, rolls her eyes, and softly moans a throaty "Ummm." She looks up at me, cocks her head, coyly smiles, and says, "Is this foreplay?"

ACKNOWLEDGMENTS

My beloved wife, DL, was an active participant for over fifty years in the dine, wine, and travel adventures described in this memoir. She deserves credit for assistance in recalling events and correcting some details I may have misconstrued. She also conducted the first editorial review to revise the spelling, grammar, and general layout of the story.

I credit my daughter, Alison, for encouraging me to undertake this project. She has written two novels, so I was also grateful for her creative advice. As I documented my early years in this memoir, I thought of Alison's repeated appeals for me to put into words some record of my pre-Alison life. She seemed to enjoy the verbal stories I related about my youth, but she chided me to put the stories in writing for posterity. At her prodding, I believe I have partially complied with her request, albeit through a prism of dine, wine, and travel.

In the spirit of my mantra, "dine, wine, and travel," allow me to offer some nonspecific acknowledgments. I feel compelled to recognize all chefs, past and present, famous or anonymous, who have contributed to the culinary arts. Their accomplishments and creativity have given my life immeasurable pleasure. Likewise, I bless the effort of untold winemakers over thousands of years who have transformed Vitus-vinifera into the ultimate liquid food I consume every day. And lastly, I commend the tourist services, tour guides, travel agents, and luxury cruise lines that have afforded me nearly infinite exposure to the wonders of worldwide travel.

ABOUT THE AUTHOR

It would be difficult, maybe impossible, to overstate Vincent DiLoreto's passion for gourmet food accompanied by fine wine. He finds great sensual satisfaction in consuming an exquisite meal, but that satisfaction is considerably amplified by the preparation of that exquisite meal. The great French chef Jacques Pépin famously said, "Food, for me, is inseparable from sharing. There is no great meal unless it is shared with family or friends." Vincent concurs with Jacques Pépin. To be the gatekeeper for such an event and for a chef or dinner host to be able to say "I'm preparing a meal that is bringing people together" is truly awesome. Vincent believes that whether it is an intimate romantic dinner with someone special or a large holiday gathering with family and friends, good food is the glue that strengthens bonds, creates friendship, and offers memorable milestones on our path through life.

CPSIA information can be obtained
at www.ICGtesting.com
Printed in the USA
LVHW011223010622
720195LV00007B/146